ISIS

CONTAINMENT & DEFEAT

ISIS
CONTAINMENT & DEFEAT

Next Generation Counterinsurgency - NexGen COIN

ARNOLD SCHUCHTER

iUniverse®

ISIS CONTAINMENT & DEFEAT
NEXT GENERATION COUNTERINSURGENCY - NEXGEN COIN

iUniverse books may be ordered through booksellers or by contacting:

iUniverse
1663 Liberty Drive
Bloomington, IN 47403
www.iuniverse.com
1-800-Authors (1-800-288-4677)

ISBN: 978-1-4917-8413-6 (sc)
ISBN: 978-1-4917-8414-3 (e)

Library of Congress Control Number: 2015919828

Print information available on the last page.

iUniverse rev. date: 01/06/2016

CONTENTS

INTRODUCTION vii

PART I
Fighting the Islamic State (ISIS/ISIL)

Chapter 1 The ISIS Threat & Middle East Geopolitics 3
Chapter 2 Ending the "Endless War" in Afghanistan 32
Chapter 3 Syrian Political Chess Match – US in Checkmate ... 41
Chapter 4 Iran's Nuclear Deal, Proxies & The Persian
           Gulf Region 55
Chapter 5 Sisi's Egypt & Gaza's Plight 75
Chapter 6 The Middle East & EU Migration Maze and Mess ... 84

PART II
Lessons Learned

Chapter 7   Wishful Counterinsurgency Thinking 99
Chapter 8   Hail to the Commander-in-Chief 111
Chapter 9   US I.Q. Tests 122
Chapter 10 To Surge or Not to Surge................................... 130
Chapter 11 Lessons Learned in Iraq.................................... 143
Chapter 12 Lessons Learned in the Anbar Awakening 153
Chapter 13 Kurdish Wild Cards... 172
Chapter 14 Lessons Learned in Yemen 181
Chapter 15 Lessons Learned in Libya & Benghazi.............. 194
Chapter 16 Terrorism Threats from Central America &
            Mexico 210

PART III
NexGen COIN

Chapter 17 Next Generation Counterinsurgency
(NexGen COIN) 235
Chapter 18 ISIS Containment Strategy & Protected Safe
Havens 249
Chapter 19 COIN Revisited and Revamped 264
Chapter 20 NexGen COIN: Strategies 274
Chapter 21 NexGen COIN: Protected Safe Havens 294
Chapter 22 NexGen COIN: Frontline Advisors/
CyberWarriors 311
Chapter 23 NexGen COIN: Empowering Bottom-up
Leadership 327

BIBLIOGRAPHY 333

INDEX 337

INTRODUCTION

Recent terrorist attacks in Paris, Beirut and on the Russian Metrojet over the Sinai Peninsula have thrust national security to the center of the 2016 presidential election race. With terrorism elevated to the most pressing concern of voters, the key question becomes which candidate will be best prepared to serve as America's commander-in-chief. The choice will become even more important for voters when they realize, as pointed out repeatedly in this volume, that the president of the United States makes all of the most important national security, foreign policy, military and anti-terrorism decisions.

Presidential candidates will be forced to show voters that they really understand what they are talking about on the subject of fighting, containing and defeating ISIS. Who would you, American voter, trust to put together strategic and military strategies and an alliance of nations to fight ISIS and other terrorism? Which candidate(s) really understand geopolitics and military planning and have demonstrated stellar leadership capabilities? Does candidate x, y or z really know what they are talking about on the subjects of counterinsurgency warfare and fighting ISIS?

Recent terrorist attacks by ISIS may transform Syria "peace talks" in Vienna, bringing together 17 nations, including the US, Russia, Iran, Turkey, the EU and the Arab League, to discuss Syrian President Assad's political future, into strategy sessions on how to contain and defeat ISIS. The future of President Assad no longer will be the most important issue on the negotiating table but his fate will become part of a strategy for dealing with ISIS in Syria, Iraq and elsewhere. Identifying Syria's "moderate insurgents" (the "good guys" versus the "bad guys") also will become part of "peace talks" in Vienna. Central to Vienna and other discussions about attacking ISIS, however, will be President Obama's risk averse refusal to put boots-on-the-ground in Syria, Iraq or Afghanistan as part of an anti-ISIS coalition effort.

It is one thing, in the words of President Francoise Hollande of France, to defiantly declare the ISIS attacks in Paris "an act of war" and quite another to define the "pitiless response" in terms of coordinated strategies. These strategies have been lacking thus far from the US and other countries involved in the war on ISIS, including Russia. The goal that the US, its allies, Russia and Iran can agree on is a unified and relentless campaign to crush ISIS at its Middle East and African sources. Achieving this goal will require ramping up multinational intelligence capabilities and, most problematic, unprecedented intelligence sharing. In addition, leaders of nations engaged in the Syria peace talks will have to agree to provide sufficient humanitarian relief and protection to displaced persons in the Middle East to enable these people to remain safely in their home countries. Achieving the goal of preventing ISIS from using social media to spread its evil messages will be much more problematic.

Congress and the American public have been left baffled, and increasingly distressed, by what the Obama administration is trying to do in Syria in both the near- and long-term. In the aftermath of ISIS terrorist attacks in Paris and Beirut and the downing of the Russian jetliner over the Sinai Peninsula, distress and anxiety among American voters increasingly is turning to fear that undoubtedly will permeate the presidential election campaign in 2016. The "what's next" question understandably is on everyone's mind. ISIS has shown its readiness and capability to strike beyond areas in the Middle East that it controls in Iraq, Syria and increasingly in Libya. These attacks are extremely hard to anticipate or prevent, especially in Europe that has opened its borders to refugees and migrants from the Middle East and North Africa.

For many years the Islamic State (ISIS) has been preparing for a civilizational showdown in the Middle East between Muslims and "crusaders." Traps for America have been laid in a strategy concocted by Al-Zarqawi that for years has been hidden in plain sight, not unlike *The Selected Works of Mao Tse-tung* that laid out the strategy and tactics that the Communists followed in Southeast Asia. Al-Zarqawi's strategy can be found in *Idarat al-Tawahhush* or the *Management of Savagery*.

In the last few years the world has witnessed or heard about an unending stream of macabre ISIS executions shown in graphic detail on YouTube and reported in social media for consumption by aspiring jihadists and others. In addition to attracting jihadists, the political goal of these seemingly senseless and barbaric acts of ISIS cruelty has been domination of the populations in Iraq, Syria, and elsewhere through fear and intimidation, including "prophetic" messages about destruction of "apostate" Muslim regimes that will be built back up and transformed under a caliphate. As for America, the ISIS goal has been to draw the US into open warfare somewhere in the Middle East, not just into proxy warfare. This would enable ISIS to achieve its goal of humiliating a "morally corrupt America" and its soldiers on the battlefield.

In recent years changing and severely challenged leadership in Baghdad, Damascus, Beirut, Riyadh, Ankara, Cairo, Tripoli and Sanaa have consistently made decisions about dealing with the threats of terrorist groups that raise suspicions about their actual political aims. Each new intervention and action in the Middle East that aims to solve or ameliorate terrorism threats seems to lead to new ones and new vulnerabilities to the advance of the Islamic State. Who knows who is doing what and for what reason(s) to contain ISIS? What's working to stop ISIS and what's not and how do we know?

If the US intelligence community has answers to these questions, they are not sharing them with either Congress or the American public. This means that the American public really has no idea what's going on in the Middle East and whether any progress is being made in the fight against ISIS and other Islamic terrorists.

For nearly two years, people in the US trying to follow the evolution and relationships of al-Zawahiri's Al-Qaeda and ISIS in the Middle East have seen the emergence of a battle for supremacy between their global jihadist movements.

In late July 2015, retired Gen. John Allen, President Obama's top envoy working with other nations to fight the Islamic State, told the Aspen Security Forum that ISIS's momentum had been "checked strategically, operationally, and by and large, tactically." We now have reasons to question the veracity of that statement which, at the time, unexplainably contrasted with Defense Intelligence Agency (DIA) assessments that painted a grim picture about how little the Islamic State had been weakened over the past year, that the US's yearlong campaign had done little to diminish the ranks of ISIS's committed fighters, and that ISIS had expanded its reach into North Africa and Central Asia.

The US intelligence community has been its own worst enemy and should be one of the biggest national security concerns for the American public. Every since 9/11 there have been good reasons for the US government and the American public not to trust or depend on threat assessments by the US intelligence community. For the purposes of COIN planning, the US should have serious questions about what the intelligence community provides in the way of key insights about US and also ISIS operating environments (OE) in Syria, Iraq and elsewhere.

Al-Qaeda rejected ISIS early in 2014 because its new leader, al-Baghdadi, refused to stay out of Syria. The Al-Qaeda affiliate in Syria, Jabhat al Nusra, has been fighting ISIS. Now, surprisingly, al-Zawahiri seems to be reaching out to ISIS, even while calling ISIS's "caliphate" illegitimate, saying that all jihadists in Iraq and Syria should cooperate in the fight against a common enemy. While saying that his ISIS rival, al-Baghdadi, has split the Muslim community, Al-Zawahiri goes so far as to say that he would cooperate with ISIS to fight the "crusaders," the Alawites, the Shia and other "enemies of Islam."

There is no way of knowing at this time whether cooperation between Al-Qaeda and ISIS actually is possible. If it did happen, it would have bad consequences for the Assad regime as well as the current US strategy of recruiting moderate insurgents, undermining coalition efforts to regain and control territory in northern Syria. Most important, Al-Qaeda and ISIS joining forces could be a wild card in any US and coalition strategy to deal with Islamic extremism in the Middle East and anywhere else, including Latin America, and also would be a wild card for Iran's ambitions for building its sphere of influence in Syria and elsewhere after sanctions are removed.

In the context of this development, it's not a surprise that conspiracy theories abound about every new Al-Qaeda and anti-ISIS decision and action. Even as the United States-led coalition of now 62 nations (including the European Union and the Arab League) to fight ISIS grows, has conferences, issues press statements, etc., it is still unclear what military, humanitarian and political backing actually is being provided by this coalition in the fight against ISIS, what successes they are having, and even something as comparatively straightforward as what exactly constitutes being a member of this coalition.

Realistically, sectarian, tribal, religious, jihadist and other conflict, disorder and chaos in the Middle East and North Africa is unlikely to improve significantly in the foreseeable future. In the midst of it all, ISIS will seek to take and hold more territory, proselytize and recruit more jihadists. Potential opposition forces exist, the so-called "moderate insurgents," that are unlikely to be melded together into cohesive anti-ISIS forces without a strategy and financing, fully supported by the US and its anti-ISIS coalition and especially Middle East members. This strategic anti-ISIS effort has to include a long-term commitment to security and protection, training, communication technology and military supplies and equipment, air support, and also humanitarian support for displaced persons.

Announced with great fanfare, the Pentagon program to train "moderate Syrian insurgents" to fight ISIS provides a classic example of why the US, no matter how important the counterinsurgency mission and how much money is spent, fails to perform successfully in recruitment, screening, and retention of insurgents and, perhaps most important, conveying the vital message that America knows what it is doing in the fight against both ISIS and ruthless dictators like President Bashar al-Assad of Syria.

In the summer of 2015, the United States and Turkey announced their joint plan to create an "Islamic State free-zone" in northern Syria, using warplanes flown from Turkish air bases and to secure the area freed of ISIS with a ground force consisting of US –trained Syrian insurgents. The Pentagon had spent the past year trying to find recruits in Syria to fight ISIS. After recruiting more than 1200 insurgents that were willing to join the program, the vetting process to root out "extremists" reduced the number who qualified to about 55. What the US discovered in the process was that most of the recruited insurgents were dedicated to fighting Assad, not ISIS, the comparative newcomer enemy in Syria.

Worse still, in an almost Keystone Cops episode, the Syrian army defector who recruited many of the insurgent-trainees for the US mission, together with his deputy and several of the trainees, were abducted by the Nusra Front in Syria near the Turkish border. The Nusra Front, the Islamist extremist affiliate of Al-Qaeda, designated by the US as a terrorist organization, also is an ISIS rival that for more than four years has fought Assad in the Syrian civil war. The Nusra Front has routed several US-backed insurgent groups (Syrian Revolutionaries Front and Harakat Hazm) in the last year. In Washington, several current and former senior administration officials acknowledged that the attack and the abductions by the Nusra Front took American officials by surprise and amounted to a significant intelligence failure.

Making the whole US effort along the Turkish-Syrian border even more complicated, at the same time the C.I.A is running a covert training program for fighters battling Assad's security forces. The insurgents trained by both US programs became targets of the Nusra Front. Both US programs have a common problem: working with Americans makes recruits a target not just of the

Islamic State but also of the Nusra Front. Gen. Petraeus even has suggested trying to induce members of Nusra to leave that group and join the US training program for "moderate insurgents." Rather than providing a viable new answer to offset the litany of U.S. insurgent recruitment failures, Petraeus's idea is unworthy of a remarkable senior US military officer who has redefined 21st century counterinsurgency (COIN).

The Pentagon, the CIA and military experts like Petraeus and others have known everything worth knowing about the violent insurgency in Syria that began as a non-violent, Arab Spring-inspired revolt against the tyranny of Assad's Baathist regime in 2011. They have known for at least four years that Al-Qaeda in Iraq (AQI) was one of the major forces driving the insurgency in Syria fighting both pro-Assad security forces and the Islamic State of Iraq and the Levant (ISIL). Insurgents in Syria cannot be recruited to just fight ISIS. After fighting Assad for years, most insurgents and their leadership also don't see the need for more training. The Pentagon would have to revamp its anti-ISIS strategy to include fighting pro-Assad forces and providing "safe-zones" for insurgents under no-fly zones to protect them from attacks by Assad's forces, Russian airstrikes, and ISIS.

At some point, as it tries to figure out which insurgents are moderate and which ones actually are terrorists, the US will have to decide how to deal with the Nusra Front in its "safe-zones" strategy. Abu Mohammed al-Golanim, leader of the Nusra Front, has made it clear that Nusra's main mission is to fight the regime of President Bashar al-Assad and Hezbollah supporting him. But there is plenty of evidence confirming that the Nusra Front is as much, perhaps even more, of a threat in Syria than ISIL. Human Rights Watch argues that the Nusra Front was "responsible for systematic and widespread violations including targeting civilians, kidnappings, and executions". The Nusra Front and ISIL share a common ideology and goals. The Nusra Front also wants to set up a caliphate and impose Islamic law and brutal sharia justice. The Nusra Front sees Iran as the main obstacle to its goal in Syria: to topple Assad and take over Damascus after Assad falls.

In each country in which Islamic extremists attract local civilian populations, it is because they portray themselves as upholders of righteousness by comparison with corrupt, authoritarian governments that lack legitimacy. In both Syria and Iraq, the response to ISIL has been a security-focused military strategy that has fed regional and local sectarian violence and the proliferation of sectarian militias filling security vacuums. Western support for supposedly "moderate insurgents" fighting against Assad's forces has exacerbated sectarian rifts, as Shiite militias have engaged in reprisals against Sunnis.

Lurking in Obama's mind and others advising the White House is that ISIS's predecessor, Al-Qaeda, was defeated at the cost of thousands of American lives and billions of dollars. After Americans left Iraq, Al-Qaeda terrorists have been reincarnated again in a more brutal and powerful manifestation. Haunting Obama is the question of how to avoid a repetition of costly past mistakes. Unfortunately lessons from the past have not taught the US and its allies how to avoid past failures or provided a strategy to defeat the Islamic State.

Apocalyptic and brutal ISIS seems to thrive on being attacked. In Syria, in order to enlist thousands of Sunni insurgents to attack ISIS will necessitate the removal of Assad. It will not be possible to enlist Sunni insurgent forces in Syria against ISIS on the ground while Assad remains in power. The US, Russia and Iran need to come to an agreement to remove Assad.

In addition, as a core part of a strategy to defeat ISIS, it's imperative that Saudi Arabia cease to support radical religious ideology and Islamic fundamentalist causes in the Gulf and Middle East which feed jihadists groups like ISIS. For the Saudis, jihadists are a proxy force fighting Iranian influence. Muslims in the Middle East will not become part of the solution to Islamic extremism without a sustained effort by Muslims to offer constructive alternatives to extremist versions of their religion. ISIS is thriving on a combination of Islamic extremism and the failure of Middle Eastern governments, both of which are turning young men radical in Muslim communities.

The strategic question for the US and secondarily its anti-ISIS coalition is how, while coping with and overcoming its own serious credibility problems, to intervene in escalating local and regional sectarian-based violence and local militarization that typically follows political and sectarian lines. Operating in alliances with Saudi Arabia, Turkey and various countries in the Gulf Coordinating Council (GCC), the strategic challenge becomes even more complex since each of these countries has their own strategic and political agendas that do not align with those of the US or insurgent allies in Syria, Iraq and Yemen. For example, some anti-Assad militias are being funded in Syria by Saudi and the GCC that in Iraq are labeled as "terrorists."

The US strategy has to redefine its train-and-assist missions into a strategically and tactically effective counterinsurgency strategy that, building on everything learned historically from COIN campaigns, seeks political compromises among insurgents, sectarian and ethnic groups versus reliance on winning military battles. This will take time. How much time, no one can predict. During this time, it will be essential to develop local insurgent capabilities in Iraq, Syria, Yemen, Afghanistan and Libya that, with protection and safety, can contain ISIS and other violent extremists, and hold and build civilian-military safe havens, sheltered by no-fly zones, with the assistance of forward-deployed advisors, armed with real-time intelligence, and supported as needed with timely and effective airstrikes and intelligence, surveillance and reconnaissance (ISR) sorties.

The strategic challenges in Syria have become even more complicated with the intervention of Russia in support of the Assad regime. Russia is backed by Iran and Hezbollah, its main proxy ground force in Syria. Russia has attacked insurgent fighters backed by the US that undoubtedly have been battling Assad's government as well as ISIS. Russia has dismissed the Pentagon's program to train and equip insurgents as ineffectual. If Russia is conducting airstrikes against insurgents that they define and target as "terrorists," the US has to protect its insurgent allies by adopting and supporting a safe havens strategy that includes no-fly zones.

President Obama has ordered the deployment of fewer than 50 commandos to help coalition forces coordinate with local troops in northern Syria. The White House stressed that this is not a "combat mission." The troops would train, advise and assist local forces in order to intensify lagging U.S. efforts against the Islamic State. The White House has emphasized that U.S. special operations forces will not move to the front lines, not go into battle with local forces and not call in airstrikes. U.S. forces would only help coordinate operations, planning and logistics.

Even this modest escalation of U.S. involvement in the fight against the Islamic State and other jihadist groups generated push back and criticism in the media from "experts" who interpreted it as "mission creep." None of these "experts" criticized the White House decision based on the lack of a strategy for both transforming its failed training and equipping mission in Syria and failure to provide assistance to tens of thousands of displaced Syrians. The next generation COIN (NexGen COIN) strategy in this volume proposes such as strategy – safehavens protected by no-fly zones – that deploys U.S. special forces, including frontline advisors armed with advanced information technologies, to protect and assist local forces and displaced civilians, and to contain ISIS in Syria and elsewhere.

Recently Gen. Joseph F. Dunford Jr., chairman of the Joint Chiefs of Staff, met with his top commanders during a stop in Iraq and told them to broaden their thinking and map out new ways that the U.S.-led coalition can put more pressure on ISIS fighters. What he did not say to his commanders was to look really closely at the lessons learned in Iraq, Afghanistan, Libya, and Yemen. For example, local forces supported by the U.S. are still struggling to retake the Iraqi city of Ramadi without reference to how, more than 10 years ago, an offensive led by Col. McFarland and his "Ready First" Brigade succeeded against one of the strongest Al-Qaeda strongholds in the Middle East.

Any strategy for containing and defeating ISIS has to include a safe haven strategy for displaced persons and refugees in the Middle East. More than 8 million Syrians and more than 2 million

Iraqis are internally displaced. Almost a million Yemenis have returned to Yemen from Saudi Arabia and Africa, and more than 300,000.are displaced in Yemen.

In Syria, Iraq, Yemen and elsewhere the International Organization for Migration (IOM) already is using SAS Institute's Big Data predictive analytics system for migrant tracking, humanitarian border management (HBM), systematic and continuous needs assessment of refugees and asylum-seekers, support for emergency response, management and recruitment of job seekers, community capacity-building, migrant return and reintegration assistance, and to manage coordination of assistance to displaced persons and migrants through data sharing. The strategy for NexGen COIN includes a partnership with IOM to collaborate on providing humanitarian services to displaced persons seeking refuge in safe havens.

This volume attempts to provide everything that American voters and their presidential candidates need to know about: all aspects of ISIS history and operations in the Middle East and North Africa; strategic next generation counterinsurgency (NexGen COIN) options for the US and its allies to fight ISIS; key lessons that should be learned for NexGen COIN planning from past and current US engagements in Syria, Iraq, Afghanistan, Libya and Yemen; the geopolitical context for NexGen COIN strategies and decisions covering Russia, Iran and its proxies, Saudi Arabia and the Gulf states, Turkey, the Kurds, and Egypt; and the potential consequences of the nuclear deal with Iran that frees up its funds frozen by sanctions.

Let's be clear that we all share the desire to obliterate ISIS. That said, the main purpose of this book, published during a presidential election year and in the aftermath of mass terrorist murders in France, Lebanon and Egypt, is to inject as much understanding and reality as possible into the debate about containing and destroying ISIS. Inevitably much of the political rhetoric about declarations of war and military action against ISIS is mostly just political noise and ventilating genuine and justifiable emotions. The key question in all of these reactions is,

ARNOLD SCHUCHTER

in addition to sustained airstrikes on ISIS targets, what is the right kind of strategic response and how would it work in the near- and long-term.

This view sounds much like President Obama recent remarks that military action has to be part of a broader strategy that the United States and its partners will pursue over many years. The key difference is that Obama, and also his post-9/11 predecessors in the White House, engaged in wars and counterinsurgencies in Iraq, Afghanistan, Syria, Libya and Yemen that did not have a broader strategy, their military decisions were based on misconceptions about how to fight the "enemy" and, in the instance of Iraq and Afghanistan, when and whether the wars were "won." In the past year, the United States has carried out more than 8,000 strikes against ISIS targets in Syria and Iraq, without any success in containing or defeating ISIS, and yet President Obama's strategy going forward is that there will be many more airstrikes.

More US ground forces will be needed to implement the proposed NexGen COIN strategy. But most of these ground forces can come from countries in the region with the backing of air power, intelligence, logistics and other support from the United States, France, Russia and other countries. Creating a unified effort to contain and defeat ISIS will not be easy and will take many years. The United States, Russia, Iran, Saudi and other governments have to figure out and agree on a strategy to contain and destroy ISIS, shut down its revenue streams, a political settlement to end the Syrian civil war and a "political transition" for Assad without alienating countless insurgent groups and destabilizing Syria further.

Historic sectarian animosities and geopolitical conflicts still prevail in the Middle East and Gulf region and overshadow every strategy for political stabilization or military action. Arab countries are divided on who really is the main enemy other than Shiites. Saudi Arabia, for example, is more concerned with Shiite Iran and its proxies and toppling Bashar al-Assad of Syria than fighting ISIS, although ISIS also is a threat to the Saudis. Turkey's main focus is to put down the separatist Kurds and secondarily removing

Assad. The fact that the Turk's enemy, the Syrian Kurds, is the only force in Syria containing ISIS is a problem for Turkey. The Syrian and Iraqi Kurds are focused on defending and expanding their borders and not defeating ISIS unless they threaten that goal. Iraq's government is primarily interested in protecting and preserving its Shiite-majority rule.

In retaliation for the Paris massacre, President François Hollande has expressed France's outrage with fighter jets sent to strike Islamic State targets in Raqqa, Syria. Russia joined France with its own bombing raids, airstrikes and cruise missiles. Irrespective of Russia's motivations, other than retaliation for ISIS bombing of the Russian Metrojet, both France and Russia presumably have taken the first steps in rallying the international community into a common cause based on a unified strategy. Presumably this will include passage of a United Nations Security Council resolution formally authorizing the use of force against the Islamic State. It may also include a NATO decision to invoke Article 5 of its treaty which obligates the alliance to defend its members under attack.

These important steps will still leave open the question of an effective strategy that includes both escalation of America's involvement and ways to significantly reduce the crisis of displaced persons in Syria and flow of refugees and migrants from the Middle East and Africa to Turkey and Europe. Parts I and II of this book cover most of what policy makers and strategists need to know about the factors in each Middle East and Gulf country that have to be addressed in developing a strategy aimed at containing and destroying ISIS and enabling displaced persons and refugees to remain in their home countries. Part III of this book, NexGen COIN, the abbreviation for next-generation counterinsurgency, incorporates all of the insights and lessons learned discussed in Parts I and II.

On a positive note to conclude this introduction to a book that may seem overly critical of the leadership and decisions made by US military commanders, at various times I refer to Col. Sean MacFarland as my model for remarkable COIN leadership in the Ramadi and Anbar campaign against Al-Qaeda. Col MacFarland now is Lt. Gen. MacFarland. Recently, without much fanfare, Defense Secretary Ashton Carter put Lt. Gen. Sean MacFarland in charge of the coalition fighting ISIS in Iraq and Syria. Carter's appointment followed justified criticism of the Obama administration's failed counter-ISIS campaign that, stretching from the White House across Defense and State Departments and the intelligence community, lacked coordinated leadership.

Instead of three generals responsible for different aspects of the counter-ISIS campaign, MacFarland will serve as the single commander of counter-ISIS activities in both Iraq and Syria. Additionally, Army Maj. Gen. Darsie Rogers, a Green Beret who was previously commander of the Army's 1st Special Forces Command at Fort Bragg, will take over as commander of U.S. special operations forces in the Middle East. Rogers has commanded Special Forces in Iraq numerous times over the past decade. Rogers will take command of U.S. Special Operations Command Central, or SOCCENT, located at MacDill Air Force Base, in Tampa, and co-located with U.S. Central Command (CENTCOM) which overseas operations in the Middle East.

PART I
FIGHTING THE ISLAMIC STATE (ISIS/ISIL)

CHAPTER 1

The ISIS Threat & Middle East Geopolitics

Many people, including most American voters, are asking themselves the questions: "Where did ISIS come from? How did it manage to conquer so much territory and do so much violence and damage to so many people in such a short period of time?" For those people who pay attention to the news, ISIS captured the city of Mosul, the capital of Iraq's Ninewah province more than a year ago, in June 2014, with only about a thousand of their foot soldiers against about 30,000 American-trained Iraqi soldiers and policemen, who then abandoned tens of millions of dollars in American equipment. And that was only the beginning of a surprise insurgency by a murderous theocratic jihadist group that has evolved out of a complex history covering several incarnations over more than a decade.

ISIS is engaged in a blood holy war. Targets include Shiites, various minority sects and other apostates, including American "crusaders" and their Zionist allies, and also innocent civilians. If anyone has any doubts about the ruthlessness and dangerousness of ISIS, they only need to look at the recent double suicide bombing in a busy shopping district in a mostly Shiite residential area of southern Beirut that killed dozens of people and wounded hundreds. Since Hezbollah maintains tight security control in the district, the suicide attack highlights not only Lebanon's vulnerability to the murderous wrath of the Islamic State but the vulnerability of virtually every neighborhood anywhere else.

Add this attack to several others, one on the same day and another in the same week: in the same day, shootings and several explosions in different locations erupted in Paris killing at least 40 people and wounding dozens while dozens were taken hostage; in the same week, the Islamic State's bombing of a jetliner full of Russian vacationers from the Sinai Peninsula in Egypt. The shootings in Paris occurred near the former headquarters of Charlie Hebdo, the satirical newspaper where shootings by Islamic militants in January traumatized France.

Shocking as it may seem, Osama bin Laden might qualify as a moderate in the fanatical spectrum of ISIS leadership. Just as Al-Qaeda terrorism took root in Syria, ISIS has been flourishing and developing in fertile conditions created by Assad's Alawite regime surrounded by a victimized Sunni majority. In Iraq ISIS supporters are a Sunni minority victimized by the ethnic cleansing of Iranian-built Shiite militia groups and other Shiites in control of the country. ISIS's capital and the headquarters of its military forces, Syria's Raqqa, houses its sophisticated intelligence-gathering, recruitment, and communication and propaganda operation, dedicated to destroying nation states and reestablishing a caliphate.

The roots of the Islamic State (ISIS/ISIL) can be traced back to the late Abu Musab al-Zarqawi, a Jordanian who set up Tawhid wa al-Jihad in Jordan in 2002. A year after the US-led invasion of Iraq (2003), Zarqawi pledged allegiance to Osama Bin Laden and formed Al-Qaeda in Iraq (AQI). AQI expanded into a militant network for the purpose of resisting coalition occupation forces and their Iraqi allies. After Zarqawi's death (2006), AQI created the Islamic State in Iraq (ISI). Abū Bakr al-Baghdādi became the leader of ISI in 2010. In addition to focusing on Iraq, ISI joined the rebellion against President Bashar al-Assad in Syria.

In April 2013, Baghdadi announced the merger of his forces in Iraq and Syria and the creation of "Islamic State in Iraq and the

Levant". When announcing the formation of ISIL, al-Baghdadi stated that the jihadist faction, Jabhat al-Nusra (Nusra Front), that had been an extension of ISI in Syria, would now be merged with ISIL. The leader of Jabhat al-Nusra, Abut Mohammad al-Julani, rejected the merger and appealed to al-Qaeda's emir Ayman al Zawahiri who declared that ISIL should be abolished and that al-Baghdadi should confine ISIS to Iraq. Al-Baghdadi dismissed al-Zawahiri's ruling.

At the end of December 2013, ISIS did shift its focus back to Iraq and, aided by tribesmen and former Saddam Hussein loyalists, took control of Fallujah. In January 2014, ISIL expelled Jabhat al-Nusra from the Syrian city of Al-Raqqah and made it ISIS's headquarters. In June 2014, ISIS overran Iraq's second largest city, Mosul, and then advanced southwards towards Baghdad. When ISIS burst on to the scene, seizing large swathes of territory in Syria and Iraq, it also became notorious for its brutality, including mass killings, abductions and beheadings. ISIS demanded that Muslims across the world swear allegiance to its leader, Abu Bakr al-Baghdadi.

On 29 June 2014, ISIS announced the establishment of a worldwide caliphate with Al-Baghdadi as Caliph. By September 2014, ISIS controlled much of the Tigris-Euphrates river basin, an area as large as the United Kingdom. ISIS forces grew to include about 30,000 foreign fighters from as many as 80 countries, with the majority probably from nearby Arab countries, such as Tunisia, Libya, Saudi Arabia, Jordan and Morocco.

In roughly a dozen years, ISIS/ISIL has surpassed Al-Qaeda as an international jihadist movement, but still is only one among many terrorist groups that threaten the US and the international community. The US and its global partners share the common goal of degrading ISIS's capacity to wage insurgent warfare and expand territorial control in Iraq, Syria and elsewhere. But they have not achieved success thus far by supporting Iraqi security forces and moderate Syrian opposition to ISIS, countering ISIS's social media messaging, stemming the flow of foreign fighters, and enhancing intelligence collection.

ISIS's capacity to wage war includes access to and the capability of using a wide variety of small arms and heavy weapons, including truck-mounted machine-guns, rocket launchers, anti-aircraft guns, portable surface-to-air missile systems, captured tanks and armored vehicles, including armored Humvees and bomb-proof trucks originally manufactured for the US military. ISIS has established a supply chain that ensures a constant supply of ammunition and firepower for its fighters.

ISIS's funding resources are unknown but very substantial. Last year, the US Department of the Treasury's Undersecretary for Terrorism and Financial Intelligence, David Cohen, in a speech at the Carnegie Endowment for International Peace in Washington, said: "[ISIS] has amassed wealth at an unprecedented pace and its revenue sources have a different composition from those of many other terrorist organizations." ISIS doesn't "depend principally on moving money across international borders," he said, but "obtains the vast majority of its revenues from local criminal and terrorist activities." ISIS's broad and lucrative financial portfolio generates millions every day from countless revenue streams, including the sale of crude oil and refined products, robbing, looting, extortion, special taxes, raiding banks, selling antiquities, controlling sales of livestock and crops, selling sex slaves, and others.

When ISIS proclaimed its caliphate, in 2014, it already had established sources and amounts of financing that were unprecedented in the world of global terrorism and criminality, except for the drug cartels of Mexico and Central America. In addition to its financial resources, the real threats from ISIS are that: it is not just a terrorist organization in one country or location but a federated organization; and it includes large numbers of foreign fighters that in many instances return home. For example, about 6000 foreign fighters in ISIS have been Europeans and now about 1500 are back home; an estimated 7000 ISIS fighters came from Russia; and about 300 from the United States.

It should come as no shock to either Egypt or the international community that an ISIS affiliate called Sinai Province claimed responsibility for the recent crash of an Airbus A321 operated by a Russian carrier that was bringing holidaymakers home from the Sinai Peninsula. Egypt has been a dangerous place for years. Egypt's President Sisi is well aware of the dangers from extremists in the Sinai, Libya and elsewhere. Egypt claims that it has been warning the international community to do more to tackle the spread of terrorism. As indicated in the chapter on "Sisi's Egypt," counterinsurgency assistance to Egypt from the US and other Western countries has been complicated by Egypt's crackdown on political opposition groups, like the Muslim Brotherhood, in the name of counter-terrorism.

Whether or not Egypt's Western "partners" have been taking its warnings about terrorism threats seriously enough, US and other intelligence agencies have been monitoring the network of ISIS affiliates and reportedly did intercept "chatter" between ISIS leaders in Syria and the Sinai Province that boasted about bringing down the Russian jet. Even with Western intelligence agencies monitoring ISIS leadership and UK telephone surveillance of Egyptian militants in the Sinai Peninsula, the terrorist attack on the Russian jet was not prevented. The crash of the Russian charter jet provides yet another post-9/11 wake-up call for aviation authorities in the US and around the world to the fact that most major airports are extremely vulnerable to terrorists employed as ground workers that have not been sufficiently vetted or screened along with their carry ons when reporting for work.

Until a terrorist attack like the one near Sharm el-Sheikh made headlines, most people were unaware that: as many as a thousand Egyptian soldiers, police, and civilians have been killed in terrorist attacks in the Sinai Peninsula since 2011; Islamic extremists shot down a helicopter in January 2014 over the Sinai using a man-portable air-defense system (MANPADS); and jihadists carried out a suicide attack against a tour bus of Korean pilgrims in the Sinai. More than 20,000 tourists from the UK and 80,000 Russians vacationing annually in Sharm el-Sheikh apparently have been oblivious to these and other terrorist events in the Sinai Province conducted by an ISIS affiliate, the Islamic State of the Sinai (Walayat al Sinai) that, over a the last four years, has become one of the most dangerous extremist groups in the

7

world. The Islamic State of the Sinai has drawn on resources and expertise over these years from other ISIS affiliates, presumably including for the purpose of the attack on Russian Metrojet Flight 9268.

Financing and ideology provide the potential for ISIS's affiliate network in the Middle East and globally to become extremely dangerous and destructive on an unprecedented scale and not just in terms of human lives. In addition to its seizure of energy assets in Iraq, with the fifth-largest proven crude oil reserves in the world, and in Syria, ISIS also has obtained a vast amount of steady financial support from private donors, heavy taxation and extortion levied on its captive populations, seizure of bank accounts and private assets in lands it occupies, ransoms from kidnappings and the plundering of antiquities excavated from ancient palaces and archaeological sites. Estimates of ISIS's cash and assets from various sources far exceed $2 billion.

Financing sources of the ISIS jihadist network have provoked conspiracy theories and rumors that extend from the Assad regime buying electricity and gas from ISIS to US and other multinationals trying to buy protection for their Middle East energy assets. But what has been known for several years, and confirmed by US State and Treasury departments, is that Persian Gulf countries, America's allies in the Middle East, have been major sources of funding for Sunni terrorist groups in Syria such as Jabhat al-Nusra and also ISIS. Wealthy citizens in the Gulf States and Saudi Arabia have contributed hundreds of millions of dollars to extremists in the Syrian conflict. Qatar and Kuwait especially have been singled out as terrorist financing sources by the State Department's annual Country Reports on Terrorism.

Financing of ISIS and other jihadist groups by wealthy individuals in Persian Gulf countries has continued even after the US Treasury Department imposed financial sanctions on Kuwait and Qatar. For many years, Qatar openly financed Hamas, designated by the US as a terrorist organization. Enforcement of actions in Gulf States against terrorist financing has been lacking. Gulf States have viewed payments to ISIS and other jihadists as a form of insurance to protect their own security. Kuwait, for example, has a Sunni majority that is not happy with the nation's governance and also its failure to support Sunnis under attack in Syria. Fund-raising in Kuwait for jihadists also has been driven by powerful Sunni clerics that Kuwaitis have been reluctant to offend.

In other words, in country by country in the Persian Gulf a variety of political factors have favored continuation of ISIS financing and limited the ability of the US to restrain financing of jihadists through a complex array of opaque channels. For example, individuals in Gulf States have used the Internet to launder funds to ISIS through "charities" with funds disguised as humanitarian aid. Donations from individuals in Kuwait to jihadists in Syria have amounted to hundreds of millions in cold cash without any paper trail. A great deal of dark money also has been transported to ISIS by and through criminal networks from Turkey into Syria.

In addition to these various illicit fund-raising campaigns, ISIS looted 12 bank branches when it took over Mosul, Iraq, and the bank vaults in Tikrit, which contained an estimated total of $1.5 billion. Now Afghanis making withdrawals from banks in ISIS-occupied cities are "taxed" up to 10 percent. In the ISIS headquarters of Raqqa, Syria, and other cities controlled by ISIS, all goods coming into and out of the city are taxed. ISIS taxes people transporting anything and everything throughout its "caliphate." Every shopkeeper and street vendor has to pay a monthly fee to stay in business.

The systematic looting and trading of antiquities and artifacts has become an ISIS business worth hundreds of millions of dollars. Most of these antiquities are moved through black markets in Turkey, Jordan and Iran. Not quite as lucrative but close is the hundreds of thousands of tons of stolen wheat, barley, and rice stored in dozens of captured silos that is sold to people living in ISIS territory. Everyone living in ISIS-controlled territories in Iraq and Syria become part of the totalitarian ISIS marketplace, including thousands of people kidnapped and held for ransom, and women and girls forced into marriage or sold into sexual slavery (unless they convert to Islam).

The lootings, bank robberies, ransoms, taxes and fees, selling sex slaves, extortion, contributions from wealthy individuals, and other sources of funding for ISIS's day-to-day operations and war machine are dwarfed by its oil trafficking, even with the price of oil declining dramatically in 2015. Before the decline in global oil prices, ISIS was earning up to $50 million a month from selling crude from oilfields under its control in Iraq and Syria. Thus far US airstrikes have failed to shut down ISIS's oil sales that are its largest single source of continual income. ISIS has imported equipment and technical experts from places like Turkey to keep its oil industry running, including equipment for extraction, refinement, transport and energy production.

At its peak ISIS operated around 350 oil wells in Iraq with a combined production capacity of 80,000 barrels a day, just a fraction of Iraq's total production of around 3 million barrels a day. ISIS controls over 250 oil wells in Syria of which more than half are operational. That represents about 60 percent of Syria's production capacity. As much as 30,000 barrels per day is extracted from Syria and shipped to Turkey. Around 10,000-20,000 barrels of oil per day produced in Iraq is sent to refineries in Syria. ISIS's management of its oil fields, refineries and distribution of oil has become increasingly sophisticated. ISIS sells crude to smugglers far below-market prices, sometimes as low as $10-$25 a barrel. Smugglers in turn sell to middlemen, for example, in Turkey, that move the oil to tankers for resale.

Every American voter should know by now that the next US president not only will have to deal with the Islamic State but, based on commitments made along the campaign trail, will have to do so on his or her very first day in office. Fortunately there's plenty of time left in the political campaign for candidates' ideas about warfare with ISIS to be more fully developed. Otherwise, however, time to deal with the Islamic State of Iraq and all of its terrorist successors is running out.

ISIS closely resembles a virulent disease, life threatening and deadly, spreading on the ground in the Middle East, North Africa and elsewhere, and "airborne" through social media. No matter how many times ISIS tries to shock the world with beheadings and other butcherings and executions of prisoners and "apostates," the world has not been shocked enough, except in rare instances, to fully mobilize and sustain campaigns to destroy, not just repudiate, the jihadist organisms causing the disease that has been spreading for two decades.

Equivalents of the horrific terrorist attacks of September 11, 2001 on New York and Washington occur almost every day somewhere in the Middle East, sanctified by an ideology that justifies killing and destruction all over the world. These brutal acts of terrorism usually don't make headlines and get the attention of American voters. An exception was the explosion of Russian Metrojet 9268 in the air over Egypt on October 31, 2015 which made headlines and got the attention not only of the White House and American voters but the Transportation Safety Administration (TSA) in the US and the aviation industry around the world, all of whom know that their airports and airplanes are more or less as vulnerable to terrorism as Sharm el-Sheikh in Egypt. In the US, for example, tens of thousands of ground workers at the nation's airports are not screened and vetted by TSA. ISIS terrorists have explosive devices that a radicalized ground worker could place in a cargo hold of inbound US flights.

Moscow's responses in the past to violent terrorism by Chechen Islamic extremists within their own borders has been overwhelming targeted force. If anyone doubts Putin's and Russia's reaction to terrorism, and what it means for their invasion of and support for Bashar al-Assad in Syria, revisit Russia's retaking of Moscow's Dubrovka Theater occupied by Chechen terrorists during the 2002 hostage crisis. Even Russia's own citizens would not be spared in order to deal with terrorism at home. What Putin was determined not to do about Chechen terrorism was to respond in a half-hearted way. In Russia or Syria, Moscow wants to avoid any perception of weakness in response to terrorism, but also avoid provoking widespread Islamic terrorism within Russia's own borders, knowing that as much as 20% of his country's population is Sunni Muslim.

In addition to a post 9/11 reawakening of the world's aviation industry to its vulnerability to terrorism in airports and on airplanes, the tragic fate of Russia's Metrojet highlighted that the deadly disease of ISIS terrorism comes in different forms in different countries, and that responses to ISIS by the US and its allies or Russia have to be shaped by different strategies in Syria, Iraq, Afghanistan, Libya, Yemen, Egypt and elsewhere. All of these responses should have one central strategic goal – contain and destroy ISIS while protecting civilians, especially in key population centers, and enabling them to remain safely in their homelands and avoid migration.

In every country where ISIS is flourishing, however, the most difficult strategic challenge for containment and defeat of ISIS will be how to fundamentally change governance in these nations. For example, Jihadists and ISIS flourishing in the Sinai Province has been as much the fault of the Egyptian government, that lost the people's trust, support and loyalty, as the success of ISIS radicalization. The same conclusion holds true for other countries in the Middle East and Africa. Syria, Iraq, Libya, Afghanistan and Yemen provide ample proof of the critical important of what counterinsurgency (COIN) strategy terms "nation-building" and restoring the legitimacy of national governance. The same holds true for US and coalition forces engaged in fighting ISIS. If they are viewed as fighting Islamic extremists and occupying territory on behalf of corrupt, ineffective, and hostile political regimes, it becomes impossible to mobilize support from local insurgents.

In June 2010 Gen. McChrystal was relieved of his command. He and some of his staff had made "controversial" comments about the Obama administration in a *Rolling Stone* interview. At virtually the same time, after eight years of war and on the brink of failure, McChrystal had forced the White House to rethink its strategy in Afghanistan. He warned the White House that the war in Afghanistan would be lost if a great many more troops did not arrive in the next 12 months. McChrystal also made it very clear that the Afghan government was too corrupt to support the US mission. More important, however, lost in the controversy with the White House, was McChrystal's strategic and radical change in how US troops needed to operate in Afghanistan.

McChrystal said that protecting the Afghan people is more important than killing the enemy, even if that means US troops taking more risks. "This is something that takes a tremendous amount of understanding. What I'm really telling people is the greatest risk we can accept is to lose the support of the people here," McChrystal explained to correspondent David Martin of CBS News. "If the people are against us, we cannot be successful. If the people view us as occupiers and the enemy, we can't be successful and our casualties will go up dramatically." As the author says in "Lessons Learned in the Anbar Awakening," Col. Sean MacFarland, commander of the Ready First Brigade, said essentially the same thing about the battle for Ramadi, Anbar Province and Iraq in his candid interview with Steven Clay.

In countries throughout the Middle East and Africa, as diverse as Saudi Arabia, Libya, Algeria, Nigeria, Yemen, Afghanistan and Pakistan, chapters of ISIS have been able to promise freedom from tyrannical regimes and the creation of a just society, even though they delivered cruel dictatorships. Nevertheless, there are differences in ISIS chapters from country to country. ISIS in the "Sinai Province" is very different from ISIS in, for example, Iraq and Syria. It consists mostly of local groups of jihadists, including many Bedouins and their tribal leaders, that grew out of long-standing grievances with the Egyptian state that have grown in recent years. One of these jihadist groups, called Ansar Bait al-Maqdis or "Champions of the Holy House", dedicated to battling Israel, claimed responsibility for several bombings of a main gas pipeline that connects Egypt with Israel and Jordan.

When Abdel Fattah Sisi took power as president of Egypt in 2013, he launched a crackdown on jihadist groups in the Sinai that further alienated the local population. This led to the emergence of "Sinai Province" (Wilayat Sinai) that grew out of and supplanted Ansar Bait al-Maqdis. Since the Metrojet crash, we have learned that Wilayat Sinai operates autonomously but became an ISIS affiliate that pledged allegiance to the main ISIS group located in Raqqa, Syria. Although small, what Israeli and other intelligence agencies have learned from recent attacks by the group on Egyptian military installations is that Wilayat Sinai appears to be run by professionals skilled at planning and highly effective and organized for carrying out attacks. Countless ISIS affiliates in Syria, Iraq, Afghanistan, Libya, Yemen, and elsewhere are developing the same capabilities with assistance from ISIS headquarters in Raqqa.

At the same time that battling ISIS and other jihadists in the Middle East and North Africa is becoming a more urgent priority for the European Union (EU), by necessity the EU has had to focus more planning and resources on stopping or slowing the flow of displaced persons, refugees, asylum seekers and migrants from these regions to Europe. Many Africans are leaving their homelands because of repression and conflicts. Thus far in 2015, more than 150,000 people are estimated to have crossed the Mediterranean from Libya to Italy. The largest single group is from Eritrea and others come from Nigeria, Mali and the Sudan. Many Africans have been migrating for economic and political reasons other than warfare and the threats of terrorism. Strategies for battling ISIS and Islamic terrorism in any country have to include strategies for significantly reducing the flow of migrants to Europe for any reasons.

Recently the EU announced a 1.8 billion euro fund (roughly $2 billion) for African countries from which migrants originate in an effort to provide incentives for young Africans to stay home, acquire skills and education, start businesses and find jobs. Europe also has adopted punitive measures to prevent migration and human smuggling from Africa. The overarching problem for Europe is that although keeping out economic migrants is an urgent political priority, Africa needs to provide ways for many millions of frustrated young Africans who have no job prospects to find economic opportunities elsewhere that are not available in their countries. The same could be said for young people in Iraq, Afghanistan and elsewhere in the Middle East.

The pressure for quick and decisive action by the next president is likely to grow in 2015-2016 propelled by: continued territorial expansion of ISIS in the Middle East; the likelihood of a growing European refugee and migration crisis; escalating tensions with

Russia over its aggressive military actions in Syria; Iran's support for its proxies in the aftermath of its nuclear deal and relief of sanctions; intensification of the civil war and humanitarian crisis in Yemen and related conflicts between Saudi Arabia, the Gulf States and Iran; and not least of all the likely continued meltdown of government forces in both Iraq and Afghanistan. Periodic responses of the Obama administration to any and all of these factors have been weak and, in the context of the root causes, absurd.

Former Secretary of Defense Robert Gates doesn't mince words when he talks about the foreign policy and defense responses of his former boss, President Obama, the Pentagon and its enormous dysfunctional bureaucracy, and Congress. Read his very forthright memoir, *Duty*, for fascinating insights and details. After serving six presidents in the CIA and National Security Agency (NSA), his opinion on defense strategy and tactics should count for presidential candidates and voters in 2016. In response to the now suspended $500 million US plan to train Syrian rebel fighters outside of the country to fight ISIS, Gates bluntly said in an interview with the Fox News Channel's "Special Report" that it was "nuts."

The Obama Administration and the Pentagon have stumbled from one Syrian strategy and setback to another. The White House's good intentions included doing something to significantly reduce the vast flow of Syrian refugees and displaced persons. "The only way you can staunch the humanitarian flow, the humanitarian disaster, is through some kind of a safe haven and I think that that's achievable," said Gates. The author agrees with Gates to a point. A safe haven strategy has to be accompanied by a political solution for President Assad's Syria, which has become much more complicated and unpredictable with Russia's recent military engagement, but also possibly even more feasible.

The White House and the Pentagon recently decided to deploy 50 members of US special forces to guide greatly increased airstrikes against ISIS in support of moderate insurgents in northern Syria. The White House's decision is too late and the projected number of special forces are too small to make any real difference in the Syrian battlefront, especially with the Russian air force supporting Assad's ground forces, Hezbollah and the Iranians. In addition, the White House's plan does not include a strategy for containing ISIS or, in lieu of no fly zones, creating protective safe havens in Syria's borders with Turkey and Jordan to shield both insurgents and displaced civilians.

Protected safe havens (or safe zones) for Syrians displaced from their homes by the civil war could protect civilians from attack while they remain on Syrian soil, and thereby presumably (no guarantees) would reduce the flow of refugees from Syria to neighboring states and to Europe. Already 4 million Syrian refugees are in Turkey, Lebanon, and Jordan according to the United Nations High Commissioner for Refugees. A protected safe haven also would provide a sanctuary where moderate Syrian rebels could train and from which they could conduct operations against both the Assad regime and the Islamic State. Safe zones on the ground would require ground forces for protection and no-fly-zones above. The US does not have the ground forces to secure safe zones and is unwilling to create no-fly zones.

With the skies above under control, the main challenges for protecting safe havens are on the ground. Attacks or infiltration on the ground, bombardment by artillery, rockets and missiles are even more of a threat than air strikes by either the Syrian regime or the Soviets "by accident." In addition to close air support, safe havens need aerial surveillance. Other than supplies and services for displaced persons and refugees, the biggest and most expensive requirement for safe zones would be a large commitment of competent ground forces to protect borders and police the area.

One of the main criticisms from insurgents leveled at the US and coalition forces is that they refuse to provide anti-aircraft weapons and yet provide no safety from air attacks. That complaint was being made before Russia's military commitment which raises the specter of potential long-range rocket and ballistic missile attacks. In addition to providing a refuge for besieged civilians, safe havens should provide safety for Syrian opposition forces seeking to escape from air attacks. Safe havens would need protection by anti-tactical ballistic missile systems such as the US Patriot, in addition to effective defenses against shorter-range artillery rockets and even cruise missiles fired from ships either in the Mediterranean or Caspian Sea.

A logical area for locating safe zones might be the roughly 1,800 square mile "Islamic-State-free zone" along the Turkish border with Syria to which Turkey and the US agreed in July 2015. But that 60 mile-long area along the Turkish border sooner or later could turn out to be insufficient in size to absorb displaced persons and refugees heading there not only from Syria but also from Iraq and Afghanistan displacement and elsewhere. In addition, establishment and support for the Islamic-State-free zone becoming the location or a network of safe havens would depend on continuing political and military support from a very ambivalent Turkey.

Safe havens cannot work without no-fly zones. Because of its pivotal connection to safe havens or safe zones for civilians in Syria, no-fly zones unquestionably will become one of the top – and most controversial -- issues for candidates and voters in the 2016 presidential campaign. The White House and its national security team have been assessing the pros and cons of safe havens and no-fly zones in terms of potential unintended consequences and serious escalation of conflict in Syria. The White House has stressed the difficulty, complexity and cost of setting up a no-fly zone in Syria and rejected that option in favor of "strengthening a moderate opposition."

The White House's position in part was in response to comments made in June 2015 by Russia's Foreign Ministry spokesman, Alexander Lukashevich, that Russia will not permit no-fly zones to be imposed over Syria, and also in anticipation of trying not to antagonize Moscow before joining Russia at the negotiating table to plan a "political transition" for Syrian President Bashar al-Assad.

Sen. Marco Rubio (R-Fla.) has said, in an interview with CNBC's John Harwood, that he would be willing to risk going to war with

Russia in order to enforce a no-fly zone in Syria. Doing nothing, Rubio has argued, would only embolden ISIS and increase the number of refugees coming out of Syria. "I am confident the Air Force can enforce that," Rubio said of a hypothetical safe zone in Syria. "I believe the Russians would not test that. I don't think it's in the Russians' interest to engage in an armed conflict with the United States."

Rubio isn't the only GOP presidential contender to voice support for establishing a no-fly zone in Syria. Former Florida Gov. Jeb Bush, former Hewlett-Packard CEO Carly Fiorina, and Sen. Lindsey Graham (R-S.C.) have done so as well. For these candidates there is no conviction that Putin will back down when faced with US imposition of a no-fly zone to protect safe havens for civilians and insurgents. Their position is that the US cannot cede to Putin (and also Iran) the role of dominant geopolitical power broker in Syria and the Middle East. Many military experts, however, don't agree with the aggressive opinion of these presidential candidates that the US has no choice other than to impose a unilateral no-fly zone at a time when Russian aircraft are already present in the sky over Syria.

Former Secretary of State Hillary Clinton has said that she supports creating "a no-fly zone and humanitarian corridors to try to stop the carnage on the ground and from the air." Sen. Bernie Sanders (I-Vt.) said that he opposes imposition of a no-fly zone because it could get America "deeply involved in that horrible civil war and lead to a never-ending US entanglement in that region." At the moment, therefore, it appears highly likely that establishing a no-fly zone in support of safe havens will be front and center as a foreign policy in forthcoming presidential debates and, very possibly, on the president's desk on the first day in the Oval Office.

Based on his experience working for both George W. Bush and Obama, Gates agrees with Barack Obama's White House that the US's role in the Syrian war "should be limited." The key issue for the next president pertaining to Syria and the Middle East will be American boots-on-the-ground and creation of one or more safe havens supported by no-fly zones. Gates was emphatic about one of these issues: "I would not put [US] ground troops in Syria."

What Gates learned from his time as secretary of defense was that wars are much easier to get into than out of and that presidents and their national security advisors, when confronted with tough challenges on foreign soil, are "too quick to reach for a gun." Gate's nemesis in Washington was, and still is, ideologues on the left or right who view American military intervention as a first option. Gates is critical of Obama for political leadership failures but also appreciative of his understanding that there are limits to what the greatest nation on earth can do with military power.

According to Gates, the worst fallacy in presidential and defense decision-making is that US military engagements, such as in Iraq, Afghanistan and Libya, start without any clear exit strategies. They also start by making decisions about the use of military force without looking analytically and dispassionately at critical past lessons learned from realities on the ground. Not enough questions are asked in the NSC decision-making process about 'what if our assumptions prove wrong.' Gates quotes Petraeus at an early stage in Iraq saying, "Tell me how this ends." Questions not asked in defense and national security decision-making often are more important than seemingly brilliant answers.

Russia's airstrikes in Syria have unexpectedly moved Putin to the front of a roster of foreign policy issues for voters and 2016 presidential candidates. Russia's political and military intervention in Syria qualifies as a strategic "game changer" even though Russia has provided financial and military support to Syria and Assad for many years. In a strategic and geopolitical context, it's really difficult to know what Putin has in mind for Syria and Assad going forward. Putin's military support for Assad means that, and the Russians already have shown, he will ruthlessly attack insurgent opposition to Assad that mainly consists of Sunni Muslims, which constitute the vast majority of Syria's population.

Russia has supported the Assad regime for many years. But the latest effort to save Bashar al-Assad sends a really important and timely message to other countries in a region in which states are collapsing and despots, that also were former US allies, like Qaddafi in Libya and Mubarak in Egypt, lost America's support. While the Obama administration shows extreme caution in its Middle East policies, Russia aggressively asserts itself. Even Middle East and Gulf countries that don't agree with Russian military actions in Syria are impressed by Russia's military intervention.

At the very least, Russia's intervention is likely to strengthen Assad's hand in any future political settlement and, even if Assad is pushed out, it will strengthen Russia's role in shaping Syria's future. With ISIS as the excuse, Russia may have acted very quickly in Syria because Assad's military position was rapidly weakening, but Putin probably had other goals in mind, like showing other countries in the region that Russia stands behind its friends.

Reminiscent of the story of Ramadi in the Great Awakening discussed later, changing the core US message to locals became a catalyst for significantly increasing their support in the battle against Al-Qaeda: instead of Americans saying that "the US will leave as soon as possible," the message was changed to "we'll stay until the job is done – and cover your back come hell or high water!" Arguably the strategy behind Russia's message of steadfastness and decisiveness in support of Assad in part is aimed at Egyptian President Abdel Fattah al-Sisi, who has visited Moscow four times since taking power in 2013. Even Saudi Arabia's leadership, which opposes Russian support for Assad, has visited Putin and signed cooperation agreements in various fields. Israeli Prime Minister Netanyahu has visited Putin to work out security agreements to protect Israel in the aftermath of Assad's downfall.

For Russia the financial cost of its strategy in Syria has been minimal and the benefits potentially considerable. Even while attacking insurgents in Syria along with ISIS, Russia broadcasts the message internationally that it is committed to dealing with jihadists that increasingly are terrorizing Pakistan, Indonesia,

Yemen, Morocco, Afghanistan, Saudi Arabia, Bangladesh, Tunisia, Egypt/Sinai, and also Russia in the Caucasus. In contrast, seemingly muddling along, the US is trying to figure out: how to fight ISIS without supporting jihadi groups; support Kurdish fighters without alienating Turkey; get rid of Assad without direct action and any vision for Syria's future; and avoid more costly military and political quagmires resembling Iraq and Afghanistan.

Russia's campaign, like so much else involved in the Syrian civil war, could have serious unintended consequences for Russia and the Assad regime. Putin's protection of the Assad regime's pro-Iranian Alawites/Shiites, verifiably accused of genocide, not only is likely to alienate the rest of the Sunni Muslim world, but also Muslims in Russia and the Caucasus that have been joining ISIS in large numbers. Supposedly the threat posed by Chechens and Islamic extremists in Russia's Caucasus are part of Putin's rationale for military invasion of Syria to attack Islamic extremism.

Russia has fought two wars against Islamist separatists in Chechnya. Concerning for Moscow is that several commanders from the Emirate Caucasus in Chechnya and Dagestan already have switched their allegiance to ISIS. Putin may be somewhat comforted that thousands of jihadists from Chechnya and Dagestan are leaving Russia for Syria. What is Putin's post-ISIS end-game strategy, assuming that his defense of Assad is successful? There are not many Sunni Muslims in Syria that could be recruited to support a Putin-engineered post-Assad regime.

From Moscow's perspective, its eyes may not be focused as much on what ISIS is doing in Syria or in the Sinai peninsula as much as on Russia's North Caucasus region where recently militants in Dagestan, Chechnya, Ingushetia, and Kabardino-Balkaria declared allegiance to ISIS and its Caliph, Abu Bakr al-Baghdadi, and established the Islamic State of the Caucasus. The ISIS governorate in the Caucasus called Wilayat Qawqaz is challenging the existing al-Qaeda affiliate, Islamic Emirate of the Caucasus, formed in 2007. ISIS has vowed to liberate Chechnya and the North Caucasus from Russia and depose Putin. A YouTube video produced in the ISIS capital of Raqqa included a Russian speaker, jets and military equipment that all came from Russia. "This message is for you, Vladimir Putin!" said the fighter. "These are the aircraft you sent to Bashar [Assad], and we're going to send them to you. Remember that!"

With Russia's military and political intervention in Syria, the rapid removal of President Assad no longer is on the negotiating table. The political solution for Syria and its "political transition" for President Assad are primarily in the hands of Moscow and its Iranian allies. Iran, a key part of Assad's military and financial support for many years, may not continue to participate in the peace negotiations, depending on the future involvement and behavior of the Saudis. The United States has NATO countries, including Turkey, as allies in the Syrian peace negotiations but Saudi Arabia and members of the Gulf Coordinating Council (GCC) definitely would rather not negotiate with Iran and will not accept anything less than Assad's immediate removal from office.

Closely watching negotiations on Assad's "political transition," Syrian insurgent groups that have been fighting Assad (not ISIS) for years understandably could conclude that, after promising aid for years that never arrived in sufficient amounts, the US is preparing to join with Russia and Iran in shaping a political outcome for the Assad regime that marginalizes them. In the forthcoming Vienna peace talks, Russia, Iran and the US each will submit lists of which insurgent groups qualify for participation. In the final analysis, Russia and Iran may hold the trump cards for selecting "qualified" insurgent participants in future peace talks. Ironically it is Russia, Iran and its proxies that are battling Syrian insurgents on behalf of protecting Assad who has killed more than 250,000 Syrian innocent civilians and rebel opponents of his regime.

Any negotiated US-Russia collaboration that supports Assad at the expense of insurgents is likely to further radicalize them, potentially driving more of them to join forces with the Islamic State or other extremist groups. Depending on the nature of a U.S deal with the Kremlin, it also could send a message to Muslims, and certainly to those from the Caucasus and in Afghanistan, that what the Islamic State has said is correct about the West being the enemy of Muslims. The US very badly needs an end-game strategy for Syria that avoids these pitfalls.

The Obama White House has consistently refused to engage in the war against Assad's regime in Syria and to put boots on the ground in support of insurgents fighting both ISIS and the Assad regime. The US has relied instead on thousands of airstrikes against ISIS and in support of Kurds and rebel forces fighting both ISIS and Assad. By agreement with Turkey, the US now is basing warplanes at Incirlik air base in Turkey to make it easier to increase strikes against ISIS in northern Syria and Iraq.

In its air campaign, the US has relied heavily on air support from its Arab allies and minor contributions from other Western allies, including Britain, France and Australia. As the US recently intensified airstrikes against ISIS in Syria, sending two dozen attack planes to its new Incirlik base in Turkey, support from both Arab and Western allies has virtually vanished. Persian Gulf states mostly have been focused on supporting rebels fighting the government of President Bashar al-Assad of Syria. Now Saudi Arabia, the United Arab Emirates (UAE) and Jordan have shifted most of their aircraft to their fight against Iranian-backed Houthi rebels in Yemen. Bahrain and Qatar only occasionally fly over Syria. Western allies do not intend to move jets from their air bases to Incirlik. France flies out of Jordan and the UAE. Britain has had no bombing missions in Syria, just intelligence, surveillance and reconnaissance flights.

More concerning for the White House is the failure of Turkey, a vital NATO ally in the Middle East and the coalition-led war against ISIS and jihadists, to support the US's battle against ISIS in northern Syria. Instead, before and in the aftermath of the electoral victory of Turkish president, Recep Tayyip Erdogan and his Islamist Justice and Development Party (AKP), Turkey has focused on battling their nemesis, the Kurds in Turkey and Syria. Syrian Kurds have taken over large areas in northern Syria and established self-government in the area that they call "Rojava." For Turkey, ISIS is only a secondary enemy compared to the Kurds and the possibility that they will attempt to expand Iraqi Kurdistan to the Turkish border with Syria and west of the Euphrates.

Following a suicide bombing in July 2015 in the Turkish-Syrian border town of Suruc that killed 33 pro-Kurdish activists, in October the worst terrorist attack in Turkish history, also targeting pro-Kurdish activists, happened in Ankara. The Turkish government appears to have done nothing to followup on these acts of terrorism and has reiterated that the Kurdistan Workers' Party (PKK) is the worst terrorist threat to Turkey.

For Turkey's political leaders, the PKK and ISIS have basically the same aim – to destabilize and undermine Turkey. The PKK established the Kurdish Democratic Union Party (PYD) as an affiliate in 2003. Several years ago the US designated the PKK as a terrorist organization. For the United States, making its battle against ISIS in Syria much more complicated is the fact that its strongest military ally is the Kurd's People Protection Units (YPG), formed in 2004 by the PKK's affiliate, the PYD.

In July 2012, the Assad regime moved out of most Kurdish-majority areas in northern Syria. The YPG took control of this territory with the intention of establishing a "Western Kurdistan" in "Rojava," all along the Turkish border, east and west of the Euphrates. In this swath of border region live Kurds, Turkmen and Arabs. The YPG has a fighting force estimated at between 30,000 and 50,000. The YPG wants and needs more heavy weapons in order to seize more territory from ISIS in northern Syria. Turkey opposes Kurdish advances in northern Syria and the US or other sources providing heavy weapons to the YPG. The Turks are fearful that these weapons will end up in the hands of the PKK. Ankara has no intention of allowing the PYD-PKK to create a "Western Kurdistan" along its southern border. Arab nationalists living in northern Syria also oppose the PYD's advances, even if the Kurds are pushing back ISIS.

Consequently, trying to navigate both Turkey's opposition to the PYD-YPG and Arab concerns about encroachment on their territory, the Obama administration recently announced support for a new rebel umbrella organization called the Democratic Forces of Syria (DFS), which includes the YPG, the Syrian Arab Coalition and other rebel factions in the Turkish border region. A goal of this new alliance is to cut the connection between the ISIS "capital" of Raqqa and its stronghold to the east in Iraq's Mosul. Washington's formation of the DFS had to include an agreement with Ankara to prevent Kurdish forces from occupying Syrian territory west of the Euphrates and also not to supply Kurds with heavy weapons.

Three years ago, in a CBS 60 Minutes broadcast, the daring and remarkable journalist Clarissa Ward made her way through hell in Syria's Aleppo to interview radical Islamist fighters. Three years later more or less disorganized groups of Syrian militias are still fighting against both Assad's forces and ISIS. Insurgents still need heavier weapons and also anti-aircraft weapons. Ward has made nearly a dozen trips to Syria since the civil war broke out in 2011. Clarissa recently moved to CNN, but basically nothing has changed in her reporting on Syria except for a major increase of Kurdish fighters trying to drive ISIS out of northern Syria and, perhaps most important, their use of hand-held devices capable of giving coordinates for enemy positions to coalition aircraft, that were provided as part of a joint US-Kurdish operation. Otherwise in Ward's latest trip to northern Syria, not alike three years earlier, she found fighters still using a collection of home-made mortars and hunting rifles.

Much of Aleppo, another of Syria's historic crown jewels, has been reduced to rubble. As Ward tells us, local insurgents and Kurds in Aleppo have been reinforced by foreign fighters, many of whom are radical Islamists. The rebel fighters show no optimism in response to the latest White House announcement about the US sending special forces to Syria to support the so-called new alliance, the Syrian Democratic Front. The Alliance is in name only. The rebel forces tell Clarissa that they mainly need the US to provide ammunition, radios, heavy weapons and more American airstrikes.

The Alliance is trying to take back territory from ISIS that consists mostly of Arab areas. Most of the Alliance's fighting power comes from Kurdish militias. Since Turkey is opposed to Kurdish fighters and especially the YPG operating near its southern borders, the Alliance will be limited in fighting for cities like Raqqa, the Islamic State's headquarters in Syria. The Kurds are well aware of this issue, but also are aware that their disorganized and untrained Arab rebel partners cannot be relied on as effective allies on the battlefield. As for Arab rebel fighters, they worry about the YPG's close ties to the Kurdistan Workers' Party (PKK) which the US and Turkey list as a terrorist organization.

Thousands of Kurdish fighters have come to Syria from Iraq, Turkey and Iran. For Arab rebels from northern Syria, these Kurds are foreign fighters. But the Kurdish fighters number more than 40,000 and hold most of the more than 280-mile-long frontline with the Islamic State while the Syrian Arab Coalition has only about 5,000 fighters. For these Arab tribal militias, in a very real sense they have ISIS and Assad's forces on one side and Kurds on the other. After four years of fighting, the insurgents are worn down. US special forces joining them some day on the battlefront means much less at this time than uniforms, ammunition, shoes and other basics for survival.

Next to resolution of the civil war in Syria, Russia's intervention in support of President al-Assad, and the future role of Iran and its proxies in Syria and elsewhere in the Middle East in the aftermath of the nuclear accord, the latest phase of the Afghanistan debacle will have to get priority attention from presidential candidates and American voters in 2016.

In Afghanistan, ISIS is emerging as a major terrorist threat along with a resurgence of the Taliban. The Taliban ruled Afghanistan from 1996 until 2001 when the US and its allies, including the Northern Alliance, drove them into Pakistan. The Taliban regrouped in Pakistan and returned as an insurgency targeting Western troops and the Afghan state. The United States has been trying ever since 2001 to end the longest war in its history and figure out what it has accomplished in Afghanistan.

It took the Taliban's recent attack on the city of Kunduz and the rapid retreat of pro-government forces to make the White House and the Pentagon "nervous" about leaving Afghanistan entirely in 2016 and to "look carefully at other options." The collapse of Kunduz undermined confident assessments previously issued by US senior commanders about the impressive performance and leadership of Afghan forces. The US still has no strategy for Afghanistan other than keeping thousands of American troops in place, which is not a strategy. Pakistan continues to support the Taliban and refuses to use its influence to pressure them to engage in peace talks.

President Mohammad Ashraf Ghani's National Unity Government has been weak and achieved little progress delivering on its reform promises, the Afghan economy has collapsed, the security situation has deteriorated, Afghanis have lost their trust in the government and its leadership, and peace negotiations with the Taliban have stalemated. Pakistani and Afghani intelligence services signed a memorandum of understanding to keep the Taliban and other terrorist groups in check which has not been fulfilled.

Kunduz's fall to the Taliban was almost inevitable as the result of poor Afghani leadership in Kabul, and Afghanis know it. For the Taliban's new leader Mullah Akhtar Mansour, the seizure of Kunduz was intended to send a strong message about the renewed potency of the Taliban to the people of Afghanistan. Unfortunately the temporary seizure of Kunduz not only resulted in many Taliban casualties but also widespread criminality, pillaging and looting, and damage, thereby staining Mansour's intended message. One unintended result will be more legitimacy for ISIS that already has a strong foothold in eastern Afghanistan.

The Taliban not only are at war with the Afghan government and its inept security forces but with each other, fighting over leadership succession, even as ISIS expands its control of various parts of the country. For two years, the Taliban's leader, Mullah Mohammad Omar, was secretly kept in a hospital in Karachi. It was not until July 2015 that the Afghan government announced that Omar had been dead for two years, precipitating a Taliban leadership crisis. Mullah Akhtar Mansoor assumed power after the announced death of Omar. Mansoor quickly was challenged by a breakaway Taliban faction led by Mullah Mohammad Rasool who was joined by local ISIS militants and others from as far away as Syria. ISIS already controls a number of districts in eastern Nangarhar province, bordering Pakistan, and has established a rapidly growing presence in Zabul province where the Taliban succession conflict broke out.

The US has about 10,000 troops in Afghanistan. Keeping US forces at this level is not a solution. Afghans are losing more and more patience with their government. Thousand of demonstrators filled streets in Kabul recently to protest deteriorating security, targeted violence and the Ghani government's incompetence. The Taliban may not be viewed by the Afghan people as saviors, but an ineffective and corrupt government remains a poor comparison. The serious misbehavior of the Taliban in Kunduz did not cast them as a good alternative to the Afghan government. Nevertheless the Taliban are regaining ground in many of the same areas where US forces suffered heavy losses to the Taliban during more than a decade of combat.

The US has not shown any strategy to prevent Afghanistan from following the disastrous path of Iraq where last year the Islamic State overran major cities and large swaths of countryside. In northern Iraq, it is only Kurdish forces backed by American airstrikes that is preventing further expansion of ISIS and, at the same time, cutting jihadist supplies lines from northeast Syria to Mosul, Iraq's second largest city. Iraqi government efforts to retake Ramadi in the Sunni Arab heartland of Anbar Province are stalled since ISIS has had more than a year to fortify their positions. Using suicide bombers, improvised explosive devices (IEDs) and houses rigged with explosives, ISIS effectively defends its more than 600-mile front shared with the Kurds. The US has been slow to equip and train Kurds who complain that they need more antitank missiles to defend against suicide vehicle attacks.

From Syria and Iraq to Afghanistan, local forces opposing ISIS, other jihadists and the Taliban repeat the same criticisms against US-coalition forces of support that is too little and too late. The encirclement of Kunduz, for example, actually began two years ago when American military forces began pulling out in the fall of 2013. Within minutes after US special forces left, the district governor was assassinated and the police had abandoned their bases. The Taliban started implementing a systematic effort to not only undermine local government and law enforcement but, and this is most important, to change its own local governance behavior in ways that exemplified a more lenient Taliban that was more responsive to ethnic (Tajik, Uzbek and Turkmen) conflicts and issues.

In a sense, the Taliban attempted to apply Mao's message to insurgents about the importance, in addition to decisive military action, of countering the government in power with a strong religious or ideological message. For the Taliban regaining territory in Helmand province and elsewhere in Afghanistan, the message has been: "We are all fighting side by side under one banner, which is Islam. We are struggling for Islam not for any particular ethnic group." Serious misconduct in Kunduz, however, contradicted both the Taliban's original raison d'être, after the collapse of the communist regime in 1992, and their most recent message about changing their local governance behavior.

Foreign terrorists -- Tajiks, Uzbeks, Uighurs, Chechens and others – flowed into Kunduz over the past two years. The US and the Kabul government have known about it and were warned for two years that the province was moving towards collapse. Per usual government officials in Kabul assured local officials that reinforcements would come if and when needed. The American commander in Afghanistan, Gen. John F. Campbell, asked in May 2015 about the Taliban's military strategy, seemed almost dismissive. "If you take a look very closely at some of the things in Kunduz and up in Badakhshan, they [Taliban] will attack some very small checkpoints," he said. "They will go out and hit a little bit and then they kind of go to ground," he added, "so they're not gaining territory for the most part."

By comparison with Syria, Afghanistan or Iraq, Yemen is not a priority foreign policy concern for voters and presidential candidates. However, it is equally imperative that the US modify its support for the Saudi coalition's aerial campaign in Yemen that has killed thousands of civilians, according to credible reports by human rights groups. US policy-makers have to figure out a constructive alternative role for the US in resolution of the civil war in Yemen. Fighting in Yemen has forced more than 1.5 million people to flee their homes, according to UN agencies. Although Syria's refugees and displaced persons dominate news reports, as a percentage of the population the number of displaced persons in Yemen and their conditions actually are much worse.

President Obama has expressed some mild criticisms to Saudi King Salman about "errant" Saudi-led coalition airstrikes that have bombed hundreds of homes, markets, refugee camps and hospitals. In late October 2015 a Saudi-led coalition, supported by the US, leveled the only functioning hospital in Yemen, serving a population of 200,000. This bombing came just three weeks after the deadly US strike on the trauma center in Kunduz. In Yemen more than 50 medical structures have been damaged or destroyed by airstrikes since a US-backed and Saudi-led coalition launched a devastating air campaign in March 2015. In the same month, at least 12 hospitals were bombed in Syria. Physicians for Human Rights have documented attacks by the Assad regime on 313 health structures killing almost 700 health personnel in Syria.

President Obama apologized for the deadly attack on the Kunduz hospital. In addition to verifiable violations of international law, US support for air attacks on hospitals and other medical facilities in the Middle East should become an important issue for Americans in the 2016 presidential campaign. Neither the Saudis nor the US have issued any apologies or acknowledgements of responsibility for bombing Yemen's hospitals. On the contrary, a US military spokesman responded: "We are confident that the intelligence and advice we pass on to Saudi Arabia and other coalition members is sound, giving them the best options for military success consistent with international norms and mitigating the potential for civilian casualties," said Cmdr. Kevin Stephens, a US military spokesman in Bahrain. "The final decisions on the conduct of operations in the campaign are made by the members of the Saudi-led coalition, not the United States."

In addition to providing intelligence, munitions and midair refueling to Saudi coalition aircraft engaged in bombing Yemen, the Obama administration also is providing US warships to help enforce a blockade in the Gulf of Aden and southern Arabian Sea to prevent weapons shipments from Iran to the Houthis, Shia rebels that are engaged in a bloody uprising against the Saudis. This sea cordon, however, also cuts Yemen off from imports of basic commodities including food and fuel, adding to the nation's extreme miseries. Since 2011, without any review of benefits or outcomes, the US has provided Yemen with more than $300 million for humanitarian programs and another $500 million for "transition to democracy" programs and projects that have been impossible to accomplish while the current civil war goes on. In the meantime, the US recently doubled the number of advisors to provide enhanced intelligence for the Saudi coalition's airstrikes.

The US has no strategic plan in place to end hostilities in Yemen or to restrain the Saudi-coalition from killing a great many more civilians. Destruction of key infrastructure has left millions of Yemenis without access to clean water or electricity, and a quarter of the country's health facilities are shuttered, according to the World Health Organization. There is no US plan to work with Saudis to remedy this disaster as outbreaks of dengue fever, malaria and other treatable ailments have become deadly for large numbers of Yemenis. "The humanitarian situation is nothing short of catastrophic," Peter Maurer, president of the International Committee of the Red Cross, said after a recent visit to the battered country. "And it is getting worse by the day."

CHAPTER 2

Ending the "Endless War" in Afghanistan

There was a time, seemingly ages ago, when Afghanistan was a war that almost everyone wanted. They wanted revenge for 9/11. It was a crusade against the Taliban regime and Al-Qaeda. America needed the war as protection against international terrorists like Osama bin Laden and Al-Qaeda. Very few voices were raised in opposition when Obama surged U.S. troops to about 100,000. The number of U.S. troops actually was wildly out of proportion to the enemy. The cost was enormous -- $100 billion just in 2011! But soon the war in Afghanistan turned into a painful and futile experience. From saving Afghans, the imperative became get American soldiers home – as fast as possible.

It's entirely possible that presidential candidates in 2016 and their advisors will feel compelled to present their own versions of an "Afghanistan Plan" to the voting public, if only to highlight their foreign policy credentials. Certainly Afghanistan deserves as much attention as it possibly can get in presidential campaigning crammed with policy and position papers on domestic and international issues. For this purpose, with the benefit of the 20-20 lens of hindsight, it would be useful to briefly look back to December 2009 when President Obama laid out his "Afghanistan Plan" in just 4 succinct minutes.

The core goal of the President's strategy was "to disrupt, dismantle, and defeat al-Qaida and prevent its capacity to threaten America and our allies in the future." In addition to "denying al-Qaida a safe haven," Obama enunciated four additional goals: "reversing the Taliban's momentum"; "strengthening the capacity of Afghanistan's security forces and government so that they can take lead responsibility for Afghanistan's future"; withdrawing 10,000 US troops from Afghanistan by the end of 2009; and "… that the 33,000 "surge" troops approved in December 2009 will leave Afghanistan by the summer of 2012." By moving the US mission from combat to support, Obama declared, the government of Afghanistan would be enabled to move "towards full responsibility for security across Afghanistan by the end of 2014."

As 2016 approaches, roughly six years later, only one of Obama's goals has been achieved -- reduction of US troops in Afghanistan. The "strategic partnership" between the US and Afghanistan and their bilateral cooperation in the areas of security, economic and social development, and institution building have failed to produce stabilization or security. Between 2006 and the end of 2009, when the President announced his Afghanistan Plan, the Taliban actually had made a dramatic comeback after being driven from the country in 2002. Security had steadily deteriorated. Without any specific reference but as the basis for Obama "Afghanistan Plan," the White House and Congress had yet another new strategic plan for Afghanistan in 2010, this one formulated by General Stanley McChrystal, Commander of ISAF and US Forces.

The McChrystal military plan for Afghanistan was comprehensive, covering much more than just military strategy. But the military strategy component had great value not only for 2009 but for 2016 and beyond, and not just for Afghanistan but also for Syria, Iraq and any country in the Middle East struggling with terrorism and ISIS. The McChrystal plan's goals, which strongly resonate with the author's counterterrorism strategy, applied to the Taliban but could apply equally well to ISIS: halt the progress of the Taliban; reverse it, especially in key population areas; and do whatever is possible and necessary to regain the initiative. Instead of focusing military and support resources on targeting enemy combatants, the focus of the counterinsurgency effort should be providing security for the local population.

The central concept of McChrystal's strategy is that, crucial to the success of counterinsurgency against jihadists in any country, is building local support and loyalty by enhancing security and normal life in key population centers. The chapter on "Lessons Learned in the Anbar Awakening" explains why this strategy was the key to US military success in Operation Iraqi Freedom, in Ramadi, Iraq, 2006-08. Like Operation Iraqi Freedom, however, and much like the strategy for Afghanistan proposed by Gates to Obama that is described in *Duty*, a significant US ground presence was required to make counterterrorism work.

A US ground presence was essential, argued Gates, in order to deny the Taliban, al-Qaeda or any other jihadists the ability to hold or control major population centers, to degrade jihadist capabilities and to stabilize Afghanistan, Iraq or any other counterinsurgency battleground long enough to train local security forces and provide reassurance to local populations that they can stay put and lead normal lives. Gates confirmed McChrystal's request in 2010 for increased troops in Afghanistan, but reduced the number from 40,000 to 30,000 and urged flexibility going forward.

Bringing an end to America's longest war – which has lasted as long as WW I, WW II and the Civil War combined -- killed more than 2300 Americans and wounded another 20,000 is an admirable goal. But the war in Afghanistan will not end – it will go on. Reducing the number of American troops from 10,000 to anything less is more of a symbolic gesture than a meaningful number. Only one of the goals remaining for U.S. troops can be accomplished with this number of boots-on-the-ground in Afghanistan: protecting the American embassy in Kabul and maintaining operations at Bagram Air Field to the north of Kabul, the main American hub in Afghanistan, and at bases outside Kandahar in the country's south and Jalalabad in the east. The other two U.S. goals -- training the Afghan national army and support for the army against terrorist groups -- are beyond the capacity of remaining American troops.

Afghanistan's President Ghani needs all the help he can get from the United States and NATO allies. The recent fighting in Kunduz exposed the limits of both foreign forces in Afghanistan and Afghan soldiers. Just a few hundred Taliban soldiers forced thousands of Afghan soldiers and police officers to flee from Kunduz. The U.S. no doubt will continue its drone war in Afghanistan that has been successful in killing targeted Taliban and Al-Qaeda militants, but also killed hundreds of other people categorized in warfare as "collateral damage."

An "endless war" -- with no plan or strategy for stabilization of Afghanistan and dealing with rising security threats in Pakistan – deserves to end. With the threats of both ISIS and the Taliban growing, security in Afghanistan is likely to unravel further in the future. Without a strategy for effective counterinsurgency warfare in Afghanistan, the presence of a limited U.S. force there really doesn't matter, including for the national security of the U.S. "I will not allow Afghanistan to be used as safe haven for terrorists to attack our nation again," said President Obama.

Six years ago, President Obama declared that "We must reverse the Taliban's momentum" and strengthen the capacity of Afghanistan's security forces so that they can take lead responsibility for Afghanistan's future." Not only has that goal not been reached, the Taliban insurgency is stronger than at any time since the American invasion in 2001. And now the Islamic State (ISIS) is gaining ground in Afghanistan against the Taliban and Afghan civilians are fleeing the spiraling violence.

According to data compiled by the UN supplemented by interviews, the threat level in about half of the country is either "high" or "extreme." The UN has evacuated four of its 13 provincial offices around the country for security reasons. Districts with extreme threat levels either have no government presence at all or the government presence is reduced to only the district capital. In all, 27 of Afghanistan's 34 provinces had some districts where the threat level was rated high or extreme.

In his recent testimony to the Senate Armed Services Committee Gen. John F. Campbell said: "The Afghan security forces have displayed courage and resilience. They're still holding. The Afghan government retains control of Kabul, of Highway One, its provincial capitals and nearly all of the district centers." According to Afghan officials interviewed by the UN, Gen. Campbell's report about Afghan security was untrue.

Highway One, for example, a ring road connecting all of Afghanistan's main cities, suffers from repeated Taliban ambushes and roadblocks. Insurgents repeatedly cut the highway in the Doshi and Baghlani Jadid districts of Baghlan Province. Few government officials now dare to use the highway. In many districts that are nominally under government control, government forces hold only the government buildings in the district center and are under constant siege by the insurgents. The police have been trapped in those buildings without a way to escape. According to Wali Dad, the police chief in Charchino, his 400 police officers have been surrounded and pinned down there for months.

In Wali Dad's opinion, quoted by the UN, "The government is failing in their governing, and it's better to let the Taliban rule." Likewise in Oruzgan Province, in southern Afghanistan, where four of its five districts were rated under extreme or high threat. "We had 570 policemen in Khas Oruzgan District, but now only 75 men remain and all in the district center; the rest have been killed, surrendered or escaped," said Abdul Hameed, the deputy district governor. "We are still begging for survival, but we get no attention from the central government. If the situation remains the same, the district will fall to the hands of the Taliban."

The Taliban have been a largely Pashtun-based insurgency and strongest in Pashtun-majority areas in southern and eastern Afghanistan, with some pockets in the north, such as Kunduz. According to United Nations data, the Taliban insurgency also has increased in many parts of the country where there had been little Taliban presence in the past, including some areas in the north. "We have had fighting in 13 provinces of Afghanistan over the past six months, simultaneously," President Ashraf Ghani said last month in response to criticism after the fall of Kunduz.

This is not to say that Afghanistan is hopeless and shows no progress. In fact during the last 14 years, according to the World Bank there has been real GNP growth, new businesses have been growing, school enrollment increasing from one million children to 8.7 million, including a very large increase of girls, and a huge increase in teachers. But these and other gains are constantly under threat. Al Qaeda training camps are operating in the country. The Taliban is gaining momentum. The national unity government has been challenged by infighting and a recalcitrant Afghani Parliament. Corruption in the public and private sectors has not been restrained. And the Afghan government continues to rely on "strongmen" and local police under their control for security. Against this backdrop, President Obama's commitment to keep U.S. troops levels at around 10,000 does not respond to conditions on the ground. Afghanis know this and are leaving the country in droves for Turley and Europe.

With all eyes on fighting ISIS in Syria and efforts by the U.S. to remedy its ineffectual military response, Defense Department officials have not mentioned lately that, 14 years after the U.S. invasion of Afghanistan, the Taliban are fighting for or are back in control of at least one-fifth of the country. Most recently, the bombing of a Doctors Without Borders hospital in Kunduz has been headline news, but this tragic event was part of a widespread offensive by the Taliban in northern Afghanistan that is part of a multifront attack that includes several southern Afghan provinces. The Taliban's simultaneous attack on both northern and southern Afghanistan has significance for several reasons:

- it is deeply straining Afghan security forces that in many areas have been surrounded and cut off from resupply;
- the Taliban are determined to capture Lashkar Gah, the capital of Helmand Province, and to control Helmand because the province accounts for nearly half of the Afghan's opium poppy cultivation;

- a former Taliban stronghold, the Helmand district was a major focus of the American troop surge more than a decade ago and, once again, as Taliban fighters grow in numbers, Afghan soldiers and their officers feel abandoned by their government, have run short of ammunition and fuel, do not have the heavy weapons that they need, lack logistical and air support, lack helicopters for resupply over long distances and medical evacuations.

The Afghan Defense ministry persists in denying all of these problems. Although Afghan forces outnumber the Taliban, as in Kunduz, the advantage in numbers has not translated into strength on the battlefield because of poor leadership and corruption among commanders, reportedly selling weapons, ammunition, and fuel, which leads to demoralization of soldiers and police. Afghan soldiers and police see their choices as getting killed, surrendering or fleeing, leaving weapons and ammunition behind for the Taliban to gather. All of this undermines the local Afghan population's trust in government forces.

The failure of regular Afghan forces to combat the Taliban has led the Afghan government to rely on irregular militias, many quietly U.S.-funded for years, even as President Ashraf Ghani has pledged to disarm them and their strongmen. These militia leaders have deepened ethnic divisions in Afghanistan, weakened the central government's influence, and undermined any vestiges of the US's signature effort in Afghanistan to build a capable army and police force. In part this trend prompted President Obama to cancel the withdrawal of US troops. However, with Afghanistan seeing the spread of territorial control by the Taliban, ISIS, and warlords and their militias, the U.S. keeping some 10,000 troops in Afghanistan obviously is nothing more than a political gesture.

Long before the Afghan government announced (Oct 16, 2015) plans to expand and "nationalize" its Afghan Local Police (ALP) and militia network and, virtually the same day, President Obama called off the U.S. troop pullout, Afghanistan was facing a fierce Taliban offensive in a wide swath of its northern provinces. There was no indication that either decision was connected to the other.

But the Obama administration and its National Security Council (NSC) had to be aware that President Ghani would call on key warlords and countless others, for military assistance, and that forming additional ALPs would be extremely risky and probably even counterproductive. The Ghani decisions also contradicted previous assurances from Afghan officials that security forces were holding their own against the Taliban. In a sense Obama's announcement merely confirmed that conclusion. The Kunduz capitulation pounded a final nail into the proverbial coffin.

By yielding security control to irregular forces, Afghanistan was turning back the clock to the 1990s when feuding militia commanders created chaos and a bloody civil war. Some of the commanders, "strong men" otherwise known as warlords, now hold senior government positions and will guide the Afghan's mobilization and rearming of militias: Hajji Mohammad Mohaqiq, a former militia commander and now the country's deputy chief executive; vice president, Abdul Rashid Dostum; and the governor of Balkh Province, Atta Muhammad Noor. As has happened in Afghanistan's past, and actually never stopped happening for decades, local "strongmen" will form rival militias, now funded by the central government.

Reflecting diminished confidence in the Afghan Army and police forces, in theory creation of nationalized police and militia forces will replace a patchwork of militias around the country, provide better training, and much more accountability to the Afghan national government. Whereas in the 1990s northern provinces were the heart of anti-Taliban resistance, in the recent past the Afghan Army has been losing ground to the Taliban that seem determined to carve out territory in the mountainous north. The collapse of Kunduz, a city in the north near the border with Tajikistan, spurred the government to adopt its plan, which involved a complete about face on dismantling local militias.

Gen. Campbell said that he was skeptical of any plan that involved paying warlords to deploy their men. "I think if they're looking for people that have volunteered to protect their villages, you know, that's one thing," he said. But if the government's plan involved

39

"going to a warlord and saying, 'I need to take you, and pay you and move you, and go do something here,' that's a completely different thing," he said. General Campbell himself did not have a better solution that he was prepared to discuss. For Afghan's leadership, relying on militias for self-defense clearly is a last resort. A little known fact, that Gen. Campbell certainly knows and that contradicts his comments, warlords and their militias have been key U.S. allies in fighting the Taliban and al-Qaeda: warlords operate some of the largest U.S. and NATO contractor security forces in Afghanistan. There are more than 200 warlords and their militias in Afghanistan which is one of the country's best kept secrets.

CHAPTER 3

Syrian Political Chess Match – US in Checkmate

Russia must be gloating that the Pentagon's program to train insurgents in Jordan and Turkey has failed. Revelations that that the program had only "four or five" trainees, rather than as many as 5,400 fighters this year could not be better news for Russia. Per usual, speaking on condition of anonymity, the Pentagon admitted that "Training thousands of infantry was not the right model." One of the many questions being asked about the Pentagon's insurgent recruitment and training fiasco is why it took so long to recognize that fighting Assad, not ISIS, was the main priority for literally thousands of insurgent groups in Syria.

The US then announced an alternative strategy to equip as many as 5,000 Syrian Arab fighters that would join more than 20,000 Kurdish fighters in an offensive backed by coalition warplanes to battle the Islamic State in Raqqa, their headquarters in Syria. One would have thought that this plan was approved by Turkish officials, especially since Turkey considers Kurdish militants their enemy. The surprise, however, was that Turkish officials also expressed concerns to Russian officials, suggesting that both Russia and the US are supporting Kurdish militias that have been the US's most important ally in fighting ISIS. Now it appears that Russia is even competing for the allegiance of Syrian Kurds.

This is not the first time that supposed agreements between Turkey and the US have lost Turkish support. The US Turkish "ISIS-free zone" created in northern Syria's Aleppo Province no longer seems to be operational. The timing of this about-face is bad. Assad, Russia, Hezbollah, and possibly the Iranians are organizing an offensive from Homs northward to the Aleppo area.

With everyone's attention focused on Russia's extremely aggressive intervention in Syria, Russia's recent political moves in Iraq, and Iraq's responses, were barely noticed. What did provoke headline news was the intelligence and security cooperation pact between Russia, Iran and Syria that Iraq's Defense Ministry also signed. Inevitably the signing of this agreement caused speculation about Russia's strategy and intentions. Some observers connecting the dots are seeing the possibility of Moscow seeking to form a non-Western coalition in the Middle East.

Russia established an intelligence operations room with Iran and Syria inside Baghdad's Green Zone, which also houses America's embassy. Iraq recently had the audacity to reject a US request not to open its airspace to Russian flights heading for Syria. Adding insult to injury, Iraqi Prime Minister Haider al-Abadi asked Russia to expand its air campaign from Syria to include ISIS targets in Iraq. A senior Abadi official then talked about negotiating a military alliance with Russia. After expending hundreds of billions of dollars and thousands of lives, Iraq reaching out to Russia obviously is disturbing for the US. Abadi complains that the US has not used its air power to protect Iraqi forces fighting ISIS. Abadi is not happy with the pace of America's effort in Iraq to fight ISIS.

Russian Foreign Minister Sergei Lavrov told the press that Russia was helping the fight against Islamist insurgents in Iraq with the consent of the Baghdad government. He added that Russia also was cooperating with Iraqi Kurdistan in the fight against terrorism. Russia's recent moves are further steps in longer-term political and military interventions to significantly expand its footprint and influence in the Middle East. As context, let's not forget that the

USSR was involved with Syria practically from the day it was formed in 1946 and has been a political, economic and military supporter of the Assad family for four decades.

Foreign minister Adel Al-Jubeir could not be clearer about Saudi Arabia's view of Bashar al-Assad's future: there are no circumstances where Bashar al-Assad can remain in power – whether his exit is through politics or by force. Turkey also has been unequivocally clear about Assad's future. Both Turkey and Saudi Arabia also have been equally clear about their opposition to Russia's intervention in Syria and its consequences: both have said that Moscow's support for Assad and its bombing campaign in support of his regime was a "big mistake." Both Sunni Muslim powers support the moderate opposition in Syria.

All of this talk about Russia's disruptive role in the Syrian conflict has been fed by a geopolitical undercurrent that rarely surfaces in the media, and is likely to become increasingly important as a factor in Moscow's future Middle East policy and relationships with Saudi and the Gulf region: the growing oil competition between Saudi Arabia and Russia. The wild card in the future of Russian-Saudi oil competition will be Iran after sanctions are lifted and it re-enters the global oil and gas market. Russia's strategic intentions are to partner with Iran in the development of export routes through pipelines across Syria and through Syrian ports. But like Russia's other strategies for expanding its energy export channels and markets, the outcomes are uncertain.

The Saudi share of the European crude market has been dropping for decades and Russia's has been growing. Whereas in the 1970s, Saudi Arabia sent half of its oil to Europe, the Soviet Union built pipelines from West Siberian oil fields to European markets, forcing the Saudis to switch to Asian markets where demand at better prices was growing. Then, with the European Union trying to reduce its reliance on Russian energy, Poland starting to import heavily discounted Saudi oil and reached an agreement with Lithuania, Latvia and Estonia to build a natural gas pipeline to and from the Baltic States.

The Eastern European goal is future independence from Russian gas supplies. In the interim, Saudi gained Eastern European customers with its heavily discounted prices. At the same time, in Asian markets Russia has become a serious competitor to the Saudis, reinforcing the Saudi's price war aimed at increasing market share. In the perspective of competition for energy markets, Saudi Arabia and the Gulf states are at war with Russia, a war that for all of the combatants could be more consequential than the Syrian conflict.

As part of Russia's strategy, and this is just speculation, Russia will seek to block the Saudis from establishing energy export routes in Syria. Russia wants a much larger share of the European oil and gas market which it has been losing to Saudi in recent years as Saudi sells its energy products at a steep discount. Saudi is becoming very aggressive about its oil export competition with Russia. Just as President Vladimir Putin tries to restore Russia as a major player in the Middle East, Saudi Arabia is starting to attack Russia's traditional stomping ground by supplying (rather dumping) lower-priced crude oil to Poland.

Opposition to the Russian bombing campaign has intensified a rapprochement between Turkey and Saudi Arabia that seems to have gained pace over the last months. Possibly behind the closer relationship between these two countries is their respective relationship with Russia in the sphere of international energy trade. In addition to escalating Russia-Saudi energy export competition, Turkey and Russia announced a deal in December 2014 to construct "Turkish Stream" – four strings of gas pipelines, only one of which would go into Turkey, and the other three would pass through Greece to the European market. This deal has stalled recently for a variety of reasons and provides Turkey with one more reason to draw closer to its Muslim brother, Saudi Arabia, rather than Russia.

In a December 2014 meeting, Putin promised the Turks to sell them gas they already were receiving at a 10.25% discount. Turkey wants the discount before signing the pipeline deal with Moscow. Putin wants a signed deal for all four pipelines before giving Turkey the discount. Sixty percent of Turkey's gas comes from Russia to generate 45% of Turkey's electricity. Putin also wants Turkey's help to negotiate gas deals in Europe. Russia also needs help selling the three other pipelines to European customers. Turkey has not agreed to either of these demands.

The political, economic and energy production and distribution relationships between Turkey and Russia, Russians and Saudi Arabia and the Gulf States, Russia and Iran, Iran and Saudi and the Gulf States, and all of them with Central Asian oil producers resembles a rubik's cube puzzle game. Any move by any player sooner or later results in counter-moves by all the other players. For example, one of Turkey's strategic economic goals is to become a regional energy hub. Central to that goal is the Trans-Anatolian Natural Gas Pipeline (TANAP), a natural gas pipeline from Azerbaijan through Georgia and Turkey to Europe. It will be a central part of the Southern Gas Corridor which will connect the huge Shah Deniz gas field in Azerbaijan to Europe through the South Caucasus Pipeline (SCP). For both Azerbaijan and Turkey, this project is of enormous importance. Construction of the pipeline began in March 2015 and completion is expected in 2018.

The State Oil Company of Azerbaijan Republic (SOCAR) owns almost 60% of TANAP and Turkey owns most of the rest. Iran apparently wants to buy a stake in TANAP. This opens up one of the most interesting aspects of Iranian energy and economic development. With all of the political back and forth about Iranian economic benefits from the lifting of sanctions, rarely is it mentioned that the Iranian Revolutionary Guard Corps (IRGC) has de facto control over Iranian oil and gas business and Iran's involvement in any regional gas business deals, including with Turkey.

The IRGC stands in the way of Turkey or any foreign company seeking access to Iran's gas resources or taking a stake in gas development that impacts on Iran. Further complicating the situation, if Iranian natural gas along with Azerbaijan gas begins flowing into European markets through TANAP, Moscow will have another major natural gas rival that, in the instance of Iran, was supposed to be a strategic ally.

Iran has an estimated 137.6 billion barrels of oil, about 10 percent of the world's total proven reserves. It ranks third in proven oil reserves after Saudi Arabia and Canada. Iran is the fourth largest exporter of crude oil with 40. But as a result of mismanagement, inefficient infrastructure to extract gas, lack of an adequate pipeline network and other reasons, Iran will need to attract the interest of international energy companies. Based on the schedule in the Joint Comprehensive Plan of Action, sanctions will probably be lifted sometime during the first quarter of 2016. Following that, it will not be easy for Tehran to meet its long-term goal of producing 6 million barrels of oil per day. Nor will it be easy for Turkey to make strategic energy deals to fulfill its goal of becoming a regional energy hub

Iran's massive South Pars offshore gas field is shared with Qatar, with about one-third in Iran's territorial waters in the Persian Gulf. South Pars also includes 23 oil fields that Iran intends to develop in the next three years. If anyone has any questions about where Iran will be investing proceeds from the lifting of sanctions, South Pars itself will absorb a minimum of $70 billion. Sanctions against Iran have stood in the way of development of the South Pars gas field, the world's second largest proven natural gas reserve.

Further complicating Russia's execution of the pipeline deal is that Qatar, with the third largest gas reserves in the world, also is a big competitor for Russia, with the advantage of shipping liquefied natural gas anywhere in the world, bypassing land routes. Russia currently ships gas to Europe through Belarus and the Ukraine, but can't rely on that continuing. Facing a dramatic global drop in gas prices, Russia may not have enough capital to build the alternative four pipelines. Nord Stream 1, a Russian pipeline, and now the $11 billion Nord Stream 2, under the Baltic Sea, will double supplies of Russian gas to Western Europe, and will provide an alternative to "Turkish Stream." Germany wants "Turkish Stream" scrapped and replaced by Nord Stream I and 2. Turkey is faced by a plethora of expert international energy opinion telling it that the "Turkish Stream" project is not feasible and should be abandoned.

Russia's military strategy and tactics in Syria are not encumbered by anything like the US's political constraints. Moscow's military intervention in Syria has not strengthened US-Turkish military ties, which might have been expected since Russia historically has long been the Ottoman's most feared enemy. Putin's support for Assad's regime is comparatively clear, enabling Russia to boldly and forcefully capitalize on the ISIS threat while the US vacillates and struggles to formulate a politically acceptable and coherent strategy for fighting ISIS in Syria.

Assad's military problems and US indecision enable Moscow to increase its sphere of influence in the Middle East region from a strengthening base in Syria. For Putin's Russia, Syria arguably is an ideal platform for resurrecting its image as a power broker that, rather than the US, calls the shots on Syria's political future. Another significant motivation for Russia's intervention in Syria is its naval strategy to protect its Mediterranean base in Tartus. Tartus may be of lesser importance for Russia than the Crimea's Sevastopol, but Tartus is key to Russia's presence in the Mediterranean and important in Putin's geopolitical view of the world and Russia's place in it.

The crash of a Russian passenger jet in Egypt's Sinai, very likely at the hands of the ISIS franchise in Egypt's Sinai Peninsula, may have been retaliation by ISIS for Putin's decision to wage war against the jihadists in Syria. If nothing else, the crash dramatically refocuses international attention on President Putin's campaign to prevent ISIS from overrunning Syria and ousting President Assad. If anyone thinks that Putin will back off, in some way intimidated by an ISIS threat of further retaliation for Russia's role in Syria, they're wrong. On the contrary, it's very possible that in the future Putin will intensify Russia's role in Syria, adding more military muscle, as a boost to his image as a powerful leader in the post-Soviet world order.

If Putin did not already have a sufficiently clear and unequivocal stand against ISIS, in the future he probably will double-down on it, just at the time when the US and its allies seem to be wavering or at least uncertain about their future roles in Syria. In Putin's opinion, US-led efforts in Syria have been feeble and ineffective. For Putin, Russia's stand against ISIS is both defensive as well as offensive. Putin's regime sees Afghanistan to the southeast of Russia threatened by ISIS, adjoining Central Asian states that are very vulnerable to terrorism, and its own Caucasus region persistently threatened by its Chechen population.

For Putin, the destruction of a Russian plane with hundreds of Russians aboard will feed his propaganda machine with the perfect fuel: Russia is under siege; Russia needs to protect the safety of its people and their national interests; Russia needs to save the world from being overrun by ISIS and Muslim fundamentalism; intervention in Syria is just one part of a larger Russian anti-terrorism preventative measure; Russia must stand up to the hostile policies of the West and compensate for their weak intervention in Syria, and the like. Putin is playing his hand against the US in Syria to: protect Russia's strongholds on Syria's coast in Latakia and Tartus; preserve Russia's regional base in Syria; facilitate a political process that enables Assad to stay in control or replaces him as long as a new government protects Moscow's interests; and limit the scale of Russia's military intervention to avoid over-commitment and counterproductive consequences.

With Russia supplying air support, planning and logistical assistance, command, control communication, and intelligence capabilities, the ground war in Syria will remain in the hands of Assad's forces, Hezbollah, Iraqis, and Iranians. Previous Russian military interventions elsewhere indicate that its air campaign will consist of strikes on the ISIS chain of command and control, supply chains, and sources of financing. Moscow's advantage over the US will be the potential effectiveness of Russia's ground game that, unlike the US, includes a great many more boots-on-the-ground and special operations forces backed by sophisticated intelligence and military capabilities.

Russia will strive to avoid a quagmire and another Afghanistan-scale disaster. Problems will arise for Moscow, however, if it is unable to facilitate a political solution on the future of Assad and the Syrian government and cannot impose its political will on its allies. Worst case, the Shia coalition of Assad, Iran, Hezbollah, and Iraq may galvanize Syrian Sunnis against them, even channeling Sunni rebel fighters to ISIS and other extremist groups. Russia will seek to minimize any risks in Syria that may relate to Israeli security interests or territorial encroachment. Recent and future talks between Putin and Israeli Prime Minister Benjamin Netanyahu should clarify acceptable military and operational boundaries between pro-Assad forces, including Hezbollah, and Israel.

The knowns about the Syrian conflict appear to exceed the unknowns. Bashar al-Assad is a tough, stubborn individual who was not likely to welcome a revolutionary effort to overthrow his "legitimate" regime. For complex historic reasons, in addition to his own military forces, he had the good fortune to be supported by most Christians, Jews, Shiite Muslims, Alawites and others who feared a takeover of Syria by radical Sunni Muslims. Most important, Assad had the support of Iran and Russia. A significant factor often missed in discussions about Russia's position on Syria is that an estimated 14 percent of Russia's population (15 million) is Sunni Muslims.

From the outset of the civil war in Syria, the American position has been that the first step in resolving the dispute had to be the removal of Assad from office. That would not work. That impossible position has not changed for four years. Not just recently, but for quite some time, Putin has expressed the view that the only real chance of ending the conflict in Syria was for the United States and Russia to be joined by Iran, Turkey and Saudi Arabia to negotiate a comprehensive peace proposal. Iran supported this position.

"External players can not decide anything for the Syrians. We must force them to come up with a plan for their country where the interests of every religious, ethnic and political group will be well protected," Lavrov told Russian state TV in a recent interview. "They [Syria] need to prepare for both parliamentary and presidential elections."

In the chess match on political settlement of the Syrian crisis, Egypt and Russia have agreed to the necessity of a political solution based on the Geneva Communiqué which would guarantee the formation of a transitional body in Syria. This leaves Saudi Arabia as the strongest and most influential supporter of the National Coalition for Syrian Revolutionary and Opposition Forces (SNC), a coalition of opposition groups in Syria formed in 2012. Egypt and Saudi share essentially the same position on removal of Assad. Egypt could be influential in persuading Saudi to withdraw its military support of the SNC, which would leave Turkey as its only supporter. In the Syrian chess match, therefore, Egypt could play an important mediating role.

Only history will reveal even an approximation of the truth, but the recent decision by Russia to support the Assad regime with airstrikes and other military forces may have been a calculated strategy by Russia, with Iran's concurrence, to force a Syrian political process that leads to an end to the Syrian crisis. In support of this view, several months ago Iran outlined a four-point sequence consisting of (1) a cease-fire, (2) formation of a unity government, (3) constitutional reforms and (4) elections. Iran could have added a step (5): a concerted effort to stamp out the threat of the Islamic State.

The price of this Russian strategy, however, for which Putin has offered no apologies, has been the inevitable escalation of violence across the country displacing tens of thousands more people, intensifying the humanitarian crisis. More than 9,000 migrants a day crossed into Greece just last week, the most since the beginning of the year. As many as 100,000 people have been uprooted north of Homs and in areas around the city of Aleppo. A great many more refugees would have fled Syria but, according to humanitarian aid groups, are trying to wait out the fighting near their home villages. In addition, the border with Turkey has been closed.

The current and future dialogue between Russia, the US, Turkey, Saudi Arabia, and NATO about the future of Syria and Assad not only is significant, it could become pivotal. The key issue for all parties remains the future and role of Assad in a "political transition" in Syria. For Russia, as an absolute condition, any "political transition" has to involve Assad. Another key issue is the participation of Iran in future discussions. Russia wants Iran included; the US and Saudi are opposed. But other Russian positions, assuming that they are credible, seem promising.

Russia is using the term "partnership" with the US when discussing the process of "political transition" in Syria. The process itself, Russia says, should be transparent with international monitoring. The end result, according to Russia, should be a "unified country" with a secular government. Assad's fate should be decided by the Syrian people. Russia's position in the diplomatic chess game on Syria's "political transition" process and its outcome for Assad ('let the Syrians decide') perfectly puts the US in check.

Even more brilliantly, almost guaranteeing checkmate, Russia connects its proposal for Syria's "political transition" to the Geneva Communiqué of June 30, 2012. At the international peace conference for Syria in June 2012, participants agreed to what has become known as the Geneva Communiqué. It laid out a six-point plan intended to stop the violence and move the two sides towards a political settlement. The Geneva Communiqué calls for the establishment of a transitional governing body that would "exercise full executive powers." It says that could include "members of the present government and the opposition and other groups and shall be formed on the basis of mutual consent."

In the aftermath of Geneva 2, the focus and commitment of the international community has been on how to make a "political transition" and "mutual consent" work in Syria. The language of the Geneva Communiqué did not say President Assad must be excluded from any future transition. Geneva 2 allowed for the Assad regime and opposition groups to work out an accommodation in which Assad gets to stay in the short-term, if acceptable to Russia and the United States (and Saudi and Iran, both of which have been fighting proxy wars in Syria), but does not guarantee that Assad will remain a political player indefinitely.

Russia's decision to enter the Syrian conflict with air strikes upended the strategy of the United States and its regional and European allies and forced them to the negotiating table. By tipping the balance of power on the battlefield in Assad's favor and making it less likely that his enemies will be able to drive him out, Moscow clearly hopes to improve his position in future talks. And it appears that Russia has succeeded with this opening chess move.

Russia's next move was to win a seat at the negotiating table for Assad's main backer, Iran. That was yet another a major diplomatic victory over the US. Iran, which has furnished advisers to aid Assad's forces on the ground and supported the Lebanese Shiite Hezbollah fighting on behalf of Damascus, agrees with Russia that Syrians must pick their leader. While all of these moves were taking place, Russia was at work in the background coordinating its military action on Syria with Jordan, another important regional ally of the United States, by setting up a "special working mechanism" in the Jordanian capital, Amman. The US was forced to welcome this cooperation. US Secretary of State John Kerry said, "We have no problem whatsoever with this effort and it may even help make certain that the targets are the targets that they ought to be."

As Kerry studied the chess board, he did not rule out Iran's participation in a conference on Syria next week with Saudi Arabia, Turkey, other allies, and Russia. In diplomatic-speak he said, "We want to be inclusive and err on the side of inclusivity rather than exclusivity." Russia not only has argued for Iran's participation in peace talks, but also the "full spectrum of opposition" -- that Russia is in the process of trying to destroy.

The good and the bad news in Syria is that even with close to a thousand Russian air sorties on "terrorist installations," opposition forces appear to be holding out reasonably well but civilians continue to suffer the brunt of death and destruction. Rebels have figured out how to deal with Assad's ground forces with a combination of heavy mining and anti-tank missiles. Tens of thousands more civilians have been displaced in addition to hundreds killed. Since the US and Turkey have refused to impose a no-fly zone, they have had no impact on the ground war, over 80% of which has targeted areas held by rebels, and not ISIS and al-Nusra.

Most of the big news about Russia's military presence in Syria has focused on its bombing raids against both Islamic State positions and rebel groups opposed to the regime of Bashar al-Assad. Then came headline news about Russian warships in the Caspian Sea launching long-range cruise missile at Syrian targets. In addition, debate rages in Washington and in the presidential campaign about establishing a no-fly zone (NFZ) in various parts of Syria.

Recently Kerry asked the National Security Council (NSC) and State Department staff to examine the pros and cons of a NFZ in Syria in which military aircraft would not be allowed to enter. The goal of NFZ advocates has been to prevent the Assad regime's devastating barrel-bombing on civilian targets which has generated vast numbers of refugees and displaced persons in addition to a huge death toll. But with the entrance of Russian aircraft into the Syrian civil war, a NFZ potentially has much more controversial consequences.

What receives much less attention in the media is fact that Russia and NATO, led by the US and the UK, increasingly are engaged in all-out electronic warfare in Syria that probably will be more important in determining the outcome of rebel efforts to oust Assad than any other factor. The arrival of Russia's fighter planes captured headline news, but under the radar (no pun intended) the equally important news is that Russia has deployed its Krasukha-4 mobile electronic warfare (EW) unit to Syria, adding to its other capabilities to electronically "blind," deny or disrupt NATO's intelligence gathering capabilities and also intercept intelligence from low-orbit surveillance satellites (Lacrosse/Onyx series), various reconnaissance aircraft, and the RAF's Sentinel R1 and Reaper drones.

NATO and Russia are turning their state-of-the-art electronic technologies against each other in Syria and continuously ratcheting up their EW cat-and-mouse game. As perhaps the next best thing to a NFZ, NATO surveillance assets are able to monitor all Syrian-based Russian military aircraft activity and know the rebel groups that Russian aircraft are targeting. Russia knows exactly what NATO is doing with its reconnaissance and intelligence-gathering assets and continuously tracks all of them, including Lacrosse/ Onyx satellite positions. Each side uses automated counter-measure systems to dodge signal jamming or interception. What we don't know is how much of Russia's EW interventions aim to undermine the Islamic State and prevent its expansion. What we do know is that none of these EW assets support insurgent groups that are fighting both ISIS and the Assad regime.

CHAPTER 4

Iran's Nuclear Deal, Proxies & The Persian Gulf Region

On the eve of US approval of the nuclear deal with Iran, Iran's Supreme Leader Ayatollah Ali Khamenei emphatically stated that his country will not enter into talks with the United States outside of the nuclear deal with world powers in order to "penetrate" the Islamic Republic. Khamenei went on to say: "We approved talks with the United States about the nuclear issue specifically. We have not allowed talks with the US in other fields and we will not negotiate with them." What he was referring to was further discussions with the "Great Satan" about the Syrian civil war or any other of Iran's proxy wars. "The Iranian nation ousted the Satan. We should not let it back through the window to penetrate Iran," he said.

Khamenei indirectly was responding to remarks by Iranian President Hassan Rouhani signaling that Iran was ready to hold talks with world powers on ways to resolve Syria's civil war. Khamenei also reiterated his stance against Israel. "I say that you (Israelis) will not see the coming 25 years and, God willing, there will not be something named the Zionist regime in next 25 years," he said. Obviously, Congressional debate about the Iran nuclear deal will not shed any light on whether: the Iranians really can be trusted or not; agreeing to the Joint Comprehensive Plan of Action (JCPOA) will enable Iran to strengthen its proxy partners and their wars and expand their visible and invisible destabilizing activities; the nuclear deal with Iran will adversely impact on the US leadership role in the Middle East, North Africa or elsewhere, and its conflicted relationship with Israel.

None of these questions have any direct bearing on evaluating the merits of the JCPOA. Moreover, in all likelihood, none of these questions have clear answers that the US intelligence community, State Department or other US national security advisors can shed much light on. All that we know at the moment, which probably will be debated in connection with the Iran nuclear deal, is that economic sanctions on Iran will begin to lift when it reduces its stockpile of low-enriched uranium to 660 pounds (300 kilograms), a 98 percent reduction in its current stockpile of nearly 12 tons.

If Iranians are caught cheating by inspection of its nuclear installations, international sanctions will be reimposed. After 15 years, however, and this is the most problematic issue in the nuclear deal debate, Iran will be allowed to produce reactor-grade fuel on an industrial scale using advanced centrifuges. In that 15-year period, and conceivably long before that, say critics, Iran's economy will be so strong, especially after the lifting of sanctions, retrieval of its assets and economic gains from oil and mineral resources, that it won't matter if new international economic sanctions are imposed. In addition, Iran's nuclear installations will be protected by air defense systems bought by Iran post-sanctions with its restored and new wealth.

Although the duration of the nuclear agreement (15 years) received the most attention in Congress and the media, the real issue is that, as the years go by, Iran will need less and less "breakout time" to get centrifuges in operation and produce weapons grade fuel. Under the nuclear deal, inspectors will be monitoring production of centrifuge components for 20 years and Iran's stock of uranium for 25 years. More important than what officially, on paper, gets included in the JCPOA deal with Iran, will be Congressionally-approved supplementary US policy that says to Iran: "if our intensive, unrelenting, intrusive intelligence detects any evidence that you are pursuing nuclear weapons, we will use any means necessary, including military force, to stop it." That's not far from the statement made by US Energy Secretary Ernest Moniz to a House committee that any attempt by Iran to produce highly enriched uranium "at any time must earn a sharp response by all necessary means."

Iranian weaponization would officially and publicly get the highest US and presidential intelligence priority irrespective of who and what party occupies the White House in the coming decades. The US will draw on and share intelligence with the International Atomic Energy Agency (IAEA), but not solely rely on information from IAEA inspections to make its own followup decisions. In addition the US and its allies will do everything within their power to prevent ballistic missiles and their technology from getting to Iran or its proxies. The US will strengthen the missile defense and counterinsurgency capabilities of Israel and Gulf Arabs with a specific focus on Iran. The US will make sure, before the relief of sanctions, that P5+1 and all of its allies around the world that have been involved in Iranian sanctions are ready to implement sanctions snap-back provisions when and if necessary.

Separately, and not covered by the JCPOA agreement, but in response to the concern of every country in Europe, the Middle East, Africa and Asia, the US intelligence community and its global partners, as one of their highest priorities, will systematically monitor efforts by Iran to fund and arm its proxies and foster destabilization anywhere in the world, and will develop and implement coordinated contingency plans to deal with Iranian and Iranian-proxy activities that threaten the security interests of the U.S and its allies. All of these commitments need to be made publicly by the current or next President of the United States and also, more immediately, by any candidate that hopes to occupy the Oval Office.

Iran has the technological capability to produce a nuclear bomb. Arguably, however, what the Islamic Republic did not have over the past decades, in its own national psyche, was sufficient respect from the US and Western nations. For good reasons, as a given in their relationship, neither Iran nor the US trust each other. Iran probably has wanted transnational civilian power and respect even more than just military power. Developing nuclear power and a nuclear bomb have been a means for Iran to achieve international respect, ironically at the expense of increasing international political isolation. During P5+1 negotiations, Iran's political psyche may have been revealed most clearly in its defiant statements about the West's "colonial war" against Iran intended to keep it from scientific advancement, and also expressing a host of other grievances going back to the 1960s. Iranian dialogue with the West continued, however, even as sanctions tightened.

As Congress debated the Iran nuclear deal, Kerry probably was correct in his view that the Ayatollah was watching the proceedings with a deeply ingrained suspicion that America's untrustworthy leadership will not only reject the deal but, in the process, add additional layers of disrespect to its ruptured relationship with Iran. Kerry -- and President Obama – have been convinced that rejection of the Iranian nuclear deal sooner or later would lead to war and, at the very least, wreck potentially important opportunities to engage with Iran and also the US's Arab allies to discuss destabilizing regional issues, including Israeli security. Kerry claimed that these discussions were promised by Iran's foreign minister, Javad Zarif and his boss, President Hassan Rouhani. Of course, other than approval of the Iran nuclear deal, there is no way of proving that Zarif and Rouhani will follow-through on their commitment to Kerry. Is Iran intent on destroying Israel? According to Kerry, the Iran nuclear deal answers that question, not by pointless speculation about Iran's intentions, but rather by removing the nuclear threat mechanism for Iran's destruction of Israel.

Under JCPOA, Iran is supposed to come clean about its past nuclear activities. The task of assessing Iran's past nuclear activities falls to the International Atomic Energy Agency (IAEA). By the end of December 2015, the IAEA has to obtain Iran's road map for cooperation and report on Iran's work developing nuclear technology, including the design of warheads. Thus far the IAEA has not explained how it will obtain Iran's full (honest) disclosure.

One of the main problems facing Iran in its required response is that, in the past, it has denied previous weaponization activities; in fact, the Ayatollah has said Islam forbids nuclear weapons. Showing the level of distrust by P5+1 for honest compliance by Iran, centrifuge production will be videotaped 7x24 for 20 years. For 25 years all Iranian uranium production -- from mine to mill to yellowcake to gas to waste – will be tracked and traced. According to the international intelligence community, it is not possible for Iran to have a complete, covert, separate fuel cycle, but no chances are being taken by the P5+1 and the IAEA.

Iran has agreed to turn its worrisome Fordow facility into a research center where Iranian and world scientists will work side by side. For years experts have believed that Iran was enriching uranium in centrifuges there. Iran also has agreed to rebuild its Arak heavy-water reactor, currently the only site in Iran capable of starting production on weapons-grade plutonium, using a design that would make production of weapons-grade plutonium impossible. Iran will have to give up most of its centrifuges for the next 10 years. However, the deal allows Iran to continue enriching uranium at its Natanz facility to a level sufficient only for civilian purposes.

The devil is in the details of the JCPOA. Legitimate questions have been raised about every aspect of the JCPOA by people in the US and around the world that have the expertise to evaluate its extremely complicated provisions. Some of the most serious concerns have been that: Iran's centrifuges and its R&D program for centrifuges will not be shut down; many centrifuges will simply go into storage; uranium enrichment will continue, leading to future testing and manufacturing; in addition to enriching its own uranium, enriched uranium can be sourced from other countries for use in Iran's nuclear reactors; redesign of the heavy water reactor at Arak will delay production of weapon-grade plutonium for only 15 years, after which Iran also can acquire new heavy water reactors to produce weapons-grade plutonium; likewise, restrictions on nuclear activities at Fordow expire after 15 years; the JCPOA does not include anywhere/anytime inspections of suspected sites by the IAEA for enforcement purposes; and most important, the JCPOA dispute resolution process, which could include referral to the UN Security Council, is lengthy and lacks consequences for non-compliance and cheating.

Iran poses many challenges for inspectors who have to police the agreement and gain access not only to scientists, labs and factories, but also to many underground sites and military bases. Inspections will have to be intrusive, especially given Iran's history of evasions and illicit procurements. Approval of the deal by Congress, and scrutiny of the deal by presidential candidates should focus on how the US and the IAEA propose to effectively detect cheating and covert sites. What we do know is that IAEA inspectors will have access to the entire supply chain that supports Iran's nuclear program and will engage in continuous surveillance of centrifuge manufacturing and storage facilities.

Probably the most controversial issue in the Congressional debate on the Iran nuclear deal will be the "24-day" rule for resolving disputes if Iran refuses to give inspectors access to any suspicious site. This requirement expires after 15 years. Inspectors then can still demand to enter sites, but without any deadline for Iran's compliance. Obviously this provision does not qualify as "anywhere/anytime" access to suspected sites. If Iran refuses an inspection, the punitive action, including reimposition of sanctions, will be decided by a commission that includes Iran. Commission decisions only require a majority vote, so Iran cannot determine the outcome. But Iran has made clear that, if sanctions are reimposed, it no longer will be bound to honor the agreement.

One of the most important outcomes of the process of seeking international support for the Iran nuclear deal has been Kerry's successful efforts to gain support from the Gulf Cooperation Council (GCC): Saudi Arabia, Qatar, Bahrain, Kuwait, the United Arab Emirates and Oman. In this process, Kerry's commitments to the GCC included: providing training for GCC Special Forces; increasing intelligence sharing; forming a common front against Iranians who seek to foment trouble in the Gulf region; assistance to improve missile defenses; increased joint military exercises;

and help for the navies of Gulf States to intercept Iran's attempts to smuggle weapons and people. All of these commitments to the GCC for military support also qualify as important support for international military containment of ISIS in the Gulf region.

In August 2015, no one inside or outside of Washington was ready to place bets on Congressional approval of the Iran-nuclear deal. The most beneficial aspect of the discourse about the deal to-date has been shedding light on, and feeding speculation about, Iran's proxy strategy over the past decade and going forward. The Arab Spring, however, has added a turbulent dimension to Tehran's proxy strategy and also engendered growing Sunni-Shia regional conflicts. Saudi Arabia, Turkey and the Gulf States have been increasing their resistance to Iran-supported Assad and, even moreso, Iran-supported Houthis in Yemen. Should Assad fall from power, no one knows how the unwinding of Assad's Syria is likely to unfold, the outcome for the Tehran-Damascus alliance, the consequences for the complex Syrian insurgency, the evolution of the Iran-Hezbollah alliance and, not least important, ISIS's ascendency in Syria.

In retrospect the deal negotiated by Kerry with the Gulf Arabs for support of the Iran nuclear deal over time may be viewed as the second most important outcome of the Iran nuclear deal, especially in terms of shoring up Gulf regional alliances for future proxy conflicts with Iran. However, while the international community is mainly focused on the Iranian nuclear deal and its impact on Iran's support for its proxies in the Middle East, the shock for those investing in oil and equities in stock markets around the world, and for Saudi and other Gulf state oil producers, is that Iran has been preparing to boost oil production, just one week after international sanctions are lifted! OPEC, and also Russia, have not indicted yet that they intend to cut oil production. Iraq, OPEC's second largest oil producer, is pumping more than 4 million barrels of oil a day, even with the global decline in oil prices.

Even in wealthy Saudi Arabia, and with oil prices dropping precipitously, the government has been burning through roughly

$10 billion a month in foreign exchange holdings to help pay expenses, and has been borrowing heavily in the international financial markets for the first time since 2007. Other Arab countries in the Persian Gulf that are dependent on oil exports, including Kuwait, Oman and Bahrain, are facing fiscal deficits for the first time in two decades. The price of oil, now more than 60 percent lower than it was earlier in 2015, could remain depressed far longer than even the most pessimistic projections, and do even deeper damage to Saudi and other Gulf oil exporters. Major oil exporting countries have lost more than a $1 trillion in oil sales because of the oil price decline over the last year. In addition, Gulf oil producing states did not anticipate the weakness in China's economy impacting so dramatically on oil prices.

A global oil supply glut has been evident for some time, driven partly by a vast increase in Saudi production and growing energy self-sufficiency in the United States which, until recently, was once heavily reliant on Middle East oil. Saudi Arabia not only is producing a record amount of oil, but also is increasing the number of rigs drilling for future production. And its Gulf allies, the United Arab Emirates and Kuwait, are following suit. Even with the turmoil wrought by the Islamic State, Iraq's oil production has jumped nearly 20 percent since the beginning of the year. The surge in production may seem counterintuitive, but all oil exporters in the Middle East are competing with each other to gain Asian market share since the United States is using much less of their oil.

The global oil glut is likely to worsen after the nuclear deal with Iran is approved, potentially releasing as much as several million more barrels of oil into the 94-million-barrel-a-day global market in a year or so. Iran had the second-biggest output in OPEC before US-led sanctions. Iran's oil production could increase by 500,000 barrels a day within a week after sanctions end and by 1 million barrels a day within a month following that. Iran already is planning a conference in London in December 2015 to discuss new oil contract models with international companies. In the context of the huge drop in oil prices, and the global glut of global oil supplies, Iran's impact on oil production after the lifting of sanctions could become one of the major unintended and unexpected consequences of the Iran nuclear deal.

In the global oil sphere, the Saudis have been flooding the market in a deliberate attempt to drive down the price of oil so that American and other high-cost producers cannot compete. In other words, the US is in an unexpected oil war with Saudi in which Iran will play a role if the nuclear agreement is approved. Thus the Iran nuclear deal becomes part of US competition with the Arab region for a share of global oil revenue, and could become an unanticipated destabilizing factor in the Arab region as Brent oil prices possibly descend as low as $30 a barrel in 2016. More vulnerable than Saudi, Kuwait or the UAE in the global oil price war will be Nigeria, Angola, Algeria, Venezuela and Iraq that need oil revenues to sustain their economies and capabilities to finance their own fight against ISIS and other terrorism

As Congress debated the Iran nuclear deal, Turkey had Russia on its mind. Turkey's Prime Minister Recep Tayyip Erdogan was quoted as saying that Russian President Vladimir Putin may be ready to "give up" on Syrian President Bashar Assad. As we now know, that's far from true. Russia, like Turkey, Saudi and the US know that, barring a strategic intervention, Assad probably is on the way out. Russia is not comfortable with Assad's military support from Iran and the successes of ISIS in Syria. Putin has his own plan in mind that would provide a path to salvation and legitimacy for Assad as a member of an international anti-ISIS coalition that could even include Iran. In addition to Iran, Russia has been one of Assad's most loyal backers. Moscow wants to maintain access to a warm water port in Syria. More important, Russia does not support US-led regime change anywhere in the Middle East, including Syria, Iraq and Libya. After his GCC meeting, Kerry met with Sergey V. Lavrov, the Russian foreign minister, and Adel al-Jubeir, his Saudi counterpart, to discuss the crisis in Syria.

In addition to dialogue with Russia, the Iran nuclear deal also reopened communication between the US and Cairo, the first bilateral strategic dialogue since 2009 and after Islamist President Mohamed Mursi was ousted in 2013 by the military amid mass protests against his rule. Cairo remains one of Washington's closest allies in the Middle East. Cairo and Washington have been exploring ways to expand their security relationship. Cairo has a US commitment to receive arms valued at over $1.3 billion and already has had delivery of eight F-16 fighter jets.

With or without a nuclear deal, Iranian funds of as much as $150 billion (and possibly much less) will be returned to Tehran. After Congressional approval of the nuclear deal, the $150 billion or less will be a "bonus" for Iran. If Congress rejects the nuclear deal, the web of international sanctions will crumble and the banks that hold Iran's funds will unlock access. Will these previously frozen funds flow to Assad and various other Iranian proxies in Iraq, Yemen and elsewhere? Will it make a difference?

Assad's Syria is very dependent on money, fighters and weapons from or supported by Iran. Iran spends more than $6 billion annually on Syria. After making such a huge financial investment to keep President Bashar al-Assad in power and protect its interest in Syria, Iran will not easily relinquish its geopolitical stake. The Islamic Revolutionary Guards Corps (IRGC) Ground Forces, Quds Force, Iran's intelligence services and law enforcement forces have aided Assad's regime, and huge amounts of military supplies have been shipped in by air. Lebanese Hezbollah has supported Assad with a well-trained force. Iraqi Shia militants also are fighting in Syria in support of Assad as part of the Abu al-Fadl al-Abbas Brigade which brings together Syrian and foreign Shia fighters, Lebanese Hezbollah and Iraq-based Asa'ib Ahl al-Haq and Kata'ib Hezbollah.

Presidential and Congressional debates about the terms and implications of an Iran nuclear deal also put a secondary spotlight on Iran's proxies, like Hezbollah and supposed proxies, like the Houthis in Yemen. A tertiary light has been shed on Iran's support for Assad's regime in Syria, using Hezbollah as its proxy fighting force, and the fact that insurgent groups in Syria like Al-Qaeda-affiliated Jabhat al-Nusra are opposed to both Assad and Iran.

Removal of sanctions against Iran in connection with the nuclear deal adds enormous complications to existing complexities in the

Middle East. Tehran will reap as much as $150 billion through sanctions relief and regaining assets that have been frozen in overseas banks. These billions in proceeds for Iran from the lifting of sanctions probably will make some of the main beneficiaries: Syria's Assad; Hezbollah, the Lebanese militant group fighting (and dying in large numbers) on Assad's behalf in Syria; Shiite militias in Iraq; and Houthi rebels in Yemen. Iran's Shia proxy forces will reinforce their power and influence in the Sunni Arab-dominated region and improve their ability to compete with Saudi Arabia for primacy in the Middle East. The Saudis know and fear this probable outcome of the Iran nuclear deal.

The nuclear deal between Iran and the West will do little to change Iran's proxy strategy.

Supreme Leader Ayatollah Ali Khamenei has made it clear that Iran would continue to support its allies and proxies in the Middle East. "We will always support the oppressed Palestinian nation, Yemen, Syrian government and people, Iraq, and oppressed Bahraini people, and also the honest fighters of Lebanon and Palestine," he said July 18, 2015, in a talk after prayers to mark the end of Ramadan. Although Iran's relationship to its proxies is very much impacted by the nuclear deal, they have not been included in US negotiations, presumably in order to not introduce obstacles to consummation of the deal.

"We'll still have problems with Iran's sponsorship of terrorism; its funding of proxies like Hezbollah that threaten Israel and threaten the region; the destabilizing activities that they're engaging in, including in places like Yemen," President Obama told reporters on July 15, 2015. The president said he hoped that the deal would lay the groundwork for future discussions with the Iranians "that incentivize them to behave differently in the region, to be less aggressive, less hostile [and] more cooperative." However, he added, "we're not counting on it."

Strong concerns have been expressed across the region -- particularly in Israel and Saudi Arabia -- that Obama and the US has been more focused on successfully consummating a nuclear deal than on the threat of rising instability fostered by Iran and its proxies. The State Department's spokesman John Kirby emphatically denies this. For some time, however, American relationships with Iran have included numerous contradictions and conundrums within the GCC. In Ramadi, US troops and Iraqi security forces are relying on Iranian-backed militias to fight the Islamic State while the US strives to get the Shiite-dominated Iraqi government to enlist more members of Sunni minorities to fight ISIS. The US has no idea whether Iran will support this effort or whether the nuclear deal will embolden Iran to only support Shiite militias in Iraq, Hezbollah and Hamas fighting Israel, Hezbollah and Iranian troops defending Assad in Syria, Houthi rebels fighting in Yemen, and increased sectarian conflict around the Gulf region. Optimists see opportunities for an expanded dialogue between Iranian and American governments to ease these conflicts.

The best possibility for collaboration between Iran and the US could be Afghanistan where both the US and Teheran want to restrain the Taliban and block Al-Qaeda from re-establishing safe havens. Iran wants to prevent the flow of Afghan opium and refugees into Iran. In Yemen, where the Saudis claim that their goal is to prevent Iran from controlling the vast territory along their southern border, there's actually not much evidence that the Iranians have provided significant military support to the Houthis or exercise real control over the group. There are reasons to believe that Iran might even cooperate to calm the chaos caused by Houthis and other rebels in Yemen, but that may be just another instance of wishful thinking.

It was not long ago that Minister Mohammad Javad Zarif, Iran's lead nuclear negotiator, not only closed the nuclear deal, but he had the audacity to shake President Obama's hand at the UN General Assembly. In addition to his work on the nuclear deal, that unplanned gesture put a bulls-eye on his back for Teheran's conservatives even though the deal will result in lifting sanctions. Iran's conservatives are determined to stop "American infiltration" of Teheran.

The friendly handshake with "the enemy" was viewed with great displeasure by conservative Iranian officials. For conservatives, diplomatic and any other relationships with America threatens the Islamic revolution. Iran's supreme leader, Ayatollah Ali Khamenei, emphatically has ruled out any further negotiations with the United States. He has warned that such talks would "open gates to their economic, cultural, political, and security influence" in Tehran. In contrast are President Rouhani's efforts to lessen enmity with the West with the prospect of speeding up beneficial business deals and Zarif's efforts to engage Iran in finding a political solution in Syria. Zarif, however, in his personal history and career as a diplomat, is the exception in Iran, having spent 20 of his 55 years in the United States as a student and diplomat.

In the aftermath of the nuclear deal with Iran, we are seeing an escalating struggle for the future of Iran between the hard-line vision of the Islamic Republic and pragmatists like Zarif and Rouhani. As a strong undercurrent in the conflict is elections to the majlis, Iran's parliament, to be held in February 2016, and also for the 86 members of the Assembly of Experts that has the power to dismiss a supreme leader. Rouhani reelection seems assured but he needs a moderate parliament in order to deliver reform. Rouhani has to be careful about any efforts to improve relations with the United States.

Recent events in Iran make it clear that the Iranian battle against "The Great Satan" not only continues but may be intensifying. Iran has arrested a number of activists, journalists and artists since Rouhani's 2013 election, among them four Iranians with U.S. citizenship. This is the work of hard-liners in the judiciary and the security forces.

The U.S. and Iran have had no diplomatic relations since students in Teheran (Nov. 4, 1979) stormed the U.S. Embassy compound and held 52 Americans hostage for 444 days. On the 36th anniversary of that event, protestors in Teheran and other cities carried placards reading "political and security penetration is forbidden" while pumping their fists in the air and shouting "God damn America," and "No compromise, no surrender to U.S." These demonstrations marked Iran's "National Day against Global Arrogance."

One piece of "good news" from the Iranian protests was a statement by Iran's supreme leader, Ayatollah Ali Khamenei, saying the "Death to America" chants heard around Iran's cities were aimed at Washington's policies — not the American people themselves. "Obviously by 'Death to America,' we don't mean death to the American people," Khamenei told a group of students in Iran. "The American nation is just like the rest of the nations. It ... means death to U.S. policies and its arrogance."

Tehran's use of proxy forces dates back to the 1980s when it launched the Quds Force, as part of the Islamic Revolutionary Guard Corps, to create, train, and direct militant groups in the region to basically do Iran's bidding. The term "proxy" forces probably is a misnomer since the so-called "proxy" forces in each country are quite different and have to been examined and understood in their historical contexts. Yemen provides one of the best illustrations. Internal power politics at play in Yemen are among the oldest, most complex and dynamic in the Middle East. A weak Sunni-led central government had been barely holding onto power for decades while engaged in simultaneous and perpetual conflicts with a myriad of militant actors, many of whom the government itself was responsible for creating in the midst of tribal disputes and secessionist movements in both the north and south that could not be resolved.

As the Iran nuclear deal moved forward, Saudi Arabia repeatedly hinted that it would seek its own atomic weapons if Tehran's nuclear program was not halted. Saudi Arabia probably does not have the capability to build a nuclear weapon. Could it buy one? Possibly from Pakistan? The Saudis have bailed out Pakistan many times. But any deal by Pakistan (which has more than hundred nukes in its stockpile) to sell nukes to Saudi would be very risky in terms of producing sanctions on both countries.

Saudi Arabia, that for years has been pushing extreme fundamentalism and financing the radicalization of Sunni Islam around the world, did not have a better alternative to the Iran nuclear deal before Congress. Saudi's King Salman signaled broad support for the Iran nuclear deal in a meeting with President Obama at the

White House, while urging a tough inspection regime and snapback sanctions, and also vehemently objecting to Iran's autonomy with regard to inspections of its military installation at Parchin.

The nuclear threat from Iran resulted in a much more aggressive Saudi perspective on its own role as protector of the Sunni-Arab world, which has not received much attention from either Congress or the media. The Iran nuclear deal has given Saudi's King Salman a platform to insist that the United States help combat Iran's proxies across the region. The Obama Administration has promised increased military support for Gulf Cooperation Council (GCC) countries -- including a potential missile defense shield, previously discussed at Camp David, other military hardware, like F-15s, that Israel objects to, and building an Arab defense force.

Salman wanted more US support, beyond intelligence and logistics for the Saudis campaign against the Houthis in Yemen. Without any announcements or Congressional involvement, the US has more than doubled its advisors on the ground in Yemen, providing targeting intelligence for airstrikes and helping the Saudis in various ways to roll back the Houthis. Without any question, the US is engaged in a war in Yemen, call it a counterinsurgency, that has not been approved by Congress and that the American public knows nothing about, including US responsibility for a very large number of civilian casualties.

The Saudis used their cooperation and support for the Iran nuclear deal to extract some additional "concessions" from Obama, including more US maritime, cyber and missile defense weapons, training of Saudi's special forces, and an unspecified increase of US activities in the region to help halt Iran and its proxies in Syria, Iraq, Lebanon and Yemen. The good news is that all of these "concessions" were aimed at enabling the Saudis to improve their ability to defend themselves and limit direct US involvement in Gulf conflicts. A focus of Obama's conversation with Salman was the Saudi-led military campaign against Iranian-backed Houthi rebels in Yemen. US officials have provided intelligence and logistics support for the campaign since it began.

Civilian casualties in Yemen have become a controversial humanitarian concern for the US. Targeted by the US and using US bombs, "errant" Saudi coalition airstrikes have destroyed markets, apartment buildings and refugee camps. Many of the bombs have fallen so far from any military target that more than a thousand civilians have died in the strikes, without any objection expressed by the US. The US has been finalizing a deal to sell more missiles to Saudi for its F-15 fighter jets. In parts of northern Yemen, which is populated largely by Shiite Muslims, the bombing campaign by Sunni Saudi Arabia has forced people to take shelter in mountain caves.

Instead of acknowledging killing civilians by mistake, Saudi Arabia blames the Iranian-backed Houthis, accusing them of fighting from populated areas. Col. Patrick S. Ryder, a spokesman for United States Central Command, said American officials have asked "the Saudi government to investigate all credible reports of civilian casualties resulting from coalition-led airstrikes and, if confirmed, to address the factors that led to them." More than 4,500 people have been killed in Yemen's civil war. Hundreds have died in street battles between the Houthis and their rivals for control of Yemen's most important cities, like Taiz and Aden. In addition to the ground war, harsh Saudi restrictions on imports have deepened humanitarian suffering in Yemen, causing shortages of fuel, water and medical supplies

Iran's increased support for its proxies in Iraq, Lebanon, Syria and Yemen will contribute to the long-term regional conflict between radical Sunni-Shia theocracies. But the focus on military threats by Iran and its proxies, especially after lifting of the crippling sanctions, is missing the fundamental fact that the Arab Gulf states have an overwhelmingly superior advantage compared to Iran in both military spending and arms.

The Saudi government spends more than 25 percent of its budget on military assets (more than $80 billion in 2014). The United Arab Emirates (UAE) spends about 40 percent as much ($23 billion in 2014). Iran only spent $15 billion that year, less than half of the UAE's budget. It's not just a matter of Iran being outspent, the Gulf Arab countries have purchased, and will continue to purchase, the most modern American military hardware, such as fighter jets, Predator drones, Apache attack helicopters, Patriot air-defense systems, and the latest missiles, bombs, and other weapons.

Saudi and the Gulf states are an armed camp that holds the regional balance of power. The huge drop in oil and commodity prices will have its negative effect on the Gulf states and Iran but, with a more diversified economy, Iran may be in a better position to deal with these global trends. Now that the US is no longer dependent on Saudi oil, it may be reminding itself that most of the 9/11 terrorists came from Riyadh and that, in a real sense, Saudi is engaged in an ideological and theological war with Iran that has a long and violent history over centuries. In the 2016 presidential campaign thus far, Saudi's political and military position in the Gulf and Middle East has been cloaked by concerns about Assad (that Saudi wants unconditionally removed) and Iran in the aftermath of the lifting of Sanctions.

Saudi's current religious identity has been shaped by Muhammad ibn 'Abd al-Wahhab (the founder of Wahhabism) and his radically puritanical form of Muslim faith that declared war on all other Muslim teachings and pledged allegiance to a Caliph or Muslim leader. Adopted by Saudi's Ibn Saud in the mid-18th century, Abd al-Wahhab's teachings became the doctrine that he used to seize power and instill fear under the banner of jihad that included the idea of martyrdom to gain immediate entry into paradise. By 1790, Ibn Saud controlled most of the Arabian Peninsula and terrorized Syria and Iraq, massacring thousands of Shiites in Iraq's Karbaka in 1801. In the early 19th century, the Ottomans destroyed the Saudi state and forced the Wahhabis to withdraw into the desert where they remained for most of the 19th century.

When the Ottoman Empire collapsed during World War I, Abd-al Aziz united Bedouin tribes and launched the Saudi "Ikhwan", a reincarnation of Abd-al Wahhab's and Ibn Saud's Wahhabist insurgency. The Ikhwan succeeded in capturing Mecca, Medina and Jeddah between 1914 and 1926. Fueled by billions in oil revenues, the Saudis expanded the reach of Wahhabism throughout the lands of Islam. ISIS emerged as deeply Wahhabist, seeking to purify Wahhabism and return it to its true origins that they see as lost in the westernization of Saudi Arabia. In January 2015 former Saudi King Abdullah bin Abdulaziz passed away and was succeeded by his half-brother, King Salman bin Abdulzis. Yemen became King Salman's first and foremost foreign policy challenge and the first deployment of the joint GCC military command set up in November 2014 that notably includes Turkey.

At a Camp David meeting in May 2015 between the GCC and Obama, the president rejected the idea of initiating mutual defense treaties with Gulf states, but agreed to expedite military assistance to Gulf countries to build their capacity to deal with "asymmetric threats" related to terrorism and to assist in the development of an early warning system for missile defense -- a region-wide ballistic missile defense system. As part of this agreement, Gulf states will consult with the US before taking military actions. What this means is that the US will have to approve – and cannot deny some responsibility for -- any military actions taken in Yemen and the rest of the Gulf region by GCC members.

The relationship of the US to the Persian Gulf region and the dynamics of Middle Eastern politics are threatened and have been altered by Iran's current and future regional resurgence. The recent Iran nuclear deal exacerbated concerns in the Gulf States about Iran's growing capabilities to establish regional hegemony. These cumulative concerns have provided a very strong, negative and disruptive undercurrent for the Vienna talks on the future of Assad and Syria. At the heart of the stresses between the Gulf States and Iran, which seemingly focus on Sunni Saudi's antipathy toward Shiite Iran, may be more about the history of Iran and Bahrain and why, for much of the 20th century, the strategically located island-nation of Bahrain has seen its sovereignty threatened by Iran.

Bahrain has been ruled by the Sunni Muslim Al Khalifa family which captured the Bahraini archipelago from the Iranian-based Al Madhkur family in 1782-1783. In the 19th century, the Al Khalifa family secured its control of the territory through a series of treaties with Britain. The British had a base in Bahrain until 1971 when it withdrew from the Gulf. At that moment, the Shah withdrew Iran's claim to Bahrain. Ruled by Sunnis, more than 70 percent of Bahrain has been Shiite. In 1981 the Iranian-backed Shiite Islamic Front for the Liberation of Bahrain failed in its attempt to overthrow the Bahraini's Sunni rulers. The attempted coup and the outbreak of the Iran-Iraq War led to the formation of the Gulf Cooperation Council (GCC) in which Bahrain joined with Kuwait, Oman, Qatar, Saudi Arabia and the United Arab Emirates (UAE). The tensions between ruling Sunni elites and Shiites have periodically erupted into rioting and violence. Home to the U.S. Navy's Fifth Fleet, Bahrain was swept by protests during the 2011 "Arab Spring" uprisings in which Shiites demanded political reforms.

Without attempting to cover various cycles of protests by the Shiite majority and their outcomes, suffice it to say here that Bahrain has had good reasons not to welcome Iran's recent acknowledgement that it supports opposition groups seeking greater political and economic rights for Bahrain's Shiite community. In June 2015 Bahrain announced the recalling of its ambassador to Tehran for consultations after what it said were repeated hostile Iranian statements. More recently Bahrain summoned Iran's acting charge d'affaires to protest against Iran's Supreme Leader Ali Khamenei voicing support for "oppressed people" across the Middle East, including in Bahrain.

Bahrain also said that an arms smuggling plot by two Bahrainis with ties to Iran had been foiled. Announcing their arrest, the interior ministry said the two suspects had admitted receiving a shipment of explosives, automatic weapons, and ammunition from Iranian handlers outside Bahrain's territorial waters. One of them had received military training at a Revolutionary Guards camp in Iran in 2013. Then Bahrain recalled its ambassador to Iran after its security forces discovered a large bomb-making factory and arrested a number of suspects linked to Iran's Revolutionary Guards. As a result, Bahrain's Ministry of Foreign Affairs said it had also declared the Iranian charge d'affaires in Bahrain a "persona non grata" and gave him 72 hours to leave the country.

Envision all of this conflict between Bahrain and Iran, and support for Bahrain from the entire GCC, as the acrimonious prequel to Syria peace talks. Iran announced that it would quit Syria peace talks if it found them unconstructive, which was not unexpected. In particular Iran anticipated, and it got, "negative role" from its primary regional rival, Saudi Arabia. As could have been expected, the Syria peace talks turned into an increasingly bad-tempered series of exchanges between the conservative Sunni-ruled kingdom and its GGC supporters and the revolutionary Shiite theocracy.

Less than 24 hours after the Vienna talks, the negativity escalated in a followup regional security conference in Bahrain (minus Iran) when Saudi Foreign Minister Jubeir attacked Iranian interference in countries in the region and meddling in Lebanon, Syria, Iraq and Yemen. Iranian President Hassan Rouhani reprimanded Saudi Foreign Minister Adel al-Jubeir for criticizing Tehran. At this point, the role and patience of Iran is unclear in the next round of Syria peace talks.

CHAPTER 5

Sisi's Egypt & Gaza's Plight

After the crash of the Russian Metrojet over Egypt's Sinai Peninsula, President Abdel Fattah el-Sisi dismissed claims of responsibility for the terrorist attack by a branch of the Islamic State in the Sinai Province as propaganda aiming at harming "the stability and security of Egypt." Sisi portrayed these alarms as part of a plot by Western governments, including the US, against Egypt. Why would the US and Egypt's other Western allies try to tarnish Egypt's image? According to Dr. Alaa Abdel Wahab, an adviser to the minister of tourism, it is because they resented "the popular support for President Sisi."

This paranoia and defensive theme is not new in Egypt. Every time that Egypt experiences a crisis, it raises the specter of a shadowy foreign threat against its sovereignty or image. For Sisi, who spent years in military intelligence before he led the ouster of President Mohamed Morsi of the Muslim Brotherhood two years ago, the response and its conspiratorial mind-set reflect a lurking suspicion that the US and the UK are using the terrorist attack to expose its weakness. The fact that the US views Egypt as one of its main allies in the Middle East and Gulf region should be especially disconcerting to the White House.

The denial of a possible terrorist bombing of the Russian airplane also reflects Sisi's refusal to admit that his army has not been able to defeat and eliminate a militant insurgency in the Sinai. The news media has been prohibited from publishing critical reports about Sisi's government. After a military airstrike in September mistakenly hit a picnic of Mexican tourists and killed a dozen of them, the news media was barred from discussing the matter. Egypt has a great deal at stake in maintaining Russian and European tourism in the Sinai. Tourism in Egypt will be hurt even more as every nation in the EU either tightens or shuts down its borders in response to the terrorist attack on Paris, casting a shadow over the flow of tourists within and to Europe and Egypt.

Egypt, the most populous Arab country, just conducted an 'election without voters" that, as much as any such event possibly could, defines Egypt today. Egypt has had no parliament since June 2012. In the 2011-12 election, long queues of enthusiastic young people had lined up at the polls following the overthrow of autocratic Hosni Mubarak. With a huge percentage of the voting population young, no more than 20 percent of the voting population showed up at the polls in the recent election for Egypt's parliament, highlighting growing disillusionment with the Sisi regime since the army seized power in 2013 from Egypt's first freely-elected president, the Muslim Brotherhood's Mohamed Mursi. That was followed by the fiercest crackdown on dissenters and activists in Egypt's modern history, jailing thousands of Mursi's supporters.

President al-Sisi, the sixth president of Egypt since June 2014, came to power as a strongman who promised stability and security at a time when most Egyptians had grown exhausted from the uncertainties of the Arab Spring. Whereas Sisi described the recent 2015 election as a milestone on the road to democracy in Egypt, the low turnout undermined then-army chief Sisi's promise in 2013 of a "road map to democracy." Egyptians wanted Sisi's promised transition back to democracy, improvement of the economy and security. After four years of political turmoil, Egyptians above all wanted security. Sisi has delivered repressive security and restrictions on civil liberties. The recent anti-terrorism law in Egypt, for example, supposedly aimed at fighting jihadist insurgency, has been used to crack down on political opponents, dissidents and journalists, for "promoting false news."

President Obama has seemed quite unfazed by Egypt's lack of progress in democratic reforms, domestic policies on human and civil rights and freedom of expression. The United States has delivered to Egypt 12 Lockheed Martin F-16s Block 52 aircraft, 20 Boeing Harpoon missiles, and up to 125 M1A1 Abrams tank kits made by General Dynamics. Washington also has delivered two navy vessels, doubling Cairo's total fleet of Fast Missile Craft to four. In other words Egypt, Washington's close security ally in the Middle East, also is a very good customer for the U.S. defense industry. The US and Egypt also will resume "Bright Star," the joint military exercise suspended after the military coup of July 3, 2013.

Secretary of State John Kerry recently told Egyptian officials that they would not be able to defeat terrorism at home unless they showed greater respect for human rights and build trust with the public, but made it clear that the U.S. would not let their concerns with human rights stand in the way of increased security cooperation with Egypt, including assistance to better police the border with Libya. While defending the jailing of journalists accused of terrorist activity, Egypt's foreign minister responded that Egyptian authorities were trying to "strike a better balance between maintaining security and protecting human rights."

Egypt has used American-made F-16s and Apaches to destroy many targets in the Sinai's towns where militants were suspected of hiding, and occasionally leaving total villages in ruins. No apologies have been made by Egyptian officials for killing large numbers of innocent civilians and none were requested by Kerry. Some members of Congress, however, including Marco Rubio and John McCain, had urged Kerry to make human rights a centerpiece of his recent visit to Egypt. Kerry did reference the risk to Egypt of young protesters who have been jailed becoming radicalized while in prison, an indirect and muted reference to thousands of imprisoned secular and Muslim Brotherhood protesters.

Egypt presents an extremely complicated foreign policy story in relation to Syria, Saudi Arabia and the Gulf States, Israel and Gaza, and the rest of the Middle East. Libya is the easier part of the story of Egypt's relationships to other states in the region because it reflects former army-general Sisi's commitment to protect Egypt's security. Libya and Egypt share a porous 745-mile-long border. Since the fall of Muammar al-Qaddafi's regime in 2011, Libyan weapons have flooded into Egypt. Sisi and Egyptian security officials understandably have been extremely unhappy about this and other outcomes of the disintegration of Libya, its breakdown of law and order, and the emergence of militant Islamist groups that are thriving in lawless Libya, and even operating training camps in the desert of Derna on the Egypt-Libya border. Muslim Brotherhood members have been seeking refuge from Egyptian security forces in Libya.

It might have been reasonable to expect Egyptian military intervention into Libya. That hasn't happened for a number of reasons including the preoccupation of Egypt's military forces with its own domestic jihadist threats in the Sinai and terrorism elsewhere in the Egyptian mainland. Egypt also has been concerned about the safety and status of hundreds of thousands of Egyptian expatriates residing and working in Libya. Furthermore Libya's ongoing civil war and chaotic political affairs are really messy and unpredictable. More than that, the total focus of Egypt's security establishment, whether it involves Libya or Gaza (on its border) or Syria, has been on protecting its borders and domestic stability.

When the car of Egypt's state prosecutor, General Hisham Barakat, was blown up in Cairo, his assassination intensified existing fears and foreboding in Egypt about a new phase of violence which were reinforced when the Islamic State-affiliated Wilayat Sinai, or "Province of Sinai," killed dozens of soldiers and policemen in a raid on the town of Sheikh Zuweid the following day. Terrorists in the Sinai Province declared allegiance to the Islamic State in November 2014. A special forces operation killed nine members of the Muslim Brotherhood the same day of the Sheikh Zuweid attack. The Brotherhood called on Egyptians to rise up against President al-Sisi to avenge these deaths, further feeding fears of a spiral of violence.

Sisi's raison d'être of security and stability is quite understandable. The question is whether it is being undermined by forces beyond Sisi's control and by his approach to enforcing security, for example in the Sinai, where violent military repression feeds rather defeats insurgency. Thus far, looking forward, the U.S.'s close security ally in the Middle East has not proven itself to be a reliable counterterrorism partner.

Nor has Egypt proven to be a reliable mediator between Israel and the Palestinians (Egypt borders both Israel and Gaza), especially because of its deep antipathy towards Hamas. Egypt does have credibility with Israel and shares its security concerns and commitments. But Egypt's concerns about Islamism, terrorism and the looming dark forces of instability feed its hostility towards Hamas.

Gaza, administered by the Hamas movement, is under a tight military blockade imposed by both Israel and Egypt. The Israeli army says tunnels between Gaza and Egypt are used to supply armed factions in Gaza with weapons. The Egyptians claim they are used by Sinai-based armed groups affiliated with ISIS. Hamas emerged from the Muslim Brotherhood, which was designated as a terrorist organization after Sisi's overthrow of President Mohamed Morsi. Cairo accuses Hamas of meddling in Egypt's affairs and supporting former President Mohamed Morsi. In addition to shutting tunnels between Gaza and Egypt, used to smuggle both weapons and consumer goods, Cairo has destroyed hundreds of homes in Rafah on the Egyptian side of the Gaza Strip in an effort to quell a rebellion by fighters from the Sinai Province group.

Gaza is just a strip of land 25-miles long and 7-miles wide along the Mediterranean at the border between Israel and Egypt. Its history starts as part of the Ancient Egyptian region of Canaan. Because of its strategic location, Gaza became an important trading center for Asian, European and North African markets. Thanks to its strategic importance, Gaza's history includes countless battles for its control from the Philistines in the 13th century B.C. to Alexander the Great, whose army killed the entire male population for refusing to surrender, to four centuries under the Ottoman Empire until the end of World War I.

The major turning point for Gaza came after World War II with the British Mandate of Palestine and partitioning of the territory into separate Jewish and Arab states that led to the 1948 Arab-Israeli War. The 1949 Armistice Agreement gave Jordan control over the West Bank region of Palestine and Egypt gained control of Gaza. With the influx of Jews into newly independent Israel, Arab refugees flowed into Gaza. In contrast to Jordan that offered citizenship to many Arab refugees, Egypt did not and they remained refugees under Egyptian military rule until Israel took over the Gaza strip following the 6-day war against the Arab States in 1967. Gaza and the West Bank remained under Israeli occupation and military control for nearly 30 years.

From the first Palestinian uprising or "intifada" against Israeli rule, starting in a refugee camp in northern Gaza in 1987, Hamas was born as a Palestinian extension of the Muslim Brotherhood Organization. For Sisi, Hamas's connection at birth to the Muslim Brotherhood helps to explain his animosity. Hamas's rebellion against Israel, including terrorist attacks and suicide bombings, included demands for its replacement by a Palestinian Islamic state. The subsequent history of Hamas militancy, the creation of and conflicts with the Palestinian Authority, the second Palestinian Intifada in 2000, Israeli's continued occupancy of Gaza until 2005, Hamas' struggle with Fatah for control of Gaza, a de facto divide of the territory controlled by the Palestinian Authority between the Hamas-governed Gaza Strip and the West Bank under Fatah control, all are well documented elsewhere.

Fast forward to a recent news item reporting that Egyptian forces flooded smuggling tunnels dug beneath the Gaza-Egypt border in Rafah in the southern Gaza Strip. The Egyptians pumped water from the Mediterranean Sea into these underground passages used not only for terrorist's purposes but by smugglers bringing an estimated 30 percent of all goods that reach Gaza. Hamas has earned millions of dollars in tax revenues from these smuggling operations. Israel has imposed a blockade on Gaza in an attempt to strangle the strip's economy and undermine Hamas' ability to govern. Egyptian President Abdel Fattah al-Sisi is determined to crack down on Islamist insurgents in the Sinai Peninsula after at least 33 security personnel were killed in attacks in the region bordering Gaza. Residents of Sinai, however, claim that they rely on the smuggling trade through tunnels for their living.

Within the Gaza Strip, smuggling tunnels were dug under the Philadelphi Corridor, a narrow strip of land (about 9 miles in length) along the border between Gaza Strip and Egypt. Under the provisions of the Israeli-Egyptian peace treaty of 1979, the Philadelphi Corridor was established as a buffer zone controlled and patrolled by Israeli forces. One purpose of the Philadelphi Route was to prevent the movement of illegal materials (including weapons and ammunition) and people in both directions between the Gaza Strip and Egypt.

After the Israel-Egypt Peace Treaty of 1979, the town of Rafah, in the southern Gaza Strip, was split by this Corridor. One half of the town belongs to Egypt and the other half is located in Gaza. After Israel withdrew from Gaza in 2005, the Philadelphi Corridor was placed under the control of the Palestine Authority until Hamas seized power in 2007. Egypt and Israel closed borders with Gaza. In 2009, Egypt began construction of an underground barrier to block existing tunnels and make new ones harder to dig. In the last few years, Egypt's military has tried to destroy most of the 1,200 or more smuggling tunnels between Gaza and Egypt.

More than 4 million Syrian refugees are in five countries: Jordan, Lebanon, Turkey, Iraq and Egypt:

- Lebanon hosts approximately 1.2 million refugees from Syria which amounts to around one in five people in the country;
- Jordan hosts about 650,000 refugees from Syria, which amounts to about 10% of the population;
- Turkey hosts 1.9 million refugees from Syria, more than any other country worldwide;

- Iraq, where 3 million people have been internally displaced in the last 18 months, hosts 249,463 refugees from Syria;
- Egypt hosts 132,375 refugees from Syria.

Gulf countries including Qatar, United Arab Emirates, Saudi Arabia, Kuwait, and Bahrain have offered no resettlement places to Syrian refugees. By comparison, Egypt has been surprisingly accommodating to Syrian refugees. Even with difficulties finding decent, affordable housing and jobs, it is surprising that any Syrian refugees in Egypt would yearn to move to Gaza. A year after the 51-day war in 2014, Gaza remains decimated. More than 100,000 Palestinians remain homeless. Israel sustains and tightens its blockade, preventing essential construction materials and supplies from entering Gaza. Gaza's border with Egypt is also frequently closed and smuggling tunnels in Gaza's south have been systematically destroyed, further blocking transit of supplies needed for both sustenance and reconstruction.

Of the 1.76 million people living in Gaza, 1.26 million are Palestine refugees. Years of conflict and the tightened blockade have left 80 per cent of the population dependent on international assistance. The United Nations Relief and Works Agency (UNRWA) sustain 1.3 million refugees. Over half a million Palestine refugees in Gaza live in eight Palestine refugee camps. The scale of human loss, destruction, and displacement caused by the third conflict between Hamas and Israel within seven years was catastrophic. Tens of thousands of Palestine refugee houses were totally demolished or suffered severe or major damage. Reconstruction lacks funding. The economy of Gaza is completely broken. Infrastructure is devastated. Gaza has one of the highest unemployment rates in the world.

Many Syrian refugees have come to Gaza (Palestine for them) after not being welcomed or able to adjust to and assimilate in Egypt. The experience of Syrian refugees in Egypt has been very mixed. But there are no refugee camps in Egypt. Most Syrian refugees live in or near Cairo. But many have chosen to flee to Europe and other host countries, including Gaza. More than 430,000 refugees from North Africa, including Egypt, and elsewhere in Africa have attempted the treacherous Mediterranean journey from Libya to Greece in 2015. Thousands have drowned trying. Many refugees from Egypt have managed to get to Gaza through the tunnels from Egypt. They are not helped in Gaza by UN and other refugee agencies, however, which are extremely short of funds and only help Palestinian refugees. Life is hard for Syrian refugees but at least they are welcomed in Gaza.

In a recent meeting with a delegation from the Committee for Foreign Affairs of the Italian Senate, President al-Sisi said that Egypt currently hosts around five million refugees from Arab and African countries. These refugees, Sisi said, are receiving the same health and educational services as Egyptians, despite the economic burden the Egyptian government carries. Al-Sisi said that Egypt doesn't abuse them or do favors for them. However, he emphasized the importance of defending the "Egyptian state," adding that "we don't want to be a "refugee state."

The United Nation's High Commissioner for Refugees (UNHCR) data shows that Egypt hosts 261,741 registered refugees, mostly from Sudan and South Sudan, Syria and Libya but also from Iraq, Yemen, Ethiopia, and Eritrea. The number of unregistered refugees in Egypt is much higher than the official registered numbers. The point is that Egypt offers refugees access to public healthcare and education but it has no procedures for offering them asylum. Of the 250,000-300,000 Syrian refugees, about 80,000 are registered with UNHCR.

CHAPTER 6

The Middle East & EU Migration Maze and Mess

Chancellor Angela Merkel's commitment for Germany to absorb as many as a million refugees in 2015 and a million or more each year for the next few years was amazing and, frankly mystifying, even though on paper seemingly justified by Germany's demographics and need for more workers. Her magnanimous gesture suggested that the huge influx of migrants would not create serious political frictions in Germany and between Germany and neighboring countries. Already, however, Bavaria has been blasting Austria for the way it has handled the flow, or rather inundation, of refugees. Small Balkan nations on the path of migration through Europe have been overwhelmed by record numbers of asylum-seekers trying to cross their borders. For example, Slovenia, just a small Alpine nation on the Adriatic Sea unexpectedly became the gateway to Europe for migrants when Hungary recently closed its border with Croatia.

Merkel and her advisors must have known that their "welcome to Germany" policy was creating a veritable migrant suction pump that would suck in new waves of migrants, not just refugees from war, and not just from Syria but also from Afghanistan and Iraq through Turkey, Greece and the Balkans. Merkel's welcome to refugees has reached literally millions of suffering people in Iraq and Afghanistan living in chaotic conditions yearning for new homes and lives. In response, we're seeing a proliferation of new ad hoc border controls, fences, and police actions throughout the Balkans and main routes to Germany trying to manage the escalating flow of migrants, while Greece struggles to find facilities to accommodate thousands of migrants arriving weekly crossing the Aegean Sea.

Many of us grew up admiring Greek heroes -- Hercules, Achilles, Odysseus, Theseus, and others and even a heroine, Atalanta -- and playwrights of Greek tragedy -- Aeschylus, Sophocles, and Euripides. Today's Greek tragedy is the refugee crisis and the heroes and heroines, none of whom will be recorded in history books, are the rescue workers and members of the Greek coastguard who have pulled tens of thousands of men, women, children and babies, including a great many drowned bodies, from the waters surrounding the islands of Lesbos, Samos, Farmakonissi, Kalymnos, Kalolymnos, Symi and Rhodes.

More than 570,000 migrants bound for Europe have crossed to Greece from neighboring Turkey in flimsy, unseaworthy dinghies and other crafts, many provided by smuggling gangs. In October alone, according to the U.N. refugee agency (UNHCR), more than 218,000 migrants crossed the Mediterranean, almost as many as in all of 2014. The numbers have far exceeded anything expected just a few months ago. The European Union has pledged to relocate about 160,000 refugees -- less than three-fourths of this October refugee influx. UNHCR estimates that more than 600,000 people crossed the Mediterranean this year.

How bad is the totally underfunded Greek rescue effort? More than 300,000 people have made the dangerous sea journey from Turkey to Lesbos this year. Most of them have landed on the north coast of the island, an hour-long drive from the main hospital at Mytilene. As a result of the drained Greek budget, Lesbos has only three ambulances in operation despite a massive daily influx of refugees. The island's ambulance workers have protested that five ambulances are awaiting repairs and that staff shortages force rescuers to work up to 16 hours at a time. In October alone, 125,000 refugees arrived on Lesbos, double the number in August. Fortunately aid organizations and an army of volunteers have joined the Greek rescue effort. But they unanimously criticize the failure of the EU and the world's aid organizations to support a country that is going through its worst economic crisis in modern times.

The International Rescue Committee (IRC) is valiantly working to improve living conditions for refugees staying in the Kara Tepe transit camp near the island's capital, Mytilene. Built for 500 refugees, the camp now shelters as many as 2,500 people waiting for permission to travel further into Europe. The IRC is increasing the number of its aid workers on the ground to 200. At the same time, however, the IRC is warning that aid groups and volunteers alone cannot fill the gap: "As governments look the other way, refugees are dying. But the response desperately needs the political will of the EU, and in particular, properly resourced and well-conceived action to ensure the humane reception of refugees," said IRC regional refugee representative Kirk Day. "The scale of the crisis demands nothing less."

In addition to the chronic refugee crisis in Greece, Merkel's open door and open borders policies have been creating havoc in, for example, Austria and neighboring Bavaria. On any given day, Austria might receive more than 10,000 migrants. Austria wants to move them across the border to already overburdened Bavaria as quickly as possible. Austria puts thousands on buses to Bavaria. Additional thousands cross the Austrian-Bavarian border on foot. For example, the German federal police in the Bavarian town of Passau recently said that 5,500 refugees had arrived from Austria unexpectedly overnight. Bavaria has borne the brunt of handling the tens of thousands of arrivals in Germany – as many as 15,000 migrants arriving on a weekend is not unusual.

The days of cheering welcomes for new migrants are over. Austria has just announced that it is building a fence along its border with Slovenia. Slovenia responded with its own threat to build a fence on at least part of its frontier with Croatia. All of this migrant-related political controversy is going on as winter approaches. And no one knows how many asylum-seekers and other migrants are on the way today or will be even in the middle of winter.

Chancellor Merkel's Christian Democratic Union political party is unhappy with the potential political ramifications of the flood of migrants. Horst Seehofer, head of Bavaria's Christian Social Union party, has demanded that the Chancellor reduce the influx of migrants in the next few days. The EU is struggling to come up with a common political and logistical solution that not only accommodates Syrian refugees but those from other Middle East and North African countries. Thus far, there is no plan that EU members can agree to.

What is being discussed by the EU is the possibility of differentiating among asylum seekers to filter out tens of thousands of people that are simply migrants trying to escape conditions in their home countries or looking for jobs and a better life. Afghan migrants, for example, who are arriving in the second-highest numbers behind Syrians, and do not qualify as asylum-seekers, would be targeted by the EU. More than 50,000 Afghans have migrated to Europe since the beginning of the year.

Discussions of U.S. – Afghanistan diplomatic and military policies almost never bring up the connection between outmigration and Afghanistan's (de)stabilization. Among the various factors contributing to outmigration from Afghanistan, the withdrawal of U.S. and NATO troops is significant because it has left a security vacuum in many areas of the country, enabling the Taliban to gain more territory throughout Afghanistan, and violence is on the rise. Afghans have legitimate reasons for fleeing these areas and seeking asylum elsewhere. In addition, many Afghans say that their new government has done little to improve their lives, which does not qualify them for asylum-seeking.

For EU countries trying to different between legitimate and other asylum-seekers, Afghan migrants pose a real problem because a great many of them can claim that their lives are endangered by the Taliban. Afghan leaders are so concerned about outmigration and the potential "brain drain" of the country's most educated and best minds that the nation's Refugees and Repatriations Ministry has launched a social-media campaign to get the message out to young Afghans in order to dissuade them from leaving for Europe.

Many of the nation's most powerful former and current political leaders also are weighing in with TV and social media messages.

The most unexpected and consequential outcome of the Syrian civil war, and the wars in Iraq, Afghanistan and North Africa, will be the mass migration to Europe and political disruption in Germany and other EU and peripheral countries. It's hard to know what Chancellor Angela Merkel had in mind when she announced Germany's open-door policy for refugees, but she certainly did not anticipate a serious political backlash, not just in the political fringes but in ever-larger parts of mainstream German society.

The question in public and private conversations in Germany today, as reflected in the country's media, is whether Ms. Merkel really knows what she's doing? Did she make a decision to open German borders with any idea, or without any idea, of the potential political and community consequences or was she optimistically just hoping for good outcomes? Ms. Merkel's central message about the influx of refugees was simply "We will manage this." She announced that a million refugees will be welcomed in Germany in 2015 and millions more in future years. Her announcement was made without knowing whether cities and towns in Germany actually were prepared to absorb these refugees before and during oncoming winter months and capable of providing even minimally adequate public services and accommodations.

Many people in Germany whose minds and hearts are with the plight of refugees still envision the possibility of a refugee crisis in Germany that potentially could destabilize the country. They see Ms. Merkel's refugee decision as a risky gamble that could upset the nation's political landscape. Already frustration felt on both the left and the right in Germany about the inundation of refugees is being expressed vociferously by fringe parties looking forward to gains in next year's elections in three federal states.

As the U.S., Russia, Iran, Saudi Arabia and a dozen other countries and international participants engage in a series of conferences to resolve the fate of Assad and Syria, refugees continue to arrive in Europe in an unceasing stream. These millions of refugees and migrants are heading for Europe in numbers not seen since WW II. The problem is that they are coming not just from Syria but also from Iraq, Afghanistan, a dozen or so nations in sub-Saharan and North African regions, and other parts of the world.

The worst aspect of the migrant problem is that the current refugee and migration crisis in Europe could get much bigger in 2016 and beyond, without any way realistically of preventing or stopping it. Added to the "migrant problem" will be the unpredictable mixture of terrorists that will flow into Europe along will legitimate refugees. If ISIS and the Taliban are not contained in Syria, Iraq, Afghanistan, and Libya, and they increase their territorial gains, a great many more refugees and displaced people will flee and, sooner or later, head for Europe any way that they can, and ISIS foot soldiers will be among them. Ms. Merkel has not addressed these possibilities and their implications which also are not part of the agenda for deciding the fate of Syria and Assad.

The failed interventions in Iraq, Afghanistan and Libya have produced millions of refugees, with more to come. A quarter of Afghans recently told a Gallup Poll that they want to leave their country and more than 100,000 said that they expected to try to flee to Europe this year. 50,000 already have done so in 2015. Some will try to enter Lebanon, Turkey and Jordan that already have four million Syrian refugees. The plight of Yemenis is worsening daily and Yemen is not much farther away from Europe than Eritrea that now is the biggest source of African refugees, but is barely mentioned in the media.

Whether or not climate change actually is to blame, Syria was in the grip of a prolonged drought when the war broke out, which contributed to displacement. For this reason, large areas of sub-Saharan Africa also were becoming uninhabitable, adding to the push factors generating large numbers of economic refugees from many different regions and problem areas. Climate change and drought have not been part of any discussions of the many prospective push factors in Middle East and African migration to Europe.

The hundreds of thousands of refugees and migrants who arrived in Greece without documents since the start of this year almost all want to travel north to countries they believe offer a better chance of safety and a new life. Up until recently, officials in countries along the way have focused on helping them travel as quickly and safely as possible to other destinations, primarily Germany. As Germany reconsiders its welcome for refugees, governments in transit countries have taken action to block off their own borders. After more than 100,000 refugees and migrants streamed across Slovenia's borders in just two weeks, camps set up to handle a few hundred people were suddenly struggling to provide food and shelter for many thousands of refugees and migrants every day! Understandably Slovenia has begged for European help.

If not soon then later on in 2015 or 2016, Germany could retract its welcome for refugees. What then? What if Merkel's grand political coalition buckles under pressure and tens of thousands of refugees are stranded in a completely unprepared Greece and tens of thousands more along transit routes to Germany? Any move to block refugees in any European country impacts on the others. The fence erected by Hungary to seal its border with Croatia triggered a crisis in Slovenia. To Germany's credit, however, the federal government is desperately trying to find shelter for tens of thousands of refugees before winter sets in. Each of Germany's 16 Länder, or states, has been assigned a quota of refugees based on factors like economic strength and population.

The civil war in Syria is being treated as an international crisis. But not the humanitarian crisis that, for example, in the U.S. is being viewed from afar as a European crisis. The magnitude of the refugee crisis spanning the Middle East, Africa and Europe is completely under-appreciated and under-estimated. For refugees, the civil war in Syria and escalating civil wars in Afghanistan and Iraq, for which the U.S. shares more than a little responsibility, are propelling tens of thousands of displaced persons to become refugees and take greater migration risks as winter rapidly approaches. Bulgaria, Romania and Serbia are getting ready to close their borders. These countries fear that otherwise they will face millions of migrants being stranded throughout their territories. Bulgaria has already built a wire fence along its border with Turkey that hosts 2.5 million refugees.

In the first 8 months of 2015, over 700,000 refugees have fled Syria, Iraq and elsewhere in the Middle East and Africa and crossed European borders, almost four times more than in 2014. Turkey is Europe's biggest "transit country" for refugees from the Middle East and Africa. Turkey itself hosts more than 2 million Syrian refugees. From the start of the Syrian civil war in 2011, Turkey has had an open-door policy for refugees, has spent billions of dollars caring for them, and now hosts the largest number of refugees in the world. The European Union and Turkey have to cooperate in many ways to somehow reduce and deal with all aspects of the flow of refugees to Turkey and from Turkey to Europe. There are two big conditional issues involved in making Turkish-EU collaboration accelerate and work: Turkey's status as a candidate for admission to the EU, and both human rights and freedom of expression issues in Turkey.

Turkey has sought to join the European Union since 2005. The EU's approval process has stalled in recent years in part because of European concerns about Turkey's human rights record and the government's crackdown on the news media and freedom of expression. Angela Merkel has long opposed Turkey's admission into the EU bloc. Faced with the refugee crisis, however, Merkel has stated publicly that she would support speeding up Turkey's EU approval process as a concession for Turkey's cooperation in trying to contain the huge refugee crisis.

Reflecting the importance and urgency of Turkey's cooperation on refugee issues, concerns among EU leaders about rights issues and increasing authoritarianism in Turkey have become muted. Amnesty International, however, continues to focus on increased violence by the Turkish government against the militant Kurdistan Workers' Party (PKK) that for many years has fought for the rights and autonomy of Turkey's Kurdish minority.

Trying to prevent illegal immigration across its borders, Prime Minister Ahmet Davutoglu of Turkey has pressed for creation of a "safe zone" in northern Syria. Davutoglu's proposal resembles, but is not identical to, the proposal in this volume for protected safe havens. Turkey's proposal for a "safe zone" in northern Syria has been met largely by silence from the U.S. and the international community because it would require inclusion of a military operation and a no-fly zone.

The political context, instability and violence in Turkey are far from the best conditions for conducting negotiations with the EU for a comprehensive refugee agreement or the Turks admission to the EU. Besides growing economic difficulties, and deep entanglement in Syria's civil war, the main factor driving decisions in Ankara was parliamentary elections scheduled for November, after election results in June that threatened to bring the governing Justice and Development Party's (AKP) to the end of its 13-year reign. The November election was unexpectedly successful for the AKP. EU eyes also are on the fighting between Turkish security forces and the PKK and the AKP's seeming abandonment of the peace process with the PKK. Concerns also have been expressed within the EU about a worst-case scenario of civil war occurring in Turkey.

Add to this mix of instability, uncertainty and various other red flags, the shock of explosions in Ankara killing and wounding hundreds of demonstrating PKK supporters. Although the AKP denies its complicity in the tragedy, fingers have been pointing at both the government and ISIS and, at the very least, charges have been made that insufficient security measures were implemented to protect the PKK demonstrators. In the aftermath of the explosions, it appears that a broad political spectrum of Turks may have become more supportive of the Kurdish community, which apparently did not have negative ramifications for the AKP in the November election. In sum, for the EU and Brussels, the violence and increasing polarization in Turkey is a serious impediment to reaching critical agreements on refugees in both Europe and Turkey and the EU membership status of Turkey.

In early October, the EU issued a "Draft Action Plan" designed to accelerate EU-Turkey cooperation in support of refugees and for managing migration. Conditions for moving forward with EU-Turkey cooperation included a credible, transparent investigation of the explosions in Ankara, and clear and strong expressions of solidarity with NATO and the U.S. on dealing with Russian air or any other intrusions into its territory. Turkey's obligations, with EU funding support, will include adopting and implementing policies, legislation and programs that "facilitate self-sufficiency and inclusion of refugees into the Turkish society ... including in particular the adoption of measures enabling refugees to have access, for the duration of their stay in Turkey, to labor market and public services including education for pupils and access to health services."

The EU's Draft Action Plan covers most of the essentials for reducing and managing the flow of refugees into Turkey and the EU, provides a broad range of humanitarian assistance to refugees, and also tries to prevent so-called "irregular migrants" who do not qualify as refugees from leaving their home countries and heading for Turkey and Europe, and includes the following provisions:

- humanitarian assistance, better living conditions and supportive services for refugees;
- alleviating Turkey's financial and other resource burdens connected to hosting millions of refugees;
- finding ways to prevent migrants from the Middle East and Africa heading for Turkey and then from Turkey to the EU, including fighting criminal networks involved in smuggling migrants;
- supporting planned resettlement programs that would enable refugees in Turkey to enter the EU in an "orderly manner";
- conducting a comprehensive needs assessment of migrants to be able to implement all of these goals, including "weakening of push factors forcing them to move to Turkey."

In addition to reducing and managing the flow of refugees into Turkey and the EU, the EU also is very concerned about preventing and reversing what Brussels calls "irregular migration,: i.e. migrants that are not refugees but have left their countries for economic and other reasons. The EU intends to discuss "irregular migration" with officials in countries from which very large numbers of "Silk Route" migrants have been flowing to Europe: Pakistan, Afghanistan, Iraq, Iran and Bangladesh. Discussions of these "irregular migrants" will include preventing ISIS terrorists from traveling to and entering Turkey and the EU.

Reporters interviewing refugees on route from Turkey through the Balkans frequently hear them say that their destination is Sweden and that they expect to be warmly welcomed. No surprise, therefore, that Sweden expects up to 190,000 migrants this year, which is putting an unprecedented strain on the country's welcome for refugees, and their welcome understandably is cooling off.

Sweden's extraordinary open-ended welcoming of refugees has been somewhat mystifying since, as a nation noted for its good sense and practically, the government did not seem to account for the potential financial and other societal burdens from the sudden influx of large numbers of desperate refugees. Recently Sweden's humanitarian spirit and good intentions were translated by green eyeshades in the Swedish Association of Local Authorities and Regions into a projection of the financial burden that municipalities will bear to cover the costs of welcoming refugees: an increase in the tax rate by 2 per cent—an average annual cost per household of about 15,000 kroner or $2,400.

This tax figure actually was quite conservative because it was based on food, housing and healthcare costs for native Swedes and not the greater needs of refugees. Some small municipalities have received the equivalent of 30% or more of their population in refugees, including close to hundreds of unaccompanied children and young people each day! Sweden's Migration Agency has said more than 30,000 of the 190,000 people it expected in 2015 would be unaccompanied children. Sweden will need an additional 70 billion Swedish crowns ($8.41 billion) over the next two years to cope with the inundation of refugees. Recently refugees have been arriving in Sweden at the rate of 10,000 per week. Tens of thousands of refugees could spend the cold Swedish winter in heated tents.

The response in Sweden, however, has not all been handwringing. Many of Sweden's most enterprising companies are turning the refugee crisis into a financial bonanza by supplying large quantities of refugee accommodations, paid for by the Swedish government. Public housing in Sweden is unable to meet the refugee demand. So private entrepreneurs are buy up housing, even evicting existing tenants, to enable units to be subdivided for refugees, generously paid for by Sweden's Migration Board. Without indulging in stories about Swedish profit-making on refugees, the Swedish government itself and its coffers clearly is a driving force behind the burgeoning refugee business. There's even talk about governmental expropriation of summer homes and other "underused properties" in order to house refugees.

No doubt Sweden's property owners can't be too happy about the idea that the needs of refugees should take precedence over ownership of private property. Sweden, that has a notable history of building new towns, is even talking about building vast new developments to provide hundreds of thousands of dwellings, as a great humanitarian effort. Some green eye-shades have done the math, however, and see the possibility of Swedes becoming a minority in their own country by 2025.

Understandably resentment and fear are running high in Sweden these days in response to humanitarian visions and their tax and other detrimental implications. Several shelters intended for refugees recently were burned down in Sweden, continuing a recent series of arson attacks that police believe are directed against arriving asylum seekers. In one incident, a children's summer camp west of Stockholm to be used for asylum seekers was set afire.

Recognizing its problems of absorbing asylum-seekers, Sweden intends to join the EU's refugee relocation scheme that would enable them to share as many as 54,000 asylum-seekers with other EU members. Sweden's refugee situation is not that bad by comparison with other countries through which refugees pour trying to get to Sweden and elsewhere in northern Europe. According to the International Organization for Migration, more than 670,000 people have arrived by sea this year, fleeing war zones and poverty in the Middle East, Africa and Asia.

Sweden, like Germany, has become a kind of suction pump for refugees. Thousands of refugees (60,000 in just a week) continue to pour into Slovenia in the hope of reaching Germany, Austria and Sweden. The comparatively tiny country of Slovenia appealed for other EU states to send police to help manage the refugee flow. Slovenia also has asked the EU for help to regulate the inflow of refugees from Croatia. Some 230,000 migrants have passed through Croatia since mid-September. Hungary has sealed off its border with Croatia and migrants from Syria, Afghanistan and other Middle East and Africa countries instead started entering Slovenia at the rate more than 12,000 migrants in 24 hours. Bottlenecks at the border are forcing thousands to sleep outdoors in Serbia, Croatia and Slovenia.

The Czech Republic is detaining refugees for up to 90 days and strip-searching them for money to pay for their own detention. Most of these refugees are heading for Germany. Bulgaria, Serbia and Romania which are threatening to close their borders if Germany or other countries do the same to stop refugees coming in. The heads of governments in Austria, Bulgaria, Croatia, Macedonia, Germany, Greece, Hungary, Romania, Serbia and Slovenia and the European Commission are struggling to figure out how to deal with the growing migration crisis during the winter and expected in 2016.

PART II
LESSONS LEARNED

CHAPTER 7

Wishful Counterinsurgency Thinking

Robert M. Gates, Stanley McChrystal, Leon Panetta, David Petraeus and all of the other past and present senior US officials that have been involved in US counterterrorism/ counterinsurgency decisions know that, at least in theory, every counterinsurgency Plan A must be accompanied by a Plan B and ideally even should have a Plan C (and maybe even a Plan D). These plans define the "endgame" of fighting extremists, whether it's Al-Qaeda, Taliban, ISIS or others.

When Robert Gates observed in his book, *Duty*, that the "outcome in Afghanistan remains to be determined," he also expressed uncertainty about "how the endgame plays out after more than a decade of war" and "whether the entire effort and all the sacrifice will have been for nothing." In his view, all that was needed to avoid the strategic mistake of the early 1990s ("abandoning Afghanistan") was "a modest continuing NATO military presence after 2014 ..." At that time, ISIS in Afghanistan was not even a glimmer on Gates' radar screen.

Since then, as a gruesome preview of brutal coming events, ISIS beheaded at least 10 Taliban militants in a remote area in Afghanistan, and jihadist groups have been locked in an intense battle for control over many northern Afghan provinces. ISIS and the Taliban have declared war – against each other!

In addition, the Afghan National Army reported in May 2015 that ISIS had taken control from the Taliban in several regions, even replacing them completely in one district, and had begun recruiting candidates to create their worldwide Islamic caliphate that includes Afghanistan. After halting combat operations in Afghanistan in December 2014, US counterinsurgency action remains just drone strikes although the US is trying, without much success, to build an Afghani air force.

There was no COIN Plan B in Afghanistan and even COIN Plan A still remains unclear or perhaps unworkable to deal with either or both the Taliban and ISIS. Afghan ground forces have been begging for air support as they face the Taliban. American airstrikes in support of Afghan forces, however, have to be approved on a case-by-case basis by Gen. John F. Campbell, the American commander in Afghanistan. Campbell has declared that ISIS's intentions in Afghanistan were "aspirational," whatever that means. Not long after that, for reasons that were never explained, he changed his mind and warned that ISIS poses a serious threat to US forces. At the same time, he expressed surprise that the Afghan army was losing trained soldiers "at an alarming rate ... in the neighborhood of 4,000 a month." Battlefield casualties? No, the "folks go AWOL," according to Campbell. He provided no reasons or speculation for the unexpected exodus of Afghan troops.

Campbell also said that the death of Al-Qaeda leader Mullah Omar (actually dead for about two years without the CIA knowing it) "could drive Taliban fighters into the arms of ISIS." US Secretary of Defense Ashton Carter then said that ISIS is merely "a rebranding of militants already in the battlefield"; in other words, ISIS is just another name conceived for marketing purposes to attract more media attention. These remarks about ISIS by Campbell and Carter, two of the most senior US military and defense officials, at best qualified as clueless and certainly did not inspire confidence in their strategic contributions to the US military or nation-building role in Afghanistan.

Reflecting these kinds of opinions about ISIS, US and NATO military leaders are still downplaying the significance of ISIS in

Afghanistan, at least as compared to ISIS in Iraq. An unnamed senior NATO official declared that ISIS "does not pose a strategic threat to Afghanistan" although NATO takes "the alleged emergence of the terror group in Afghanistan very seriously." The Pentagon views "ISIS's presence and influence in Afghanistan as in the initial exploratory phase." The Pentagon has not initiated counterinsurgency planning in Afghanistan focused on ISIS. To say that there is no consensus among US military leaders on the threat of ISIS in Afghanistan, to say the least, is an understatement.

The core Taliban message that Afghanistan should only be controlled by Afghanis, and their history of fierce resistance to foreign invasions, suddenly was being upended by the Islamic State's infiltration. ISIS envisions no nations, just a Muslim caliphate. Not only do ISIS's inroads into Taliban territory suddenly threaten to challenge US and Afghani security strategy, but it creates another potentially violent sphere of Sunni (Taliban) vs. ISIS conflict. ISIS is gathering jihadi recruits in eastern Afghanistan, touting their victories in Iraq, Syria and Libya, and also using their financial resources and Internet propaganda to attract new recruits. Afghani President Ashraf Ghani is well aware of the potential threat posed by "Daesh" (ISIS). He has confirmed the presence of ISIS cells in Helmand and Farah provinces.

The foreign fighters that make up ISIS during its recruitment phase are similar to the Taliban in terms of wanting to set up a state governed by sharia law, but are different in that ISIS does not recognize nation states and there also are serious religious differences. Most Taliban follow the Hanafi School and, for the Salafi purists of ISIS, these beliefs are fundamentally incorrect. ISIS calls Afghan locals "infidels." ISIS, therefore, is a serious threat to residents of Afghani communities, much moreso than the Taliban, and Afghanis know it.

The Obama administration may have a strategy for Afghanistan, but like America's foreign policy generally, it is not at all clear. Perhaps the most disturbing aspect of America's engagement in Iraq and Afghanistan, and Syria and Libya, however, is the seemingly woeful ignorance of top advisors in the Pentagon,

State, Defense and intelligence agencies, and the White House, about the historical and cultural drivers and other realities on the ground in these countries that would either support or limit the success of wishful counterterrorism thinking. Public rhetoric from Congress and the Executive branch has been completely at odds with realities in Afghanistan, Iraq, Syria, Libya, Yemen and the rest of the Middle East.

The United States has not known, and does not know, the kinds of insurgencies in the Middle East that it will have to fight in the future. Recent ISIS terrorist attacks in France and elsewhere may rapidly change that conclusion, but it remains to be seen. As Gates said, with admirable, unprecedented candor, "After Vietnam, our defense "experts" avowed that we would never again try to fight an insurgency, yet we have done so in both Iraq and Afghanistan ... In the forty years since Vietnam, our record in predicting where we will be militarily engaged next, even six months out, is perfect: we have never once gotten it right, not in Grenada, Haiti, Panama, Libya (twice), Iraq (twice), Afghanistan, the Balkans, or Somalia. When it comes to predicting future conflicts, what kinds of fights they will be, and what will be needed, we need a lot more humility."

Gates' own experience as secretary of defense and, from that perspective, as an observer of presidents over at least the past 75 years, led him to the conclusion that "American presidents, confronted with a tough problem abroad, have too often been too quick to reach for a gun ..." On both left and right, the failure to use military force to deal with acts of extremist and other aggression is viewed by Gates as an abdication of moral responsibility and leadership. Gates, however, at the same time argues cogently for acknowledging the limitations of military power. Gates, Panetta, and McChrystal strongly agree that, when a commander-in-chief draws red lines in the sand and then vacillates instead of acting, it sends the wrong message to both adversaries and allies and also seriously hurts the nation's credibility.

It's instructive to read about the decision-making process in 2009 regarding the war in Afghanistan. CIA Director Panetta says that, at first, he was only a peripheral participant in the debate going on in the White House because it was primarily about military solutions and also postwar stabilization aims, including denial of a refuge to Al-Qaeda. One would think that the CIA would be front and center in any NSC discussion about fighting a war in Afghanistan, one of the world's most complex and conflicted nations.

These White House conversations included questions regarding how long troops would have to stay in Afghanistan. How long it would take for Afghanistan to become a fully functioning democracy? What would be the US posture towards the Taliban? Would it be different than dealing with Al-Qaeda? Panetta advocated, without much disagreement, expanding CIA operations in Afghanistan and Pakistan to thwart Al-Qaeda.

General McChrystal argued for a significant increase in US troop strength, no less than a surge of forty thousand troops, to ensure Afghanistan's stability and train its military. McChrystal had given an interview to 60 Minutes that at least implied that President Obama was detached from the details of the war in Afghanistan. McChrystal made his case in a speech and remarks soon thereafter in London in which he emphatically endorsed an expanded troop surge. Both Panetta and Gates immediately were critical of McChrystal for not "staying on message." However, both also supported the proposed troop surge.

Biden was vehemently opposed to a troop surge in Afghanistan. Hillary Clinton was enthusiastically for it: failing to do it, in her opinion, would guarantee failure of the mission in Afghanistan. None of President Obama's military or national security advisors, however, addressed the potential implications for the political future of Afghanistan of the Taliban providing Al-Qaeda with a safehaven. Panetta's best idea was to deal with the Taliban by targeting Al-Qaeda. There was much talk about preventing lawlessness in Afghanistan, but not a single strategy discussed about how to deal with it.

Let's briefly look back to October 2009 and the war in Afghanistan that was in its ninth year. The Taliban were getting stronger than at any time since the Americans toppled their government at the end of 2001. American soldiers and Marines also were dying at a faster rate than ever before. Polls in the United States showed that opposition to the war was growing steadily. Worse yet was the lack of accomplishment in every dimension of warfare and nation-building in Afghanistan. The government in Kabul under President Karzai had proven to be unreliable and full of corruption.

In his assessment of the country, sent to President Obama, McChrystal said Afghanistan was on the brink of collapse and America at the edge of defeat. To reverse the course of the war, McChrystal asked for 40,000 additional American troops in addition to the 65,000 already there. Otherwise, McChrystal suggested, give up the fight. McChrystal confronted President Obama with a choice that he was determined not to make. McChrystal's blueprint called for an extensive American military commitment to build a modern state in Afghanistan, bring order to chaos and spend hundreds of billions of dollars more, in addition to untold numbers of dead American soldiers, and without any guarantees of success.

In addition to calling for more troops, probably even more important, McChrystal had a radically different strategy of how the war should be conducted: protect (do not randomly kill) the Afghan people; try to connect with everyone, including insurgents; and build an Afghan state a step and a stone at a time. Let's remember where McChrystal came from to Afghanistan in 2009. In 2006 and 2007, when Al-Qaeda was at its peak, McChrystal's commandos set out to destroy Al-Qaeda in Mesopotamia. He had mixed success but was convinced that his efforts to destroy the insurgency were crucial to establishing a stable Iraq. His other conclusion was that, no matter how bad the situation in a country like Iraq, success was possible with the right combination of strategy and resources.

What he learned when he arrived in Afghanistan resembled what he had learned in Iraq, only worse and more complex: not only was corruption in the Afghan government pervasive and the insurgency, supported from Pakistan, extremely strong and resilient, but most important, every valley and village was different, each with its own ethnic groups, tribes and history. McChrystal concluded that, strategically, the insurgents had to be cut off from the maximum number of Afghan people who were residing in major population centers.

In other words, make the insurgents fight their way into these cities – make these cities "safe havens" (not a term used by McChrystal). Implementation of that strategy would require a great many more troops and create a political problem for the Obama administration that had sent him to Afghanistan with completely different expectations. The second part of McChrystal's strategy involved "cultural change" in the way that Afghan soldiers and police – and US soldiers -- operated. Long-term success in Afghanistan would require that soldiers and police be trained to persuade insurgents to change sides.

In Iraq, General Petraeus was commander in a losing war against an Iraqi insurgency that was flourishing and the country was imploding with civil war. Thousands of civilians were dying every month. Al-Qaeda was carrying out large-scale massacres of Shiite civilians. Shiite militias retaliated by massacring thousands of Sunnis. Petraeus, like McChrystal, refocused troop efforts to protect Iraqi civilians in order to cut off insurgents from their base of support. Then, as a brilliant stroke, Petraeus orchestrated peace deals with tens of thousands of former fighters while at the same time building an Iraqi army.

Fast forward to Iraq today. We are seeing a replay in Iraq of mission creep without a strategy that deals with the totality of current and future threats in Iraq. The Pentagon announced on June 11, 2015, that it is considering establishment of a new network of American military bases in Iraq to aid in the fight against the Islamic State. This reversal of American (read Presidential) policy would deepen American involvement in the country.

As interpreted by the leader of the Iraqi Shia militia, Al-Hashd Al-Shaabi, the US decision to deploy more forces in Anbar province was aimed primarily at dealing with criticism for the fall of, first, Fallujah (January 2015) and then Anbar's capital, Ramadi (May 17, 2015) to ISIS. A second reason cited by Al-Hashd Al-Shaabi was that the US wanted to "steal the militia's upcoming victory." Al-Hashd Al-Shaabi proclaimed that his Shia militia had the capacity to "liberate" Sunni-dominated Anbar province without international coalition's support. Reports (difficult to confirm) say that as many as 15,000 "volunteers" had joined this Shiite militia movement and, not difficult to confirm, that it was supported by Iranians.

In addition to sending 450 trainers to establish a new military base in Iraq, aimed at retaking Ramadi, chairman of the Joint Chiefs of Staff, Gen. Dempsey, described a possible future campaign entailing the establishment of what he called "lily pads" -- American military bases around the country from which trainers would work with Iraqi security forces and local tribesmen in the fight against the Islamic State. These "lily pads" were expected to sprout across the "pond" known as Anbar Province. "Our campaign is built on establishing these 'lily pads' that allow us to encourage the Iraqi security forces to go forward and create new ones."

In both Afghanistan and Iraq, similar campaigns were carried out previously under different, less pleasant-sounding names such as "oil spot" or "ink blot." As described by retired Army lieutenant colonel Andrew Krepinevich in a 2005 article in *Foreign Affairs*: "Since the US and Iraqi armies cannot guarantee security to all of Iraq simultaneously, they should start by focusing on certain key areas and then, over time, broadening the effort—hence the image of an expanding oil spot."

The "oil spot" strategy is somewhat similar to "protected safe havens": protected bases established in hostile terrain that seek to create larger secure zones around them that include additional, networked "ink spots." The main differences between "ink spots" and protected safe havens is that the functions of the latter, in any state in the Middle East, include: training local insurgents; providing protection to displaced local populations; and the presence of frontline advisors playing multiple roles, engaged in bottomup decision-making, using advanced information and communication technology, including to control targeting of UAVs and airstrikes. Frontline advisors would manage the totality of the protected safehaven's mission to free entire regions of ISIS or any other "enemy" forces.

In Iraq this new network of American "lily-pads" is the centerpiece of a strategy to retake Ramadi from ISIS. Building on lessons learned in the Anbar Awakening, advisors will reach out to Sunni tribes to accelerate the integration of Sunni fighters into Iraqi Security Forces (ISF), which is dominated by Shiites. The Obama administration is hoping (and the emphasis here is on "hoping") that reaching out to Sunnis will reduce the Iraqi military's reliance on Shiite militias to take back territory lost to the Islamic State. Briefly here's the US strategy to retake Ramadi: (1) ISF does most of the fighting to retake Ramadi; (2) once the city is "liberated," Sunni fighters have to hold it; and (3) thereafter the "liberated" city will have to be defended by local tribes.

What is unclear is how Iraqi Security Forces (Sunni) and Shiite Hashd al-Shaabi ("Popular Mobilization" Units), controlled by Hadi al-Amiri's Badr Organization, will collaborate when the latter, as their "religious duty," already are committed to "liberate" Anbar from ISIS fighters. The 1-2-3 US plan for liberating Ramadi also is complicated by the fact that Hadi al-Amiri already has made it clear, for example, after Hashd al-Shaabi's victory in Diyala province (adjoining Iran), that it is the self-proclaimed vanguard force battling ISIS in Iraq. Accused of retaliatory atrocities against Sunnis, Amiri's Badr Organization has proven itself to be an effective fighting force against ISIS and was gathering other militias under the banner of "popular mobilization" forces.

Amiri himself has been, and will continue to be, a key factor in the campaign against ISIS. His Badr Organization is both a political party and a military force. Amiri not only is pro-Iranian, Iran was his ally in fighting Saddam Hussein decades ago, and that's important to understand and appreciate in mid-2015 and going forward. Amiri flaunts photos taken with Qassem Suleimani, commander of Iran's Islamic Revolutionary Guard Corps' (IRGC)

Quds Force, the special forces unit responsible for fighting Tehran's battles abroad.

Nouri al-Maliki was so impressed with Amiri's Badr Organization that he not only funneled support and military supplies to them, he placed all Iraqi military and security forces in Diyala province under Amiri's command. Iraq's current prime minister, Haider al-Abadi, gave Amiri (after controversy) the Interior Ministry to run which controls the federal police and intelligence agencies. All of this was done in spite of a plethora of accusations about Amiri's corruption and the unquestioned fact that he is Iran's partner in Iraq.

More than criticisms of corruption, no doubt Amiri's Badr Organization and its very close ties to Iran pose a dilemma for the US in Iraq, especially with troubling reports over the years of systematic, vicious abuses of Sunnis (that Amiri dismisses as the result of lack of proper training for his forces). The Iraqi Army's loses in Anbar province, however, further empower Amiri's militia. Amiri has his own ideas and plans for "stabilizing" Iraq. He has no apologies for the use of brute force against a jihadist enemy that has killed thousands of Iraqis with car, truck and roadside bombs.

The US's dilemma about support for Amiri's Badr Organization is exacerbated by the fact that the only other effective fighting force against ISIS in Iraq, the Kurdish Peshmerga, has no plans to retake any part of northern Iraq outside of its own borders. With the help of coordinated US airstrikes, training, arms and intelligence support, the Peshmerga controls their own territory, but has no intention of helping the US and its allies retake Mosul (city of over 2 million) in Nineveh province just to the southwest of Iraqi Kurdistan.

The Kurds do not believe that the Shiite-led government in Baghdad will reform its armed forces or persuade Sunnis living under ISIS rule to rise up and turn against them. The Kurds have concluded that they are on their own and, for the foreseeable future, will have to operate without any help from Baghdad. They are securing their borders, improving their battlefield logistics and other capabilities to fight jihadists, and presumably preparing for establishment of an independent Kurdish state, which includes oil-rich Kirkuk (also claimed by Baghdad). The Kurds are realistic in their assessment of challenges going forward, currently with more than 1000 kilometers of Kurdistan's border along ISIS's territory.

All of this puts the United States in a very difficult position in Iraq. The strongest force in opposition to ISIS outside of Kurdistan is the Badr Organization. The Badr Organization's military commander, Karim al-Nouri, told the US, the world, and specifically the Islamic State that Hajj Qassem Suleimani and his Quds Force, Abu Mahdi al-Muhandis, leader of the Kataib Hezbollah militia and an Iraqi military commander who also is connected to the Quads Force, and Hadi al-Amiri's Shiite militias all were coming to get ISIS in Tikrit. Understandably the US military had grave doubts about showing support for these Iranian-backed groups that included some militia leaders on US black-lists. Muhandis, for example, was convicted for the 1983 bombing of the US Embassy in Kuwait. But the promised results in Tikrit speak for themselves.

Tikrit, the largest predominantly Sunni city in Iraq, was lost to ISIS in June 2014. Tikrit had about 10,000 ISIS troops in it when it was attacked by Shiite militias and Iraqi forces in March 2015. About 90 percent of Tikrit's residents had fled before the battle started. In early April 2015 Tikrit was recaptured. Shiite militias amounted to roughly half of the 30,000 troops attacking the city. As many as a thousand Sunni tribesmen also participated. Quds Force commander Hajj Qassem Suleimani himself led the operation. Mayhem ensued after the month-long battle. Neighborhoods were burned down. Looting occurred throughout the city. No question that Shiite militias wanted revenge against ISIS. ISIS left behind as many as 10,000 IEDs. The US did not provide any ground support for the Tikrit operation but conducted relentless airstrikes. The US viewed the role of Shiite militias as a "cause for concern" but did not protest Iran's overt role.

The US has to come to terms with the fact that Iraq's Shiite militias all boast some degree of connection to Tehran and share an antipathy towards the US, as does the Badr Organization. They are reluctant to accept US help in the fight against the Islamic

State although Nouri, the Badr Organization's commander, has said that he is prepared to accept help from whoever offers it. Was the Badr Organization consulted on the latest US strategy for deploying "Lily Pads"? Who knows? A strategic albeit controversial case can be made for involving the Badr Organization in planning the development of "lily pads" since, like it or not, their future participation will be essential for the "lily pads" to survive and work as planned.

In September 2014 President Obama announced the launch of a "comprehensive and sustained" effort to defeat ISIS in Iraq, which did not happen. In June 2015 he announced sending an additional 450 military personnel to "train, advise and assist" Iraqi forces. That action will include embedding battalion and brigade-level special operations forces and Special Forces airstrike controllers in Iraq. That deployment increases the US military presence in Iraq to 3,550.

More than 2.6 million Americans fought in Iraq and Afghanistan. As many as a million still suffer mental and physical problems. Nearly 4500 Americans lost their lives in Operation Iraqi Freedom (2003-2014) and another 2000 in Afghanistan. The American people are understandably disinclined to see more military fatalities and other casualties in Iraq. For Iraqis and Afghanis, however, the bottomline perception is that Americans come, help and then leave. Locals fear to make any public commitments so that, after the US leaves, they may get their throats cut. Even in Afghan and Iraqi villages, locals are aware of the political talk in America that engaging in warfare in their country has been too costly and too dangerous, and that the US should cut back on its military and other support efforts.

CHAPTER 8

Hail to the Commander-in-Chief

In every presidential election, each candidate makes their best case for understanding the most consequential foreign policy and national security issues of our times. A credible candidacy in 2016 requires cogent answers to some of the most complex and confounding issues in modern history. Depending on the occasion, presidential candidates in both parties express their views with varying mixtures of vehemence, exhortation and eloquence. They typically convey great confidence in their ability to create order out of chaos, for example, in the Middle East, and correct serious mistakes made in past wars, principally in Iraq and Afghanistan.

The real challenge for American presidential leadership, however, for solving both domestic and international problems, is Washington itself, the seemingly irreconcilable partisan differences in Congress enhanced by the influence of special interests and conflicts between Executive and Congressional branches that often result from efforts by the White House to control parochial self-interests in Congress. Commitments of presidential candidates to use executive powers of the White House to change dysfunctional behaviors of both Congress and the Federal bureaucracy inevitably involve more of the very White House micromanagement that itself has proven to be a major source of conflict and disarray in Washington.

Of course, for the party that doesn't occupy the White House, correcting past strategic and tactical mistakes, and preventing new ones, including unnecessary wars, usually requires a change of administration. Presidential candidates in "the other party" confidently predict that, for example, they never would have proclaimed that Saddam possessed chemical and biological weapons and an active nuclear program. Benefitting from 20-20 hindsight, they also would have engineered a competent Afghan national army and police force and a much more effective central Afghan government. Many Americans don't realize, or understandably don't want to be reminded, that the war in Afghanistan, the nation's longest war, lasted longer than US involvement in WW II. The war in Iraq lasted longer than the Korean War. And neither war was "won." In fact, both wars are still in progress, but now are termed "insurgencies."

In Afghanistan, the goal was to prevent the Taliban from returning to power or Al-Qaeda using the country as a launchpad for terrorism. Today, however, we're seeing both the Taliban and Al-Qaeda being challenged in Afghanistan by ISIS, which wasn't even highlighted by US and other military analysts as a dangerous factor early in 2015. In Afghanistan, Iraq, Syria and Libya, establishing democratic rule and effective governance still remain remote goals. In Iraq, after losing more than 4000 American lives and damaging tens of thousands more, and spending more than $1 trillion, based on a fallacious premise for invasion, the main outcome thus far has been the strengthening of Iran's position in Iraq and the Middle East. Few if any of the military and policy strategists in the Pentagon or in countless American think tanks envisioned that outcome. The Middle East is more unstable – and unpredictable -- than ever.

Usually presidential campaign rhetoric is not the appropriate place for discussions about the nation's woeful ignorance about historical, cultural, political and other factors that govern the conduct of warfare in foreign countries, like tribalism, deep and widespread corruption, sectarian, ethnic and religious conflicts and, generally, what knowledgeable civilian and military advisors frequently refer to as complicated "realities on the ground."

A president or a presidential candidate with only minimalist objectives for dealing with chaotic conditions in Afghanistan, Iraq, Syria, Libya, and Yemen usually has been, and will continue to be, severely criticized for weakness by a host of hawkish opponents and commentators. That happened to President Obama when, for example, he announced in 2011 that the troop "Surge" in Afghanistan would be drawn down and responsibility for security transferred to the Afghans by the end of 2014. The US had let large swaths of Afghanistan fall once again under Taliban domination, which was likely to continue without interruption to this day -- except for the unexpected blossoming of ISIS in Afghanistan. ISIS now is engaged in fighting the Taliban for control of the north and other sections of the country.

When the Arab Spring arrived in Syria, early in 2011, and demonstrators demanded that President Bashar al-Assad step down, he responded with repressive force. The US imposed sanctions and the case for US and international intervention grew as thousands of Syrians were killed, but Assad's chemical weapons were the main deterrent for further US intervention. As Leon Panetta, Secretary of Defense (2011-2013, and 2011-13, CIA Director) tells the story, President Obama's advisors were against aggressive military action in Syria even though US military leaders, State, Defense, and the CIA made the case that lesser actions would not work. What the US did not have at the time was any way to coordinate and support a multiplicity of Syrian rebel opposition groups that today are at war with Assad, and each other. Consequently, Defense Department planners estimated (guesstimated?) that it would take between 75,000 and 100,000 US troops (the equivalent of all the US troops in Afghanistan at the time) to take on the Assad regime.

When Assad used chemical weapons in mid-2013, the President finally approved supplying arms to Assad's opposition. Assad defied US actions and the President finally referred the matter to Congress, for virtually inevitable defeat. Thanks to Russia's intervention, Assad agreed to removal of Syria's chemical weapons (which actually may not have happened fully yet). At the time, in 2014, the threat from ISIS was growing in both Syria and Iraq. But the US had no contingency plans for dealing with ISIS or rebel groups.

The same is true for Iraq. On June 9, 2015, retired Navy Rear Adm. John Kirby, the State Department spokesman, appeared on MSNBC after President Barack Obama acknowledged that the US lacks a "complete strategy for training Iraqi security forces," and stated that the war effort "has to be owned by the Iraqis." He added that "it could take at least three to five years for Iraq to overcome the Islamic State onslaught." Asked if the current strategy is working, Kirby conceded, "Maybe the way we're going about that needs to be changed a little bit."

In his book, *Duty*, Robert Gates said that the White House, its National Security Staff (NSS), and the National Security Council (NSC), chaired by the President, are in complete control of virtually every important detail of the nation's national security apparatus and military decision-making. After serving six presidents in both the CIA and the NSC, and as Secretary of Defense, Gates should know. The American people have frequently heard the president referred to as "Commander-in-Chief." Especially in a presidential election year, it's important for the American people to know, and really understand that, with advice and intelligence information provided by the NSC, the Commander-in-Chief they elect as President of the United States indeed is completely responsible for every important strategic military and national security decision that the US makes for today and tomorrow.

This is not a new fact of life in Washington. On the contrary, since its inception under President Truman, the NSC has been advising the President on making all major national security and foreign policy decisions and working with the President to coordinate these policies among various government agencies. Chaired by the President, the NSC includes the Vice President, Secretary of State, Secretary of the Treasury, Secretary of Defense, Chairman of the Joint Chiefs of Staff, Director of National Intelligence and, when needed, the Attorney General and the Director of the Office of Management and Budget.

According to Gates, "we begin military engagements – wars – profoundly ignorant about our adversaries and about the situation on the ground." Gates and others who should know based on their leadership experience in making key military and national security decisions warn about the dangers inherent in wishful thinking based on profound ignorance about our adversaries and the actual situation on the ground in Pakistan, Afghanistan, Iraq, Syria, Libya, Yemen and elsewhere in the Middle East and Africa. They also repeatedly warn the American public about the hazards for America and the world of the unintended consequences of decisions made by presidents in both parties and their advisors during and after ill-conceived nation-building projects.

Long before 9/11, already in the 1980s, some of the brightest minds in the military services were working diligently to change the way that warfare decisions were being made from the top down and the bottom up and even the ways that the White House, the Commander-in-Chief, members of Congress and the rest of Washington's defense establishment viewed war and the way America should fight wars in the 21st century. Everyone with any interest in the subject of counterinsurgency doctrine in the United States should read Fred Kaplan's *The Insurgents: David Petraeus and the Plot to Change the American Way of War*, which covers the extraordinary stories of both Petraeus and John Nagl who, after meeting in 1987, eventually spawned what became the basis for counterinsurgency doctrine in subsequent decades.

West Point was nurturing several renegade officer-PhDs like John Nagl and David Petraeus who were researching and putting ideas together about how to fight "small wars." The Vietnam War was on its way to conclusion. By September 11, 2001, the phrase "rapidly deployable" forces had become part of the official military vocabulary, but the focus really was on technology, especially airborne weapons like Predator drones, smart bombs, spy satellites, and aerial photos. Sec. of Defense Donald Rumsfeld's "transformational warfare" seemed to be in its ascendency.

When on March 20, 2003, President Bush announced the start of the Iraq War, two-star general and commander of the 101st Airborne

Division Petraeus was in Mosul preaching the heretical concept of "nation-building" to his brigade and battalion commanders, talking to tribal chiefs, organizing local elections, vetting candidates, getting water, electricity and sanitation systems working, and generally restoring basic services and institutions. The mission priorities in Mosul had been set by Petraeus. He was totally in charge, that is, until ignorance and stupidity exercised in Iraq and Washington in 2003-04 not only got in the way but more or less destroyed Petraeus' effort.

In addition, while breeding insurgents, Iraq still had no "nation-building" or counterinsurgency strategy. In 2003-04, Americans still knew little or nothing about Iraqi culture and, more important, Iraqi insurgency strategy. However, by early 2004, that was beginning to change, thanks to John Nagle's *Learning to Eat Soup with a Knife*, his Aussie counterinsurgency soulmate, David Kilcullen, and a couple of other very bright, dedicated, brazen military officers who, as luck would have it, like proverbial rabbits were pulled out of the hat. In addition, in 2004-05, recognition was emerging that US Special Forces were deployed in more than 150 countries dealing with everything imaginable, including fighting insurgents.

What came out of countless hours spent framing counterinsurgency plans for Iraq produced nothing basically that David Galula, the French military officer, hadn't written about many years earlier. More history and data were examined. But the key to the impact of the Iraq counterinsurgency plan published in 2005 was its timing even more than new content. Given the failure of military practices in Iraq and post-Petraeus in Mosul, a credible counterinsurgency campaign plan that might work better than conventional military action was desperately needed. In addition, as shocking as it may seem in retrospect, the Pentagon bureaucracy was only very gradually realizing that the war in Iraq had a post-battlefield "political dimension."

Late in 2005, a commitment to "stability operations" as an integral part of the US military mission in Iraq emerged from seemingly interminable discussions and revisions of position papers.

Surely it was not an immediate cure for the repeated failures of senior military and civil leadership, including the Pentagon and the National Security Council, to learn from past US military successes and disasters, and especially failures to adapt when military actions produce the opposite results intended. Over time the nascent COIN promised to help remedy the costly disconnect between general officers and what was actually happening on the ground in places like Iraq, and the prevailing military predilection for direct assault on enemy forces.

By 2011, clearly COIN in Afghanistan had not worked. The forty thousand extra troops deployed to Afghanistan could not secure territory gained in a COIN-driven surge. The government of Afghanistan itself and its corrupt interdependencies through the nation was the major problem. Large-scale, long-term "stability" operations like Iraq and Afghanistan were not working. The COIN revolution was not working. Everyone involved in various COIN braintrusts realized that it was the end of long-term "nation-building" efforts that relied on US military forces. Dealing with jihadist and other terrorist groups henceforth would focus on "innovative" non-military strategies.

Unfortunately what they read in the news media is that US efforts to help Afghanistan build an air force, at great expense, that can fight the Taliban, was planned so badly that it cannot work. The effective range of the MD-530 scout helicopters cannot reach areas where the Taliban operate. The maximum altitude with a full load of fuel and ammunition is only 7,000 to 8,000 feet which means that from the Kabul airfield these helicopters cannot cross most of the mountain ranges that encircle Kabul. Complaints about the helicopter's design, engine, lack of armor, and other problems reflected that the US had not engaged Afghan pilots in decisions about what kind of aircraft they needed to fight the Taliban.

What no one involved in reassessment of the US role and mission in post-Iraq warfare was prepared to speculate about was what kind of wars -- smaller, leaner, more agile and flexible and more technologically advanced -- US forces might have to fight. It was assumed by even the brightest military minds that the next cycles of counterinsurgency warfare would fit whatever the US military did best in terms of strategy, tactics and preconceived ideas. But let's give credit due to Petraeus that he raised the possibility that future wars might defy all previous assumptions and, without being specific, said once again that the US military, faced with an unprecedented kind of enemy, might require a whole new COIN way of looking at insurgent warfare

Petraeus, Nagle and others committed to enabling the US Army and Special Forces to fight warfare involving many varieties of insurgents had not anticipated the Islamic State (also known as *Daesh*) that uses terror and violence as a tool but mainly aims to control and govern territory. Whereas COIN had stabilization goals, ISIS was providing relative stability in formerly chaotic areas, replacing corrupt, unreliable governments with functioning regimes that refuse to allow corruption. It was as though ISIS leaders had read one or another of the COIN field manuals.

Rather than a strategy to oust the Taliban in Afghanistan, it appears that ISIS and the Taliban may be joining forces. Both are against corruption and chaos. In Iraq, Sunnis remain broadly hostile to the Shiite-controlled central government and are receptive to ISIS. In Syria, President Bashar al-Assad has presided over a civil war that has killed more than 200,000 people, dislocated half the population, and left the nation in chaos, also fertile ground for ISIS.

COIN becomes even more than a little confusing when, seemingly suddenly, our allies in Middle East COIN -- Saudi Arabia, Qatar and Turkey – appear to be supporting Al-Qaeda's official arm in Syria, Jabhat al-Nusra, ostensibly for the purpose of trying to lure Nusra away from Al-Qaeda. The distinctions between Nusra, Al-Qaeda and other jihadist groups in Syria like Ahrar al-Sham are negligible. All we know, however, is that among the countless Sunni groups that the Saudi royal family has been funding in recent years, the main criteria has been containing Iranian influence in the region, and especially in the aftermath of the US-Iranian nuclear deal.

What we don't know is the extent of CIA involvement in directing arms and funding support for what they have claimed are "moderate forces" rather than Al-Qaeda-affiliated Islamist rebels. A covert anti-Assad strategy became an anti-ISIS strategy. As for Syrian jihadists themselves, al-Nusra and others are working together with ISIL in ways that suggest that ideology is not a barrier and that convergence may be accelerating. With ISIL becoming an increasingly important priority for the US through the Middle East, there even have been unsubstantiated reports that Assad is assisting the US to target airstrikes against ISIL.

Recently Congress moved to slash funding of the secret CIA operation aimed at training and arming "moderate rebels" in Syria. Who are these "moderate rebels"? No one seems to really know. The House Intelligence Committee voted unanimously to cut as much as 20 percent of the classified funds flowing into this CIA program that has a budget approaching $1 billion a year. Members of the intelligence panel admitted that they had no idea of what will happen in the aftermath of toppling Assad's regime.

As the debate among the Obama administration's top intelligence, counterterrorism and law enforcement officials rages over which terrorist group, ISIS or Al-Qaeda, poses the biggest threat to the American homeland, there is little discussion about the porous US-Mexico border that has allowed hundreds of Islamic extremists and terrorists to enter the US without being noticed or apprehended.

Interestingly, intelligence and counterintelligence officials are asking themselves outloud whether ISIS poses a more immediate danger because of its sophisticated social media campaign, designed to inspire followers to either join the caliphate or launch attacks across the United States, or Al-Qaeda operatives in Yemen, Syria and elsewhere, including those crossing America's southern border, plotting attacks to produce large numbers of casualties.

What we know to-date is that nearly 30,000 foreign recruits from more than 100 countries have poured into Syria to join the Islamic

State, doubling the number of its volunteers in just the past 12 months. International efforts to tighten borders, share intelligence and enforce antiterrorism laws are not working to diminish the ranks of new militant fighters. These foreign fighters include at least 250 Americans, up from about 100 a year ago. A year ago, Obama succeeded in rallying support for a legally binding Security Council resolution that would compel all 193 United Nations member states to take steps to "prevent and suppress" the flow of their citizens into the arms of groups that each country considers to be a terrorist organization.

James B. Comey, the F.B.I. director and attorney general, Loretta E. Lynch both are very concerned about ISIS recruiting terrorists in the US. Dozens of terrorism-related arrests are being made around the nation and we're told that the FBI has hundreds of terrorism investigations pending across the country. Many counterintelligence analysts are more concerned about the ability of ISIS to attract foreign fighters to replace its combatants in Iraq and Syria as fast as the United States and its allies are killing them, and the fact that, unlike Al-Qaeda, ISIS controls territory, provides civil services, has infrastructure and has been earning close to $1 billion a year in oil revenues and taxes.

What should be most disturbing to the American public and its Congressional representatives is that the US government has allocated billions of dollars in counterterrorism funds, assigned thousands of federal agents, intelligence analysts and troops to combat these threats, without having a clear understanding of what actually constitutes the rising risks from the Islamic State and Al Qaeda overseas and in the homeland. Counterterrorism programs employ roughly one in four of the more than 100,000 people who work at the C.I.A. and other intelligence agencies, and account for about one-third of the $50 billion annual intelligence budget. Even with the magnitude of these US investments, most members of Congress cannot explain to the American public what these programs actually do to protect the homeland.

What we do know is that about 3,400 American troops are in Iraq helping the Iraqis fight the Islamic State, while about

9,800 US troops in Afghanistan are assisting that country's security personnel in combating the Taliban, Al Qaeda and other extremists there, including ISIS. Here again, neither Congress nor the American people have any idea about the effectiveness of these interventions, especially for containing ISIS and Al-Qaeda. No doubt questions of varying kinds about these issues will be raised in the 2016 presidential campaign, but neither Republican nor Democratic candidates are likely to shed any meaningful light on the rise of the Islamic State from the ashes of the Iraq war and Al-Qaeda post 9/11.

CHAPTER 9

US I.Q. Tests

All of the military and diplomatic decisions for action in foreign countries that qualify as "strategic," including covert actions by the CIA or national security officials, are the responsibility of the White House and its Commander-in-Chief. That's extremely important for the American public to understand. Covert plans, for example, only can be put together by the CIA with White House approval. The policy objective driving or guiding a covert plan comes from the White House. The White House, the Department of Justice, and principals and deputies of the National Security Council (NSC) have to approve the plan. The President signs-off on the plan. Congress is notified, including Senate and House intelligence committees. Holding the CIA's purse strings, in theory Congress can withhold funding for a covert CIA operation. In sum, both credit and blame for the successes or failures of covert actions taken, and not, belongs to executive and legislative leadership of the United States government, primarily the Commander-in-Chief and his (or her) national security team.

The decision to go to war in Iraq, which by the CIA's own admission was one of the biggest intelligence failures in American history, exemplifies the problems and challenges facing the White House and national policy leaders that have to rely on potentially "imperfect" (or even doctored) US intelligence to make decisions about military engagement in the Middle East or anywhere else in the world. The decisions to go to war in Iraq and remove Saddam Hussein and the pursuit of Osama bin Laden before and after 9/11 offer some sobering illustrations of and lessons learned about the consequences of "imperfect" US intelligence in strategic White House foreign policy decision-making.

In the fall of 2002, the National Intelligence Estimate (NIE) got it wrong on Saddam's possession of weapons of mass destruction (WMD). Most Americans, perhaps even most school children, know that by now. The questions about the NIE's misreading of Saddam's WMD really should focus on how the National Intelligence Council, that processes and vets intelligence information and judgments from all US intelligence agencies to produce NIEs for the White House and National Security Council (NSC), not only could be so wrong but every key participant came to the same wrong conclusion.

The entire intelligence community and the CIA got it completely wrong about both Saddam's WMD and his supposed links to Al-Qaeda. The sources of information were false and unreliable. Thus false and falsified intelligence drove the US to war in Iraq, without a post-war, post-Saddam scenario, and for reasons that have yet to be clearly explained. The participants in the decision to go to war did not speculate about potential unintended consequences of military action. No one presented to President Bush facts or arguments to the contrary, suggesting perhaps that Saddam was not an imminent threat. Congress viewed the war with Iraq as necessary for no more substantive reasons than President Bush possessed.

The Bush administration has been blamed for pushing the intelligence community to its conclusions about Saddam's WMD. But that's not the case. Think tanks, experts inside and outside of academia, the UN – everyone shared more or less the same messaging about Saddam's WMD. How could this misperception be so universally prevalent? The US went to war in Iraq in 2003 for eight long, bloody, costly years, with all parties initially believing that they were right, and without any real intelligence foundation to that opinion. So how did they all get it so wrong? The answer, which is really important because it can happen again, no matter what President is occupying the White House: assumptions morphed into firm conclusions and judgments. Scary! Biases were rampant and took control of what should have been better judgment.

Even scarier in retrospect, the intelligence community indulged in the antithesis of why we have an intelligence community, namely, facts became true if they support preconceptions. The CIA failed *Intelligence Analysis 101A* -- to rigorously question and test their facts and judgments. President Bush was given misleading information and judgments accompanied by high confidence levels. At the highest level of national security policy decision-making in the aftermath of 9/11, that's like giving an addict cocaine as an antidote to heroin.

Liberating Iraq was on the drawing board in Washington for years before 2003. The Pentagon and the CIA unquestionably wanted Hussein removed. The Republican Party's campaign platform in the 2000 election called for "full implementation" of the Iraq Liberation Act as "a starting point" in a plan to "remove" Hussein. According to George W. Bush and British Prime Minister Tony Blair, the Coalition mission was "to disarm Iraq of weapons of mass destruction, to end Saddam Hussein's support for terrorism, and to free the Iraqi people." But deep in the Pentagon, in addition to Iraq, a much broader Middle East war strategy was on the drawing board pre-9/11. According to General Wesley Clark, the former Supreme NATO Allied Commander and Joint Chiefs of Staff Director of Strategy and Policy, as described in his 2003 book, *Winning Modern Wars*, in a conversation with a military officer in the Pentagon shortly after the 9/11 attacks, he was told about a plan to attack seven Middle Eastern countries in five years "... beginning with Iraq, then Syria, Lebanon, Libya, Iran, Somalia and Sudan."

Post-9/11, President Bush was obsessed with Saddam and his WMD. No one (except apparently VP Cheney) had any evidence of a connection between Saddam and 9/11 or between Iraq and Al-Qaeda. That didn't matter. The American people also believed that Saddam was involved in 9/11 but, to their credit, they preferred a diplomatic solution. The focus of Bush and Congress was rooted in the horrific experience of 9/11 and the necessity to protect the nation from a reoccurrence or even worse. The best that can be said for the 8 years and 8 months of the war in Iraq was that it was a well-intentioned disaster.

No one in the intelligence community or any senior US national security official addressed whether and why a war with Iraq would help to suppress or "defeat" Al-Qaeda or prevent it from spreading its terrorist message or its network. What the CIA knew and thought about Saddam and his WMD at the time is still unclear. Most importantly, the CIA did not ask the right questions at the right time. The CIA helped to make links between Saddam and Al-Qaeda based on what they later referred to as "worst-case scenarios."

It's not unfair to say that America went to war with Saddam and Iraq based on gut views coated with persuasive confidence levels from respected experts and analysts. These gut views were based on out-of-date, faulty, circumstantial, unverified, irrelevant and spurious information that lacked rigorous assessment, but were authenticated by the universe of American intelligence sources. US intelligence community experts led the White House into the Iraq war debacle and its vast Iraqi and US death toll. When the CIA reviewed "lessons learned" from the Iraq war, they actually commended themselves for engaging in the self-criticism, questioning the confidence levels in their previous judgments and, with no apologies, acknowledging that they failed to collect sufficient valid intelligence.

The role of the CIA and the US intelligence community in pursuit of Osama bin Laden before and after 9/11 adds to valuable, and distressing, lessons learned prior to launching the Iraq war. For the CIA, 9/11 was a huge, game-changing wake-up call, making terrorism the all-out focus of the agency, which helps to explain their contribution to the White House decision to launch the Iraq war. In a sense the reaction of America and its intelligence community to 9/11 certified Saddam and his supposed WMD as the next US military target.

From the outset, the CIA's assessment of the terrorist threat pre- and post-9/11, and then the covert hunt for bin Laden, further illustrates the weaknesses of US intelligence operations at the time targeting Islamic terrorists. Twenty-five years later, that CIA counterterrorism mission has morphed from Al-Qaeda into ISIS. The mission was changed somewhat by the Boston Marathon bombing that added "lone wolves" to the terrorism threat to the homeland. Terrorists with WMD still ranked highest on the terrorism threat scale. What we really don't know, however, based on what's been happening in Iraq, Syria, Yemen, elsewhere in the Middle East, and also along the porous US border with Mexico, is how much better the US intelligence and national security apparatus is in 2015 for protecting the US homeland from terrorist attacks than it was before and after 9/11.

Back to lessons learned from the bin Laden story. Bin Laden was first observed by the CIA in the Sudan in 1991. They tracked his move to Afghanistan in 1996. Al-Qaeda was recruiting and training thousands of jihadists in Afghanistan. Taliban leadership was providing a safehaven for Al-Qaeda. These facts should have set off alarms in the CIA especially since bin Laden's name kept popping up at the CIA in 1996. In 1997 the CIA finally figured out that bin Laden was the head of a terrorist organization that aimed to establish a global caliphate, drive the US out of the Middle East, and topple "apostate" leaders in those countries in the region that supported the US

As chatter about these goals not only poured through US intelligence, bin Laden himself publicly announced them again and again in 1995-98. Did the CIA pick up the chatter and relate it to bin Laden's emphatically clear proclamations? Bin Laden's announced intentions to destroy the US with WMD apparently did not cause any ripples in the US national security community and also got virtually no media attention in the US. At the time, the CIA apparently was not taking either Al-Qaeda or bin Laden very seriously.

Bin Laden finally got the attention of the CIA, the media and the nation on 7 August 1998 with the bombings of two embassies in

East Africa. These attacks also briefly brought bin Laden, Ayman al-Zawahiri and Al-Qaeda to the attention of the American public. The FBI placed bin Laden on its Ten Most Wanted Fugitives list. President Clinton declared that he wanted retaliation. Two targets were selected. A training camp near Khost in Afghanistan where bin Laden was supposed to be meeting with Al-Qaeda leaders was struck by cruise missiles. Bin Laden already had left. As a matter of diplomatic protocol, Pakistan had been informed that US cruise missiles would pass through its airspace en route to Khost. As a result, bin Laden probably was tipped off. The second CIA target, a pharmaceutical factory in the Sudan, was based on failed intelligence. Both misses backfired. Instead of showing US capabilities to strike terrorists, they showed failed military intelligence judgment and execution.

The bombing of the USS *Cole*, a US Navy guided missile destroyer, on 12 October 2000, clearly was a terrorist attack aimed at America. Harbored and being refueled in the Yemeni port of Aden, 17 American sailors were killed and 39 were injured. That should have been a wakeup call for the White House and the US intelligence community, especially since the CIA had information that Al-Qaeda might attack the US homeland well before 9/11. They did not know where, when or how, but this possibility was reported to and discussed with President Bush in the months before 9/11. Foreign counterparts were contacted. As a result, terrorist suspects were arrested in a dozen countries. However, none of this led to all-out efforts to tighten security in the US

When the 9/11 attack occurred the CIA had no idea who actually was responsible; however, a CIA official traveling with President Bush guessed correctly: Osama bin Laden and Al-Qaeda. There were no national no-fly lists. Passenger manifests that were checked post-9/11 against CIA databases revealed Al-Qaeda linked passengers. Later, the 9/11 Commission faulted lapses by the CIA, FBI, NSA and especially the failure of the intelligence community to penetrate Al-Qaeda in order to discover the real nature of terrorism threat warnings circulating around the world at the time. Important aviation security enforcement recommendations made by the 1996 Gore Commission had not been implemented. The 9/11 Commission faulted the CIA for a "lack of imagination": that Al-Qaeda would hijack a plane and use it as a WMD.

To their credit, in response to the *Cole* attack, the CIA had produced a detailed counterterrorism plan to go after Al-Qaeda which, for reasons never clearly explained, they kept under wraps until after 9/11. The plan included CIA and Special Forces joining with the Northern Alliance in Afghanistan to attack the Taliban supported by precision air strikes plus Pashtun insurgents attacking the Taliban in the south and east. President Bush was told Al-Qaeda would be destroyed, along with Bin Laden, in a matter of weeks. He approved the plan. CIA officials had been to northern Afghanistan many times. The CIA's intimate knowledge of northern Afghanistan and its tribal leadership made success possible in a matter of months – not weeks – using a paramilitary operation supported by airstrikes.

Three months after 9/11, in the jagged mountains of Tora Bora that separate Afghanistan from Pakistan, bin Laden's location was pinpointed by the CIA. Al-Qaeda and bin Laden had retreated to Tora Bora. Preventing bin Laden and thousands of Al Qaeda and Talban operatives from escaping into Pakistan would have required a very large contingent of US troops. Only forty members of a US special operations force raced to Tora Bora to kill bin Laden. They failed and over the next days bin Laden and thousands of Al-Qaeda and Taliban operatives crossed into Pakistan and disappeared. The failure to prevent the escape of Al-Qaeda and the Taliban into Pakistan represented a catastrophic blunder by General Tommy Franks and, more important, failed guidance from US civilian leadership. Orders from the White House should have been to not only kill or capture bin Laden but to destroy Al- Qaeda. Instead, along with Al Qaeda, Bin Laden walked into Pakistan and disappeared for nine and a half years.

The CIA's first-hand knowledge of Afghanistan 23 years ago makes US decisions on military and diplomatic engagement in Afghanistan all the more incomprehensible. What did CIA briefings for President Bush tell him about Afghanistan? The idea that the US somehow could turn the Afghan tribal society into a "democracy" and persuade the Taliban to operate within the Afghan political system had absolutely no foundation in reality in 2002 or since then. The US mission to transform Afghanistan's society, culture and political system, which led to the longest war in US history, resembles the vision and mission behind the ill-fated Iraqi Surge.

Bin Laden could not have been more pleased about the US invasion of Iraq. It reminded him of the Soviet Union's disastrous intervention in Afghanistan. Bin Laden wanted the US military in both Iraq and Afghanistan, investing substantial resources, including many young men dying, as strategic steps towards removing the US from the Middle East. Al-Qaeda had regrouped in Pakistan, some of its operatives had scattered around Asia, and some would move to Iraq and later evolve into ISIS.

CHAPTER 10

To Surge or Not to Surge

The 2016 presidential debate has taken over the foreign policy debate in Washington. There's an intense competition among presidential candidates to voice the most aggressive military policy stance against both ISIS and Iran. The core issues are whether American ground forces should fight ISIS in Iraq and how many US boots on the ground, if any, will be required. The hawks are convinced that, by sending more troops to Iraq in 2007, George W. Bush won the Iraq War and, by withdrawing troops, Barack Obama lost it and caused not only the collapse of Iraq and the rise of ISIS, but instability or the collapse of states around the Middle East. This kind of gross oversimplification of Middle East regional history and geopolitical reality should not surprise anyone listening to presidential debates, but it's important to get the story of the surge in Iraq right rather than wrong, and to draw relevant lessons learned from what actually happened.

Roughly ten years have passed since the surge in Iraq came and went. One would think that, drawing on the recollections of military leaders and really astute first-hand chroniclers, most key take-aways and lessons learned in the story of the surge already would have been documented sufficiently to inform and shape the 2016 presidential political debate. Not so, apparently. For example, a consensus among military planners and leaders of the surge was that they could not win by force alone. If ever there was a significant lesson to be learned from the surge, that one certainly wins a prize! Next, "sustainable stability" in Iraq only would happen when the Iraqis themselves decided to stop fighting among themselves. Another clear winner!

In 2003, based on a combination of fantasies and hubris, the Bush administration and its top advisors believed that US forces could quickly "conquer" Iraq, dismantle it and remove its evildoers, and construct a new, stable and democratic country loyal to the United States. It took almost three years to prove that these misconceptions overestimated America's civil-military power. In addition, military planners and pundits learned quite a bit about the dynamics of the sectarian civil war in Iraq, how to win over Sunni insurgents without treating Shia like the enemy, and the importance of dealing effectively with Iraq's President Maliki and his inner circle who were trying to sabotage the US's well-intentioned albeit unsuccessful efforts. Even Petraeus's remarkable improvisations as commander of US forces could not compensate for the fundamental flaws and misunderstandings in the US strategy for stabilization and sectarian reconciliation in Iraq.

Maliki's government resisted support for bringing Sunni insurgents into Iraqi security forces and reconciling with Iraq's Sunnis. That should have been no surprise to anyone with real knowledge of the Iraqi government and its executive and legislative process. The government, and its ruling Dawa Party, in 2005 and before, and continuing in 2015, has been completely rigged against reform, especially reform that interferes with corruption and sectarian power. Iraq consistently ranks among the ten most corrupt countries in the world. Maliki's authoritarian style and sectarian politics fit perfectly.

Based on the law of good intentions that leads to unintended consequences, the disruptive sectarian forces that were unleashed in the aftermath of the 2003 US invasion of Iraq have not been resolved to this day and probably won't be for some time to come. No national reconciliation process in Iraq ever took place. Iraq's struggle to deal with insurgencies since 2003 and before have morphed into its current fight to retake territory from the Islamic State. Likewise, the problematic power of Iranian-supported Shiite militias a decade ago today has Iraq relying on them to fight ISIS under the name of "popular mobilization" forces, further inflaming sectarian tensions.

2006 definitely was a bad year for US forces in Iraq. Then came the Sunni jihadist bombing of the Samarra mosque, the third holiest Shia shrine in Iraq, in the Sunni town of Samara, which resulted in a steady escalation of Shia retaliation and violence. Right or wrong, the Coalition strategy had to change after the Samarra mosque bombing. More than 25,000 additional American troops were added to the 140,000 already in Iraq. What difference did the surge make? What really would matter was a change in military strategy rather than the quantity of additional troops. In hindsight the strategic change seemed obvious: securing the Iraqi population by living with the people, 7 x 24, rather than consolidating US forces on remote big bases.

At the time, it became apparent to the commanders of US forces that they were not going to leave Iraq. The US strategy of "clear and hand off" could not work and had to be changed. Much more important was the idea of promoting reconciliation between Shia and Sunnis. Surprisingly, perhaps, this idea amounted to a discovery for Petraeus in Anbar Province. By his own admission, he did not come to Iraq with this strategy in his mind. He realized one day that, with the right strategy, US forces could make a fundamental difference in predominantly Sunni Arabs areas west and north of Baghdad.

In January 2007, George W. Bush sent 30,000 more troops to Iraq. Under the leadership of General David Petraeus and Commanding Gen. Ray Odierno, US troops began focusing less on killing insurgents and more on protecting Iraqi civilians, political reconciliation, and "nation-building." At the same time, Sunni leaders rebelled against the religious fanaticism of Al-Qaeda jihadists in their midst and decided to collaborate with Petraeus's forces. A drop in Sunni attacks persuaded the Shia militia leader, Moqtada al-Sadr, to agree to a cease-fire. The decline in deaths of Iraqi civilians in 2007-2009 was really impressive. It appeared that Bush and his surge had "won the war."

Unfortunately, although sectarian violence did go down, national reconciliation never occurred. The cause was not Obama's decision to withdraw all US troops at the end of 2011, but rather Prime Minister Maliki's well-documented persecution of Sunnis which paved the way for their embrace of ISIS as their only means of self-defense. Maliki had no intention of making the Iraqi government more inclusive. Even more unfortunate, for whatever incomprehensible reasons, and in defiance of reality, at that same time Obama publicly praised Maliki for "ensuring a strong, prosperous, inclusive, and democratic Iraq." This effusive praise was made even more absurd by the fact that Maliki had tried to arrest his vice president and other prominent Sunni leaders. Ironically, instead of national reconciliation, the surge had empowered Maliki so that he no longer needed US troops to stay in power and engage in sectarian tyranny.

Gen. Odierno, the US Army's top officer, recently pushed back on the Iraq War blame game, that has dominated the GOP 2016 presidential campaign trail, saying that the US military's withdrawal from Iraq in 2011 was the Bush administration's plan all along. Odierno, formerly the senior US general in Iraq, said he was unconvinced at the time that the Iraqi parliament would have approved a longer stay for American troops had Obama administration officials successfully negotiated for it. Iraqis did not, and still do not, want an American presence, which they refer to as an "occupation."

The Iraq War no doubt will return to the headlines again and again as Republican candidates attempt to tie the US withdrawal in 2011 -- and former Secretary of State Hillary Clinton's role in it -- to the rise of the Islamic State. For example, in a major national security speech recently, Jeb Bush criticized Hillary Clinton and President Obama for removing US troops from Iraq. "That premature withdrawal was the fatal error, creating the void that ISIS moved in to fill – and that Iran has exploited to the full as well."

Gen. Odierno, who commanded troops in Iraq for more than five years between 2003 and 2010, including two years as the top American general in the country, on the occasion of his retirement, tried to correct the record at his final press conference at the Pentagon. After US troops departed in December 2011, Iraqi Security Forces (ISF) "became significantly politicized," Odierno said. He also stated that US troops leaving Iraq at the end of 2011 had been "negotiated in 2008 by the Bush administration. That was always the plan. We had promised them [Iraq] that we would respect their sovereignty," said Odierno. In addition "Keeping US troops in Iraq beyond 2011 would have required the Iraqi parliament's approval, which was hardly guaranteed."

Looking forward rather than back, Odierno expressed support for embedding American soldiers with the ISF fighting ISIS militants. "I believe that if we find in the next several months we're not making progress ... we should absolutely consider embedding some soldiers with them, see if that would make a difference," Odierno said. "That doesn't mean they would be fighting." When asked if ISIS was winning in Iraq, Odierno said: "I think ISIL has been vaunted somewhat. They have not made any progress since we started airstrikes. I think we have gained back some territory, mostly by the great work of the Kurds and some work by the Iraqi Security Forces. American combat forces could probably defeat ISIS," Odierno said, "but within months after leaving, separatists would likely rise again without political and economic improvements."

Petraeus's counterinsurgency brainstorm had spawned what came to be called the "Arab Awakening" -- the "Sons of Iraq" – that eventually included over 100,000 former insurgents. Where did the surge fit into the Awakening? The surge never anticipated the Awakening in Anbar Province. But, fortuitously, under the strategic leadership of Col. Sean MacFarland, a brigade commander with the 1st Armored Division, the surge accelerated implementation of a strategy for sectarian reconciliation that took root in Anbar Province and Ramadi in 2006. Maliki was unwilling to seek parliamentary approval for the surge strategy. The US had to remove its forces. A handful of generals and several hundred troops and support staff stayed. Well over $10 billion worth of US equipment had been sent into Iraq.

Making matters much worse, just as US forces were leaving Iraq, Prime Minister Maliki pressed charges against his Sunni Arab vice president and his security detail. Petraeus, then director of the CIA, happened to be there and could do nothing to reverse Maliki's decision. Maliki launched what became the unraveling of the surge. Sunni Arabs were disenfranchised and their leaders were targeted by their own government. Sunni military and police leaders in the surge were replaced by Shia loyalists. So much US investment, so much sacrifice during the surge and afterwards, and it made no difference to Maliki and his cohorts.

We don't know, and perhaps will never know, what US military leaders of the surge actually told Presidents Bush or Obama about what worked in the surge, what didn't work and why. We also don't know why US leadership, after so much investment in the surge, did not even comment on Maliki's decision to remove then-Sunni Vice President Tariq al-Hashimi, just the day after US troops left Iraq. Hashemi fled to Turkey in the months after the Shia-led government accused him of playing a role in 150 bombings, assassinations and other attacks from 2005 to 2011. He was convicted in absentia and sentenced to death by hanging. Iraq erupted into countrywide sectarian violence.

The US declared victory in Iraq and moved on to deal with Afghanistan. In January 2009, President Obama sent VP Joe Biden to Afghanistan on a fact-finding mission. As a former member of the Senate Foreign Relations Committee, Biden was very familiar with Afghani issues. On his return, allowing for Biden's sense of humor, he reported, "If you ask ten of our people over there what we're trying to accomplish, you get ten different answers." Clearly the bottom-line of Biden's report, at the very least, was confusion in America's policies in Afghanistan. The same could be said of Syria. As the Syrian civil war grew, Al-Qaeda in Iraq (AQI) reappeared in Syria and rejuvenated itself. ISIS also pushed back into Iraq. No one in the US military command had anticipated that the Syrian civil war would fuel both AQI and ISIS.

ISIS returned to Iraq with an assassination campaign targeting Iraqi security force leaders and members in and around Mosul, and then retook Fallujah. Former US surge leaders watched in dismay as Iraqi security forces collapsed in northern Iraq. Without competent leaders at all levels in the Iraqi chain of command, an effective counteroffensive to the ISIS offense was impossible. Fleeing Iraqi leadership demoralized rank and file. A disenfranchised Sunni population welcomed ISIS forces as the ISF collapsed and fled.

In August 2015, a coalition of Shiite militia, Sunnis, and ISF troops, with strong backing from US airstrikes and drones, began attacking ISIS in Ramadi. Like ISIS had done elsewhere, they had spent months wiring buildings for bombs and booby-trapping countless locations. Holding on to Ramadi helps ISIS to hold Mosul and maintain access to its territory in Syria. Illustrative of the organizational problems facing Iraq's military forces, the Ramadi operation has multiple chains of command: the Sunnis, Shiite militia, and the ISF. An additional issue for the Iraqis was that US military leadership had urged that recapture of Mosul, Iraq's second largest city, should be Iraq's top military priority.

In 2015 an Iraqi parliamentary report, referred to a public prosecutor, blamed former Prime Minister Maliki and his senior military and civilian officials for Mosul's fall to ISIS. The damning report said that the corruption and incompetence of Maliki, all of his military and police leaders, Mosul's governor, and other political figures was responsible for the capture of Mosul by ISIS in June 2014. For the US, the question was how this could happen after years of building, training, and equipping the ISF, and what did it mean for Iraq's security in the future.

US military leadership understandably felt angry and betrayed after so much sacrifice and doing everything that had been asked of them during the surge. How could all of the investment and seeming gains simply evaporate? No one in the US government was held accountable for the Iraq fiasco. No one in command of US forces had any idea how to govern the country in a way that replicated the dynamics of the Great Awakening so as to achieve reconciliation, province by province; reform of the ISF that Maliki had politicized; and demobilization of Shiite militias and, in the process, holding fragmented and fragile Iraq together.

In addition to the daunting challenges of fighting and containing further expansion of ISIS, add the political and military challenges still facing Iraq in 2015 under the new regime of Prime Minister Halder Abadi. Maliki and Abadi have been political enemies even though both are Shiite leaders in the Dawa party. The political climate in Iraq does not look promising for slowing the Islamic State's surge to military and political power. Especially in the aftermath of the Iran nuclear deal, the future role of Iran in Iraq's sectarian and ethnic conflicts raises additional complications and questions.

For the last several years, the fate of Iraq has become of less concern in Washington, London, Riyadh, and other countries than the terrorism threat posed by ISIS in Syria and elsewhere and the role of Iran in the Middle East. Concerns about ISIS have far eclipsed worries about Al-Qaeda in the Arabian Peninsula (AQAP) and Yemen. These concerns have been exacerbated by the threat of Iran and its proxy wars in the region, including Lebanese Hezbollah's sponsorship of Shia militants in places like the eastern province of Saudi Arabia, in Yemen, in Bahrain, in southern Lebanon, and in Syria and Iraq.

Obviously the Middle East is in a pivotal historical moment. The shape and profiles of nation states are changing dramatically. Instability brought about by the Arab Spring has contributed. Governments appear broken and increasingly unrepresentative, partly in response to the pressures of instability and security challenges. ISIS thrives on such destabilization and, as a matter of strategy, wants states in the Middle East to respond to their violence or threat of it by creating police states or using police state tactics.

A good example is Kuwait that provides a model of the kind of overreaction to terrorist threats sought by ISIS. Police state laws and tactics exacerbate existing, or in Kuwait's case, latent sectarian tensions and conflicts. Kuwait's Sunnis have supported the Al-Qaeda-affiliate, al Nusra, fighting Assad in Syria, while Shia have supported Hezbollah, fighting for Assad with Iran's support. As a result, Kuwaiti's governing elite are fearful of being trapped in proxy wars in the Gulf, Syria and elsewhere. A suicide attack by an ISIS sympathizer that killed 26 Shiite worshippers in the Grand Mosque in Kuwait City led to a Kuwait crackdown and then discovery of an ISIS "network" unconnected to the terrorist act. The government declared itself at war with ISIS.

In Iraq, the benefit of the surge has not been "victory." Paradoxically, the surge has taught the US the limits of power in Middle East interventions. Hence, and for other domestic political reasons, the reluctance of the Obama administration to put boots on the ground in Syria, once again in Iraq, or elsewhere in the Middle East. As Gen. Odierno said recently, "There is no such thing as winning in Iraq, Syria, and other failed or failing states." It's a matter of what he called "sustainable outcomes" after US troops leave.

Understandably, when discussing how they would deal with ISIS and conflicts in the Middle East, in one way or another candidates in the presidential debates of 2015-16 say that they will make the US stronger or more feared. This would require some combination of military force and diplomacy or diplomacy and military force, which presidential candidates and their advisors have yet to define as a general policy or country by country in the Middle East.

Using lessons that have been learned the hard, bloody, and expensive way in Iraq, the next US and Coalition moves in Iraq or Syria are not a matter of exercising more military power but a military-civilian consensus on the right strategy and avoiding incomprehensible bureaucratic mistakes like the State Department's decision on "debaathification" in Iraq. In Saddam Hussein's Iraq, membership in the Baath party was the requirement for state employment. After the fall of the Iraqi regime in 2003, the US-led Coalition Provisional Authority (CPA) introduced a sweeping, indiscriminate debaathification process intended to get rid of the Baath party's influence. This process led to wholesale dismissals of thousands of individuals based on their rank within the Baath party hierarchy, badly undermining Iraq's government and military, and causing widespread social and political conflict.

The challenge for Iraq, and the US pre-, during and post-surge, has been formation of a more inclusive government that has the trust of Shia, Sunni Arabs and Kurds, and that competently addresses real and perceived grievances of all three of these major groups in a transparent manner. In addition, like it or not America, somewhere in this complex process, within clearly defined limits, will have to be the future presence and influence of Iran in Baghdad. Within those limits, however, Iran cannot be permitted to train, arm, fund, and equip Shia militia extremists or have its Quds force operating in Iraq or elsewhere.

Debate about the future of Iraq has focused on both the collapse of its ISF and the possible collapse of Iraq itself. One of the reasons that it's so hard to know and forecast the fate of Iraq and the ISF is that senior US intelligence officials may have doctored or politicized intelligence analysis on the Islamic State to make ISIS look weaker than it actually is and also to make it appear that the US has been winning the battle against ISIS. The *Daily Beast* recently reported that more than 50 intelligence professionals have formally complained that their analysis of both ISIS and Syria's Al-Qaeda branch, al Nusra, were altered by leadership in US Central Command in order to make the US military campaign to defeat those groups look more successful than it actually was. Politicizing intelligence reports in Washington or at CENTCOM, the US military's command for the Middle East and Central Asia, is outrageous and implies corruption of military leadership.

All the more reason that the analysis of intelligence should be a bottomup decision-making process handled by frontline advisors whose lives are at stake, since the effectiveness of counterinsurgency totally relies on objective and accurate intelligence. We're reminded of Congress voting in 2002 for the Authorization for Use of Military Force Against Iraq bill based on faulty intelligence about Saddam Hussein's stockpile of armed nuclear weapons and close ties to Al-Qaeda. Although those claims were wrong, there's no evidence that the information was deliberately falsified, but in fact was skewed in response to political pressure. "The resulting classified National Intelligence Estimate, prepared in just three weeks time, was a rushed and sloppy product forwarded to members of Congress mere days before votes would be taken to authorize the use of military force against Iraq," states a 2004 Senate Intelligence Committee report. "As the Committee's report highlights, the October 2002 Estimate was hastily cobbled together using stale, fragmentary, and speculative intelligence reports and was replete with factual errors and unsupported judgments."

The Islamic State's target currently is Iraq. The collapse of Iraq and its inclusion in the caliphate is the goal of ISIS. The most support in Iraq for that goal has come from Sunnis who are vehemently opposed to ISIS. Sunnis are well aware of the fact that ISIS is a terrorist organization. For Sunnis, however, the Iraqi government, pro-government militias and the ISF are an even worse threat than ISIS. Starting in 2006, government forces engaged in ethnic cleansing of Sunnis. For both Sunnis and Kurds, there is little or no loyalty to Iraq as a country and certainly not the Iraqi government. Iran has exacerbated the sectarian divide in Iraq and also wants to see Iraq collapse. Arab states that are more anti-Shiite than they are anti-ISIS also have no use for the Iraqi government.

The US has to face the fact that Baghdad no long rules northern and western Iraq and most Iraqis do not respect or trust their central government and are alienated from it.

Iraq's major parties have created power and security vacuums that ISIS, Shiite Islamist militants, and criminal groups have been filling. Almost ten years ago, seeing the proverbial handwriting on the wall of history, then Sen. Biden and Leslie Gelb of the Council on Foreign Relations proposed division of Iraq into three autonomous regions, based on sect, as a way to keep Iraq from falling into unrelenting sectarian warfare. Calls for the partitioning of Iraq do not have much support in Iraq. There is no way to implement partitioning schemes in Iraq without violent upheavals as millions of non-Sunnis and Sunnis would be forced to leave their home territories. Any attempts to divide Iraq's vast oil and gas resources, already a source of controversy between Kurds in Kirkuk, Shiites in Basra, and the Baghdad government, would create even more conflict and violence.

Sayyid Ammar al-Hakim, the head of the Shiite Islamic Supreme Council of Iraq, opposes division of the country and advocates a "federal Iraq" going forward. "In order to decrease the pressures on the central government we prefer federalism," he said. "It is the only way we can live in peace, and that is why we believe that strengthening the regions and the central government at the same time would benefit us all," he added. Hakim's statement followed comments by Kurdistan Region President Masoud Barzani in Washington where he said that Kurdish independence is delayed by the war with ISIS but not derailed.

Federalism in Iraq is a long-shot. Decentralization of most of the powers and responsibilities in Baghdad to provinces and regions of Iraq might work. The central government would have to retain management of infrastructure, power, water, transportation, and the like, and control over distributing oil and gas revenue. Production and export of oil and gas could be decentralized. Provinces and regions would be responsible for housing, education, labor and other policies, and also security. Lessons learned in Anbar could be extremely helpful when it comes to planning the decentralization of security.

For decentralization to take place, constitutional changes will be required. Countless laws will have to be rewritten. Powers, roles and responsibilities at national, provincial and regional levels will have to be redefined. The Kurds, however, already have an independent nation, Kurdistan, and their own military force, the Peshmerga. Fitting Kurdistan into a federal Iraqi regime will require a great deal of work but it's possible. The result would be more of a federation than federalism. The most difficult part of negotiating such an agreement probably would be the Kurd's right to independently market oil that it produces, and a formula for Erbil and Baghdad to share oil revenues.

No one, not even a Solomon, has any strategic solution for dividing up Iraq that doesn't include countless problems that can be expected and even more unexpected ones. But Iraq does have one extraordinary example of sectarian conflict resolution that, with countless creative adaptations, just might work in Iraq's 18 provinces, without dismantling the entire nation and forcing tens of millions of Iraqis to relocate. The conflict resolution model is the Great Awakening which could have the significant additional benefit of containing the expansion of ISIS.

CHAPTER 11

Lessons Learned in Iraq

A recurring issue in the 2016 presidential election campaign is decisions that were made, and not made, in current and previous administrations in connection with wars in Iraq and their consequences for the spread of ISIS, other terrorism and chaos spreading in the Middle East. In the course of raising these issues, history tends to be either ignored or rewritten hyperbolically and responsibilities assigned or reassigned without reference to actual events and decisions. Invaluable lessons learned in US warfare in Iraq, Afghanistan and elsewhere tend to be lost.

None of that is really new in presidential election years. It happens every four years in presidential campaigns. In the 2016 election, however, Iraq wars and their aftermath revisited and debated along with containment of Iran's nuclear program and its proxies, Assad's dictatorship and the involvement of Iran and Russia, ISIS and Islamic extremism in Syria and other Middle East countries, and the rising tides of refugees, asylum-seekers and displaced persons should contribute to one of the most important and controversial presidential foreign policy debates in modern history.

Hopefully debates among presidential candidates and their policy papers will shed meaningful light for frustrated and bewildered American voters on the limits of American military power and even constraints on US international leadership. For presidential candidates the most contentious issue will be future commitments of American combat forces, boots-on-the-ground, that they would make as the president elected in 2016 and, of course, the US military price tag necessary to support these military interventions.

Effective campaign speeches have to be restrained as to how much history, complexity and substance they deliver in the attempt to address complex questions like how to effectively fight ISIS in Syria or Iraq or what to do about the Assad regime and its support from Iran and Russia. The essence of what the best scholar-military minds like John Nagl, David Kilcullen, Peter Schoomaker and David Petraeus have learned over the last half century about the potential value of next-generation counterinsurgency can contribute a great deal of substance and veracity to statements made by presidential candidates intended to capture voter and media attention.

One of these apostles of COIN, John Nagl, a really smart guy, arrived in Iraq in September 2003, as informed about insurgencies as anyone on the planet, ready to take on Sunni insurgents, but he soon learned how little he actually knew. He also soon learned that the American occupation force at all levels knew next to nothing about the local culture or language. Not so, fortunately, Major General Petraeus who was in charge of Mosul and doing a remarkably good job of "nation-building," even after the unexpected disaster of Proconsul Bremer's debaathification. Everyone from the field to Washington knew by then that the war in Iraq was going very badly, but it took until almost mid-2004 for the White House and the Pentagon to acknowledge that they were fighting an "insurgency" in Iraq. And even then, and this is important to understand, the word "counterinsurgency" could not be used inside the Bush Administration.

Understandably lessons learned in the bloody war in Iraq and its aftermath are not something that most American voters are likely think much about during a presidential campaign except when candidates are blaming each other for the mistakes or misdeeds of their party's current or previous leaders. The ways that the Iraq war story unfolds in our imperfect human memories are: it was a horrific, and sometimes heroic, tale of unintended consequences; decisions were made that unintentionally handed power over to Iraqi politicians mainly serving only their own interests and subverting the goal of creating a "democracy" in Iraq; a new Iraqi leader was chosen, Nuri al-Maliki, on the completely mistaken assumption that he would build a new, inclusive, democratic Iraq; and the Iraqi Security Forces (ISF) that the US and its coalition partners invested so much money, time and effort into training and equipping were used by Iraq's leadership, until the ISF was dissolved, to prevent the creation of democratic Iraqi governance.

In 1988 Saddam had used chemical weapons against the Kurds and left at least 180,000 missing or presumed dead. After invading Kuwait, in August, 1990, the Gulf War began in January 1991 and ended a month later without coalition forces attacking Baghdad. The US (President Bush) encouraged revolts by the Kurds and Shiites, which Saddam brutally suppressed, without US intervention. In March 2003, Saddam was given an ultimatum to leave Iraq. He refused but then fled Baghdad on April 9 as US forces entered Iraq's capitol. Petraeus arrived in Iraq knowing that there was no plan for "post-conflict stability operations." Washington (Bush, Cheney, and Rumsfeld) expected the war to be over in 2003 but it took 8 more years. Turkey unexpectedly refused to allow the invasion of Iraq from its territory. As a result, after a sudden change of orders, Petraeus had to redeploy his 4th Infantry Division from Baghdad to Mosul. In Mosul, it was Petraeus who audaciously, without permission or instructions from Washington, announced and pursued the goal of "nation-building."

Unfortunately, the new American proconsul in Iraq, Paul Bremer, heading up the Coalition Provisional Authority (CPA), without consultation (apparently even with Washington), and without any understanding of the consequences, issued two infamous directives (CPA Orders #1 and #2) that wrecked Petraeus's nation-building plan by banning members of Saddam's Baath Party from holding any government jobs and that resulted in disbanding of the Iraqi army. Bremer's disastrous "debaathification" orders threw more than 50,000 Iraqi civil servants and hundreds of thousands of Iraqi soldiers with weapons or access to them out of jobs.

Bremer thereby single-handedly accelerated Iraq's insurgency which flamed up soon thereafter, just as (December 2003-April 2004) all US armed forces departed from Iraq in the largest troop rotation in history. Replacement troops, with no training or preparation for their mission, and only about half the number of troops they replaced, arrived without any post-troop rotation/ stabilization plan for Iraq. In addition, none of the troops' leaders had any clue about the principles and tactics of counterinsurgency.

Consequently, looking back more than 10 years to 2004, the US occupation in Iraq had a major responsibility for fostering a violent insurgency. Both senior US civilian and military leaders had launched the Iraq war without a post-war stabilization plan or a viable counterinsurgency strategy.

By the end of 2006, Iraq was on the edge of civil war. Baghdad was an armed camp. Backed by Iran and other neighboring countries, including Syria, armed sectarian enclaves, insurgent groups, criminal gangs, and militias ruled, using violence to achieve their objectives. In the United States, public support for the war and the patience to transfer responsibility for security to the Iraqi security forces (ISF) were waning. President Bush, US Senator John McCain, and others believed, however, that a troop surge was necessary, as President Bush said in a televised address in January 2007, "to help Iraqis carry out their campaign to put down sectarian violence."

General Petraeus -- who became commanding general of the Multi-National Force-Iraq in January 2007 -- and Gen. Odierno, who was his second-in-command, shared responsibility for developing the new surge strategy. It's fair to say that no US or other military officers at the time were better qualified from experience in Iraq to develop the US surge - counterinsurgency strategy. Most important, they knew that US troops needed to protect civilians in Iraqi population centers and that their strategy for Iraq as a whole needed to deal effectively with the struggle between Shiites and Sunnis for local and national power and resources.

As part of this strategy, US forces were sent to the Sunni-dominated Anbar region, an Al-Qaeda stronghold, to win over tribal and other leaders. The strategy sent a critical message to the Iraqi public that US forces would try to protect them, that they should not provide sanctuary to armed insurgent groups, and they should provide intelligence to US forces.

Critical to understanding the US surge-counterinsurgency strategy is the all important, and unique at the time, political-cultural factors that led to what came to be called the "Sunni Awakening": Sunni insurgents and Al-Qaeda increasingly were competing for local and national dominance; Shiite militias supported by Iran had become a serious inter-sectarian threat; Sunni tribes were determined to protect and revenge their members killed by their Shiite enemies; and puritanical Islamic laws propagated by Al-Qaeda were not welcome in Anbar Province.

Sunnis battling Al-Qaeda also benefitted Shiites who were trying to deal with their own intra-Shiite violence. Unexpectedly, in March 2008, the US supported Iraqi Prime Minister Nouri al-Maliki's attack on Shiite militias in Basra and Baghdad that, in short, changed Iraq's political environment, brought the civil war to an end and validated a future peaceful political process. However, although it may have seemed that the surge had "won the Iraq war," there was no happy ever-after. A sustainable national reconciliation between Sunnis and Shiites would have required an Iraqi government that gained legitimacy, which it didn't, and the capacity to deliver on promised services, which it did not do.

To speed up the pace of national reconciliation, Odierno attempted to integrate Sunnis and Shiites in the Iraqi Security Forces (ISF) which until that time had been predominately Shiite. The Sunni Awakening had made Maliki and his advisors fearful that the United States was creating a Sunni army that would overthrow the country's Shiite leadership. All of the US efforts to improve ISF's sectarian balance did not allay these fears. But none of that mattered when the United Nations Security Council passed a resolution authorizing the presence of US forces in Iraq only until December 2008. In response, US and Iraqi governments negotiated a US-Iraq Status of Forces Agreement (SOFA) which would define and extend the future of US engagement in the country.

By September 2008, when General Raymond Odierno replaced General David Petraeus as the top commander of the Multi-National Force-Iraq, there was a prevalent sense among Americans that the surge of additional US forces into Iraq in 2007 had succeeded beyond expectations. With violence greatly reduced, the Iraq war seemed to be over. In July 2008, US President George W. Bush announced that violence in Iraq had decreased "to its lowest level since the spring of 2004" and that a significant reason for this sustained progress was "the success of the surge."

Basically in agreement with Odierno, Obama ordered the end of combat operations and the reduction of US troops to 50,000 by August 2010. Most important at the time, and historically, Odierno shifted the mission of the remaining US forces from counterinsurgency to stability operations and reconciliation, which focused on bolstering the ISF's capacity to protect the Iraqi people and prevent conflict between Arabs and Kurds, Shiites and Sunnis, and local provinces and the national government.

US troops were going to depart from Iraq by December 2011. The Iraqis held national elections in March 2010 and formed a government in December 2010. Shiites and Sunnis were still warring with each other. The root causes of conflict in Iraq were still very much alive. US military leadership knew all about it. At the time, US troop disengagement, not democratic institution building, was the Obama administration's priority.

In the aftermath of the surge, Iraq still qualified as a failed state. Security in Iraq had improved, but Odierno was convinced that the overriding focus of his mission should be helping the Iraqis develop a properly functioning government. To his credit, he organized his military forces to accomplish this goal and worked tirelessly with US State Department-led transition teams to improve the administrative capacity of provincial and local governments throughout Iraq. In other words, no one in retrospect could accuse Odierno of overlooking the strategic importance of post-surge nation-building, with the US functioning as a partner with the Iraqi government.

Additionally to his credit, Odierno's commitment to sectarian reconciliation and nation-building in post-surge Iraq was not just on paper and in powerpoints. He traveled to every part of Iraq to monitor progress, including training of the ISF and improving their ability to work with locals, to make sure that his commanders had an in-depth understanding of the root causes of conflict and instability in their areas, and to assess the support and assistance that each of them would need to accomplish their missions. In addition to working with Arabs, Kurds, Shiites and Sunnis to resolve communal conflicts, leaders of US forces in each area of Iraq had to work with State Department staff day-to-day to mediate and negotiate power-sharing arrangements. In northern Iraq, for example, conflicts and tensions between Arabs, Kurds, the Kurdish Peshmerga, various religious minorities, and Al-Qaeda constantly threatened stability.

All in all, it was quite amazing how Odierno and the US military command in Iraq retrained and reeducated its soldiers to transition from counterinsurgency to stability operations aimed at strengthening governance in Iraq. This included provincial elections in 2009 that brought Sunnis into local government but, clearly in 2010 and afterwards, conflict and mistrust of ruling powers still prevailed.

Five years ago, Iraq had a long way to go before it became a stable, sovereign, and self-reliant country. That is still true today. For the US, especially in a presidential election year, rather than rehashing and rewriting the past, the focus should be on what the United States can do to help bring Iraq closer to national reconciliation, build a professional civil service and nonsectarian institutions, bolster civilian control over its security forces, and prevent its government from becoming increasingly sectarian and authoritarian rather than democratic.

The political and stability challenges facing Iraq were highlighted in mid-2015 by two almost simultaneous events that presented totally contrasting views of the possible future of Iraq: remarks at his retirement by General Odierno, the former US top commander in Iraq from 2008 to 2010 and commander of the United States Joint Forces Command from October 2010 until its disestablishment in August 2011; and the plan announced by Iraqi Prime Minister Haider al-Abadi to overhaul the country's government.

On the eve of his retirement from the Army, in mid-August 2015, Odierno surprised, indeed probably stunned, many of his fellow officers and others in Washington by saying, and no one should know better, that reconciliation between Shiites and Sunnis in Iraq is becoming harder and that partitioning the country "might be the only solution." Furthermore he said that the US focus for now should be on defeating the Islamic State that had seized large portions of the country.

Why is this pessimistic view about the underlying conflict between Shiites and Sunnis especially important in the midst of the presidential campaign of 2016? Because Odierno injected informed, non-partisan reality into the debate from a US military leader who began his mission in 2006 with Iraq on the brink of civil war. ISIS at the time was not a factor. Even though he had seen Iraq struggling with Sunni-Shiite sectarian chaos for years, and dedicated his mission to reconciliation of the two communities, at his retirement he envisioned possibly even worse outcomes in Iraq's future than civil war. The shock for the political and military community was his drastic suggestion that "partition" might be the only solution.

With astonishingly widespread support, including unanimous Parliament approval, Iraqi Prime Minister Haider al-Abadi introduced an unprecedented plan in early August 2015 to overhaul the country's entire government, which also had the all-important support of Iraq's supreme Shiite religious leader,

Grand Ayatollah Ali al-Sistani. Abadi's plan would: slash layers of the bloated central government and its patronage system; eliminate high level government positions that have historically been assigned by quota to Shiites, Sunnis and Kurds; and cut spending, curb corruption and invest in crumbling infrastructure. One of the Iraqis who stand to lose their post under Abadi's plan was former Prime Minister Nuri Kamal al-Maliki, who became a vice president when he was forced to cede power to Abadi in 2014. The fact that large parts of Iraq, including Mosul, Iraq's second largest city, and Anbar are under the control of the Islamic State no doubt were important motivations for Abadi's plan.

Of course there is no way of knowing whether Abadi's plan can succeed but, in contrast to Odierno's speculation about the possible necessity of partitioning Iraq, Abadi's plan aims to strengthen national unity and reduce disenfranchisement of the Sunni minority. Both Odierno and Abadi fully understand the critical importance of reaching out to Sunni leaders in violence-plagued provinces west and north of the capital and addressing the many grievances of Sunnis.

President Obama had campaigned with the noble goal of ending the war in Iraq. The 'peace president," who was awarded the Nobel Peace Prize, was – and still is – determined to remove American boots from bloody battlegrounds and extract America from unwanted foreign entanglements. Not only is the US back at war in the Middle East but, once again, without an exit strategy, any idea of how it will end, or worse, how to engage in different kinds of insurgencies in Iraq, Syria, Yemen, Libya, and elsewhere in Africa, many of which involve Iranian proxy wars and will be impacted by a possible Iranian nuclear deal and the lifting of sanctions.

The Obama Administration, and every other informed observer of the Middle East, is well aware of the fact that deep political, social, sectarian, and economic problems afflicting the Arab world for centuries are feeding religious and ideological extremism in every Middle East country, especially among younger age groups. "Righteous responses" to pervasive injustice and grievances fuel every insurgency and decision by regional actors in the Middle East and Africa to strike out against or protect themselves from extremism.

ISIS (or Da'ash) and its caliphate feeds on all of this discontent and provides a vision of both an idealized past and future. Although American political rhetoric often alludes to the need to deal with the root causes of extremism, the scope, depth and historic dimensions of these root political, economic and social problems renders such political polemic meaningless. A strategy for dealing with ISIS needs to pragmatically address the conditions that gave rise to it that, at some time in the future, may give rise to new versions of ISIS that are even more dangerous than Da'ash because they have learned from the imperfections or failures of the ISIS model of conquest.

CHAPTER 12

Lessons Learned in the Anbar Awakening

Between 2005 and 2007, with sectarian violence in Iraq rising, local Sunni tribes joined Coalition forces to fight Al-Qaeda in Iraq (AQI) which dominated Anbar Province and Ramadi. This phenomenon became known as the Anbar Awakening ("Sahawa" – Arabic for "Awakening") which has been studied and written about endlessly by military and intelligence personnel, academics, think-tankers, and others. The Awakening offers many lessons to be learned for the next generation of COIN and creating a path to regional, provincial and sectarian conflict resolution. Another important lesson offered by the Awakening might be the key role played by inadvertency in military interventions like the surge.

In many respects, the story of the Awakening tells us a great deal about the failings, and strengths, of American military planning and leadership in Iraq. Often referred to as the model for counterinsurgency against Al-Qaeda, the Awakening was an accident of warfare against Al-Qaeda in Ramadi for which much of the credit goes to Col. Sean MacFarland, his staff and the men in his brigade. In the fall of 2006, more than a year before the announcement of the surge, Col. MacFarland, Brigade commander with the 1st Armored Division, and his men were shifted from Tal (or Tall) Afar to Ramadi, the capital of Anbar Province, 77 miles west of Baghdad. Tal Afar, in northwestern

Iraq's Nineveh Province, is located approximately 39 miles west of Mosul.

Anbar province is a vast tract of desert dotted with cities and villages, stretching from outside Baghdad to the Syrian border. Well-armed Al-Qaeda in Ramadi were in control -- and out of control. By virtue of his experiences enforcing a peace accord in Bosnia and also as commander in Iraq's Tal Afar, where he replaced his mentor, Colonel H.R. MacMaster, Col. MacFarland had learned how to use his ingenuity to reach out to tribal leaders, identify the real leaders of local factions, and negotiate power-sharing deals that, in Ramadi, had to be backed by US cash to pay insurgent supporters. MacFarland, without ever mentioning it, also was a devoted student of COIN history and strategy written and preached by John Nagl, David Petraeus and others. In Anbar, MacFarland added some of his own COIN chapters to those of his mentors.

As MacFarland tells the story, off-handedly, with amazing recall and without any bravado, the brigade's move from Tal Afar to Ramadi would have been comedic if it didn't highlight prevalent confusion and disarray in the US chain of command that fortunately didn't cost the lives of his men while in transit. Not only was the move to Ramadi a logistical nightmare, but MacFarland, not complaining, had no idea what he was going to do when he and his brigade arrived in Ramadi. The sum of his commander's intent was: "Fix Ramadi but don't do a Fallujah!"

MacFarland didn't have the combat power to do a Fallujah so the advice was unnecessary. In fact, the move of MacFarland's brigade was not just to the city of Ramadi but to Anbar Province, an area the size of New Hampshire, in which about 600,000 people lived, with about 450,000 in Ramadi. In contrast to the much smaller Tal Afar, when he arrived MacFarland learned that Ramadi had no mayor, no city council, no telephone system, no services, and roughly about 5000 Al-Qaeda controlled the city's center and had freedom of movement throughout the rest of city.

In other words, MacFarland had not been supplied with any basic intel for the move to Ramadi. Nevertheless, with a superb combination of COIN and military strategy, smart and fast tactics, UAV imagery and human intelligence, placement of outposts inside the city and in tribal areas outside of Ramadi, in former Al-Qaeda safe havens, MacFarland's troops soon killed or captured most of, as he put it, the "bad guys." With only about 5500 soldiers and Marines, MacFarland's attack strategy had included:

- isolate and control access to the city so that "bad guys" and their weapons could not get in or out;
- use "clear-hold-build" neighborhood by neighborhood in Ramadi and, when the enemy was beaten down, turn them over to Iraqi Security Forces (ISF);
- establish a strategically-placed web of combat outposts, setup overnight in the city and, as quickly as possible, in tribal areas around Ramadi, to deny Al-Qaeda its safe havens, in other words, conduct a swift, simultaneous urban and rural campaign;
- take over key facilities and locations in Ramadi to seriously disrupt Al-Qaeda operations;
- since most ISF were Shia, focus on recruiting local Iraqi Police (Sunnis) from tribal areas;
- US troops and ISF jointly conduct nightly house-to-house "census patrols" to find out everything possible about everybody in the city.

A key factor in MacFarland's success persuading local sheiks to support Coalition forces was a fundamental change in the Coalition's message: Coalition forces had been saying "Don't worry, we'll be gone soon." Al-Qaeda was saying: "We plan to stay forever and Ramadi will be the capital of our new caliphate." No tribal leader or member would join Coalition forces only promising that it would be gone soon, and thereby risk beheading or other form of death not only for themselves but for their families as well. So what became pivotal for the success of tribal recruitment and the Awakening itself was a fundamental change that MacFarland made in the Coalition's strategic message to people living in Anbar Province: "Don't worry, we're not leaving until Al-Qaeda is defeated. Come join the Iraqi Police Force and we'll stand side by side with you until Al-Qaeda is gone and afterwards."

MacFarland's brigade also brought with them valuable experience in training Iraqi Army soldiers that included "partnering" with them to train Iraqi police recruits and, in the process, building an ISF/ police – Shia-Sunni -- partnership. MacFarland had found only a few Iraqi police, not more than 100, hunkering down in a couple of little police stations, in a city of a half million. So MacFarland definitely needed more police recruits. MacFarland listened closely to what local sheiks said about the biggest impediment to police recruitment: tribal members feared for the safety of their families if they had to leave them at home in order to join the police. One of MacFarland's staff had the bright idea of putting police stations next to key tribal areas. The rest is history in the Great Awakening.

MacFarland was stunned and thrilled to learn that tribal sheiks were prepared to provide as many as 3000 of the members of their tribes as recruits for police forces. The recruits were illiterate, probably couldn't pass any physical tests and, in many instances, were underage but, most important, they were prepared to join what MacFarland named Emergency Response Units or Provincial Auxiliaries. The recruits were screened with biometrics, received uniforms, weapons, satellite phones, a one -week training course, using SEALs, and then they were paid on a monthly basis. Tribes formed their own neighborhood watches. Amazingly, it all more or less worked. There was no prior plan. Tribes simply "flipped" all around Ramadi, as MacFarland describes it.

Al-Qaeda attacked MacFarland's outposts in tribal areas on the outskirts of Ramadi, assassinated a respected sheik, destroyed homes and, worst of all, hid the sheik's body for days, a desecration of his remains. It so happened that the sheik was from the tribe that had provided most of the early recruits for MacFarland's brigade. After that, the burning of a police station and a chain of other circumstances led to a gathering of about a dozen sheiks that met with MacFarland and handed him a platform containing their commitment to form the Awakening. Members of these tribes had to overcome the recollection that, in late 2005 and early 2006, Iraqi Sunni insurgents had attempted to rise up against Al-Qaeda and were badly beaten. Sheiks had lost family members.

Intimidated tribal members were sitting on the sidelines until the Awakening happened.

In an interview with Steven Clay, published in 2013, Clay asked MacFarland: "If you had to pick one thing, what do you think is the key lesson learned about your experience in Ramadi?" MacFarland explained, "… indigenous forces are the key to winning a counterinsurgency fight and you have to accept them for what they are and not be put off by the fact that they are not like us and don't operate just like us … You know, we always ask ourselves, 'Well, are they worthy allies?' Well, you know, we need to ask ourselves that same question and I would argue that we had not been worthy allies up until that point and, certainly, our history requires a bit of a leap of faith for anybody who wants to align with the United States. Anybody who watched our experience in Vietnam kind of has to really swallow hard when we say, 'Don't worry. We are not going to leave you behind."

Another key activity that MacFarland and his civil affairs team initiated was collaborative reconstruction planning with local sheiks. Sheiks were asked for their priorities. As plans were developed for projects with a tribal council of sheiks, sheiks were told that they would decide what was to be done and by which local contractors. They also would decide on people to bring in from the outside to do work. In a move that was unprecedented for US forces, the Awakening included local control over all of the decisions for Anbar and Ramadi reconstruction planning, projects and budgets for them. Anbar and the Awakening confirmed the COIN strategy of negotiating local power-sharing and governance arrangements that brought Ramadi under control in 2006 and 2007.

Al-Qaeda's presence diminished as Iraqis reclaimed their neighborhoods. MacFarland was making it up as he went along, capitalizing on fortuitously unexpected events and shifts in local dynamics, just like Petraeus had done in Mosul and Colonel MacMaster in Tal Afar. MacFarland had looked back at his experience in Tal Afar for examples of what reconstruction and rejuvenation in Ramadi should look like. He viewed Tal Afar as a warm up and rehearsal for Ramadi. Intel fusion systems just needed to be kicked into high gear. Nobody planned it that way.

Even before General Odierno's arrival in Iraq at the end of 2006, the Awakening had become the new model of what COIN could accomplish in Iraq and elsewhere. Full development and applications of the new COIN model would require a new generation of military officers, comfortable with improvisation and interaction with unsavory, ruthless local insurgents who yesterday might have been classified as "the enemy." US forces in Anbar had learned that they had to be willing to try anything and, unlike Fallujah, don't destroy the place to save it.

MacFarland was given free rein, and that fact is not to be underestimated. Although the military chain of command periodically expressed concern and skepticism, they didn't interfere with him. Who in the US military hierarchy knew what actually would work in a region full of religious Sunnis governed largely by sheiks, imams and tribal law whose main concern was protecting their own tribes and families from sectarian violence? With 20-20 hindsight it might seem obvious to recruit tribal leaders and their members to form a police force to protect their own tribes and families from Al-Qaeda in their own neighborhoods. That's what MacFarland did in 2006-07. Iraqi security forces had more than 3,000 new recruits by the time MacFarland's brigade left Anbar in February 2007. Praised for his ingenuity, MacFarland's response was "it was just a matter of necessity, like a drowning man."

The debate about and analysis of the surge continues roughly 10 years later because one of the key foreign policy issues facing presidential candidates in 2015-16, although not phrased this way, is what lessons have we learned from wars and counterinsurgency in Iraq that will enable successful future US military and political interventions in Iraq and various other countries in the Middle East, but with only a minimum of boots-on-the-ground and bloodshed, and the maximum of beneficial outcomes? The other related question for 2016 presidential debates is what is the relevance of lessons learned in Iraq and counterinsurgencies elsewhere to containing and defeating ISIS?

Given what actually has transpired in Iraq since the surge in places like Tal Afar and Ramadi, those goals sounds like wishful political thinking. For example, tragically, in May 2015, ISIS executed 600-700 Yazidi prisoners in Tal Afar which they had seized about a year earlier along with Mosul and Tikrit. The US response was that it might use drones in retaliation, but no boots on the ground. Today the Kurd's Peshmerga is the only military bulwark against ISIS in Tal Afar and a surrounding area of approximately 150 square kilometers (58 square miles) that includes 13 villages. ISIS attacked the Kurds in the Tal Afar area in August 2014, igniting a war in which more than 1,200 Peshmerga have been killed. US-led coalition airstrikes have been working with the Peshmerga to combat ISIS in Tal Afar.

Among other things the Anbar Awakening proved that, no matter how informed and brilliant the expert advice provided to military and diplomatic leadership, there is no substitute of any kind for first-hand observation of and intimate, granular familiarity with local conditions, culture, leadership, people, and so forth. There was no intelligence source in the US or in Iraq that could convey to military and civilian personnel on the frontline, the intimate realties of Mosul, Til Afar, Anbar and Ramadi, and Baghdad that could provide the critical determinants of counterinsurgency planning. Traditional intelligence sources simply could not possibly have possessed the kind of real-time intelligence and insights that MacFarland's brigade systematically searched out and discovered through countless 7x24 local face-to-face interactions. Critical intelligence was gathered on the fly, day and night, by Petraeus, Odierno, MacFarland and their colleagues as they drew up, revised, modified, carried out and reviewed the outcomes of their counterinsurgency plans.

The Awaking was not just US and Iraqi military campaigns and Iraqi Police actions conducted against AQI. The Awakening included agriculture, infrastructure, beautification, education, and other kinds of projects planned and carried out collaboratively with locals plus hundreds of millions spent to pay Iraqi troops and workers. Military and civil project costs in Iraq were over $2 billion in fiscal years 2005-2007. The governing strategy, and measures of successful outcomes, driving all of these US military and civil expenditures, can be summed up as "local empowerment."

As for the COIN goal of building effective national governance and legitimacy, the Awakening proved the overriding importance of local control, local empowerment and local security. Another key lesson learned from the Awakening was that, no matter how difficult, tricky and frustrating the military, political and civil negotiations involved, the ephemeral goal of "nation-building" has to be balanced with, and in all likelihood, subordinated to, developing local empowerment and control.

* * * *

Let's briefly revisit the Iraq story leading up to the Anbar Awakening and the surge. It's June 2003. Saddam Hussein, tyrant-dictator-monster, looking remarkably benign and almost business-like, was on trial for committing heinous crimes. Security in Iraq continued to deteriorate. Neither US nor Iraqi forces were able to do much about it. "Building democracy" in Iraq was still a fantasy. Rifts between Arabs and Kurds, Sunnis and Shia were widening. America was still suspect among Muslims because of the perceived gap between rhetoric and reality. Iraq's US "occupiers" were soon leaving. The Coalition Provisional Authority (CPA) also was leaving Iraq, but tens of thousands of Coalition forces would remain as violent insurgency escalated.

In 2005, in western Anbar, the US military and the Iraqi Department of Defense backed a tribal force that was rebelling against AQI and AQI-affiliated rival tribes. Likewise, in 2006, tribal forces already were fighting AQI in Ramadi. These anti-AQI tribal efforts were wracked by in-fighting. Insurgent factions had no history of collaborating or confederating. Formation of a lasting anti-AQI coalition was unlikely to succeed. Credit is due, however, to U.S military leaders like MacFarland who were able, with financial incentives to locals, to promote a workable level of cooperation and civility, and calm down sectarian conflict, all of which was no small achievement.

Of special importance, most of the leaders of the *Sahawa* were not hereditary leaders (many of whom had fled to greener pastures in Jordan) but rather nontraditional leaders who had earned their leadership positions through action. For US forces, the key to *Sahawa* success, and ultimately the surge, proved to be partnering with the right local leadership. The *Sahawa* was created without the support of the Anbar Provincial government or Maliki's Shia-led government in Baghdad, and it also deviated from the Iraqi constitution. Here again, it was amazing that Col. MacFarland could persuade his superiors that *Sahawa* was the right, and indeed only, way to go forward in spite of being extremely controversial and risky.

Three years later, violence in Iraq was spiraling out of control. Tens of thousands of Iraqis had been killed. Hundreds of thousands had fled their homes. Baghdad was a sectarian nightmare. Against recommendations made by the high-powered, bipartisan Iraq Study Group, President Bush decided to surge US forces in Iraq. In November 2006, Bush informed Iraq's Prime Minister and commander-in-chief, Nuri al-Maliki, who had been in power for only six months.

Maliki was convinced that the primary cause of violence in Iraq was the refusal of Saddam's Sunni Baathists to accept Shia authority. What Bush and the US military didn't know at the time was that Iraq's debaathification program, launched after the US's 2003 "invasion," actually had collapsed Iraq and propelled many Baathists, including many heavily armed former Iraqi army officers, possessing intelligence and counterintelligence skills, to join rapidly growing jihadist groups such as Abu Musab al-Zarqawi's Jamaat al-Tawhid wa'al-Jihad. The political process in Iraq following the 2003 invasion actually institutionalized divisive sectarianism. Losers, mainly Sunnis, turned against the US "occupiers."

Maliki reassured President Bush that the strength of Shia militias was being overstated. What Maliki didn't say much about was that a US troop surge would not go down well with Iraq's partner in Teheran. However, none of Maliki's opinions seem to matter much to US military leaders at the time except for his urging US support for building Iraqi security forces (ISF). After Iraq's 2005 election, ruled by a coalition of Shia Islamists and Kurds, insurgency became a civil war between Sunnis and Shia. Foreign jihadis poured into Iraq to fight the "infidel" U.S forces. In response, the Coalition rapidly recruited the ISF along with Shia militias. Poorly vetted and trained, the ISF became part of the sectarian conflict. The prevalent US military strategy was still "kill the enemy" rather than protect the population and suppress the violence.

On January 10, 2007, against the better judgment of most senior US military officers, Bush flew to Jordan to announce the surge -- sending an additional 20,000 US troops to Iraq. Gen. Odierno agreed with Bush's decision. This was to be an ISF-led operation. As MacFarland had learned in Ramadi and Tal Afar, however, as a fighting force the ISF was unreliable. The heart of the surge was the Baghdad Security Plan focused on protecting Baghdad from terrorism. "Terrorism" in Baghdad and elsewhere in Iraq, however, primarily was a civil war between Sunnis and Shia, with the corrupt Maliki government itself very much part of the problem.

The best that could be said for the surge was that its goal was to buy time. For what? A completely dysfunctional, Shia-dominated Iraqi government to somehow bring about national "reconciliation" with the assistance of US forces, focused initially on Baghdad and its environs? Important to point out here, Coalition forces were supposed to become partners and mentors of ISF, train them to plan and implement every aspect of local operations, and patrol neighborhoods together to communicate with locals and build trust with the population and its leaders. No matter what else happened in the surge, this collaborative, locally-focused model was supposed to become the driving strategy of the surge. That was basically MacFarland's COIN model perfected in the Anbar Awakening.

In January 2007, two months before Col. MacFarland was going home, Petraeus was named commander of US forces in Iraq. He joined Gen. Odierno to try to break the cycle of violence in Baghdad and elsewhere in Iraq. The strategy, shared by

Petraeus-Odierno, was pure COIN: protect the population, build trust, use that trust to gather intelligence on extremists, learn as much as possible about and reach out to potential insurgent allies, and do whatever is possible to bolster the legitimacy of the government. As part of MacFarland's brigade, two Marine battalions already were at work on this kind of COIN operation in Anbar Province and Ramadi.

In September 2007, when testifying before Congress, Petraeus sounded almost apologetic for the lack of progress in Iraq, emphasizing that the situation was "complex" and "sometimes downright frustrating." Perhaps it was asking too much of Congress to appreciate that former Sunni insurgents had joined the Coalition to fight Al-Qaeda. Shia militia, however, unwaveringly wanted the US to leave Iraq. Explaining "national reconciliation" in Iraq to members of Congress, and how the US aimed to achieve it, was difficult at best, especially because US military and State Department leadership themselves really did not know how it was to be achieved, including how to deal with Iran working relentlessly to undermine any progress. In spite of its skepticism, Petraeus was able to persuade Congress not to pull the plug on the surge.

A year later, testifying before the Senate Armed Services Committee, on April 8, 2008, Gen. Petraeus was able to report a dramatic reduction in violence levels and civilian deaths from fifteen months before when Iraq seemed on the brink of civil war. He made little reference to the Anbar Awakening, why and how local sheikhs, disillusioned with the insurgency that had ravaged Anbar Province during the past two-and-a-half years, offered their support to Coalition forces; and the fact that, without pre-planning and official authorization, MacFarland had provided military training and money for arms and equipment to men in Anbar Province who had been their enemies just a short time before.

The Awakening strategy as applied to Baghdad, however, was not classic COIN's "clear-hold-build" but instead a much more realistic version designed for chaotic insurgency conditions in

Baghdad: "clear-control-retain." The Joint Campaign Plan divided Baghdad into more than seventy-five clear-control-retain areas to create, what we'll call here, neighborhood safe havens, not unlike MacFarland's strategy in Ramadi. A network of Al-Qaeda supply routes into Baghdad also was targeted.

The Petraeus-Odierno team was ideal to lead this kind of surge operation: Odierno handled day-to-day military operations and Petraeus covered strategic and political matters and broadly communications and media. As the master of COIN, author of its field manual, architect of Bush's decision to launch a surge, Petraeus – and also Bush -- had a great deal riding on this longshot of an Iraqi turnaround. The third key member of this remarkable surge team was Ambassador Ryan Crocker. The Petraeus-Odierno-Crocker "dream team" assembled a who's who of military, foreign policy, and academic expertise and support staff.

They would need the best minds and expertise available because even the well-documented history and analyses of counterinsurgencies in the Middle East and other regions at other times in modern history that the Petraeus team all had systematically studied and assimilated provided very few reliable formulaic answers for how, and to what extent, an occupying military power can reach out to Sunni insurgents, in the midst of a sectarian civil war, turn them against jihadist extremists, and persuade them to accept an inevitably imperfect power-sharing deal. However, one of the few successful examples of co-opting really "bad guys" that worked turned out to be paying Sunni insurgents for military, policing and project work. Here again, the rationale seems obvious in hindsight but putting local "bad guys" on the payroll was not part of the original surge strategy.

We do know that at least a few foreign policy experts raised questions and concerns in the Oval Office with President Bush before the surge decision was made at the end of 2006. But even though there were no good answers and really not much of a basis for optimism, Bush overrode pessimism and naysayers and authorized a surge anyhow.

The White House's vision of the mission for the surge was not based on any understanding of what actually was happening in Anbar Province or insurgencies elsewhere in Iraq and what that would mean for dealing with Iraq's civil war and achieving the goal of "national reconciliation."

No one involved in the White decision-making process had any idea that Sunni insurgents in Anbar or elsewhere in Iraq would view "infidel US occupiers" as the lesser of evils compared to Al-Qaeda in Iraq's (AQI) brutality. Nor did the White house and Pentagon decision-makers realize that US military intervention would be viewed in Anbar Province as a source of protection against Iran-supported Shiite militia's murderous violence, and in Baghdad it would be viewed as the last hope for a mitigation of Shia-controlled corruption and refusal to share power.

In other words, the surge was not just counterinsurgency versus insurgency that would, even in a messy manner, follow the COIN manual and model. No one inside or outside of the White House and National Security Council (NSC) could have anticipated, first, the Awakening itself, and that, in 2007, it would migrate from its unexpected inception in Anbar to a bold, planned effort in Baghdad full of complex military, political and logistical challenges. Also not anticipated in Washington's launch of the surge was the paranoia of Iraq's Shia Prime Minister and his obsessively intransigent opposition to "reconciliation" and sharing power with Sunnis and Kurds. And of course no one foresaw the later emergence of ISIS.

All of these unforeseen factors together, and others, suggest that the mission and vision behind the surge were based on the right intention – increasing Iraq's capability to manage its own internal security – but was doomed to fail delivery on its goals. In hindsight, a moral of the surge story is that, without any support from the Iraqi government, the US tried to cure more or less incurable, deeply imbedded sectarian, ethnic and political rivalries. Even the most minimal localized process of sectarian "reconciliation" in Anbar was rescued from utter failure only by a series of completely unanticipated circumstances and events that became known as the Awakening. The moral of the story also includes the misconception that the surge could improve the legitimacy and capability of the Iraq government to perform competently.

Measuring success of the surge by growth of the Iraq government's respect for the US and its military presence also would fail the test of negotiations between Iraq and the US on the Status of Forces Agreement (SOFA) in 2008-09 which resulted in refusal by Iraq to sign such an agreement and its condemnation of the US in the media. For Maliki, U.S, forces represented nothing more than an unwanted limit on his power. Thanks to Maliki, SOFA called for the removal of all US forces from Iraq by the end of 2011.

As 2009 started, the American people were running out of patience with "Bush's war" in Iraq. After his inauguration, President-elect Obama ordered the end of the war in Iraq. However, he started his own surge in Afghanistan, sending another 35,000 troops there. Combat operations in Iraq would end in August 2010 and 50,000 US troops would remain in Iraq in advisory roles. US forces immediately started to move toward partnering with and advising ISF.

By mid-June 2009, ISF had assumed responsibility for security in cities. In a sense it was a landmark event, but lacked any contextual strategy for creating a better future for Iraq. In June 2014, ISF quickly disintegrated in Mosul against an outnumbered ISIS contingent that took possession of all US equipment supplied to that city during the surge. The only beneficiaries were the Kurds whose Peshmerga forces could take control of disputed territories nearby, in addition to controlling Kirkuk's oilfields. Nowhere in the surge's exit plan was the emergence of ISIS anticipated or the fact that the Kurdistan Regional Government would face and control a 600-mile border with ISIS.

Both the good and bad news about the Anbar Awakening and its aftermath is that it did provide an adaptable template for COIN strategies in Iraq, Syria and elsewhere, but with the critical caveat that the historical and cultural context and other very specific factors in Anbar that resulted in tribal forces engaging with

Coalition forces were not likely to be present elsewhere. COIN principles and the COIN model, with greater emphasis on local control get high marks, but the next generation of COIN will have to be augmented with advanced high-tech data-gathering and analytical tools to support decision-making by frontline advisors in concert with their insurgent partners.

Based on the invaluable lessons learned in the Anbar Awakening, effective implementation of COIN principles in the Middle East or elsewhere in the future will necessitate a high-tech, data-centric operational model designed to enable US Special Forces to learn as much as possible about, reach out to and engage potential insurgent allies, protect them and their families from ruthless Islamic extremist killers, build durable trust, use that trust to gather intelligence on extremists, and do whatever is possible to bolster the legitimacy of state, provincial and local governments. This will require knowing literally everything about what those governments at various levels are doing, the way they are doing it, and the outcomes – and all of it in real-time. In addition, these COIN tools have to enable the Coalition to mount a sustained media offensive to counter ISIS as it increasingly engages in a sophisticated multimedia Internet-based communication and propaganda war with the West and states in the Middle East.

We often hear the words "strategic vision" in reference to what one presidential administration or another lacks or a presidential candidate promises to bring to Washington for dealing effectively with the Middle East, China, or other regions of the world or turbulent countries, especially pertaining to national security and foreign policy issues. "Strategic vision" rarely has emanated from the White House under any presidency, especially when presidents are basically coping with foreign policy decisions made by previous presidents, such as Obama inheriting the surge and the aftermath of Iraq wars from Bush, Nixon inheriting Vietnam from Lyndon Johnson, Dwight Eisenhower inheriting Korea from Harry Truman and other such examples.

Rather than being on the lookout for a president's brilliant "strategic vision," voters should gravitate to a president who, with the right advisors and in-depth advice, aims at shaping and scaling US military-civil interventions, and how American power should be used, in ways that do the most good solving well-defined problems and leveraging opportunities, and also doing the least harm in the process, with an all-important eye always on the lookout for unexpected events, accidents, miscalculations, and human behaviors.

The Iraq war and various surges were based on a misdefinition of Iraq's interconnected political and sectarian problems which was not followed by leveraging lessons learned in the Awakening about a potential American soft power pathway to transforming sectarian conflict into collaboration. After U.S forces inadvertently created what came to be known as the Awakening, that did not change military-civil strategy in Iraq until it was too late. However, broadly changing US military strategy on the ground in Iraq would have necessitated a change of national Iraqi political leadership, which did not happen until 2014-15. Regime change was not part of the original US intervention strategy, even though Iraq's paranoid president Maliki was convinced that it was the U.S goal.

In this context, President Obama's conviction that the US should reduce its historically massive military and political investment in the Middle East has merit because it is not the size of the US footprint and investment in any region or country in the Middle East or elsewhere that ultimately is of consequence but rather knowing what the US is trying to accomplish militarily and diplomatically, and also having the right people in place to execute strategies and plans.

The strategy of requiring, not just urging, allies in the Middle East, including Iraq, that we'll call "an ally in transition," to take responsibility for their own security, with limited US assistance, as specifically requested, together with terms and conditions, is vital to the U.S not becoming overextended in multiple interventions in the region. The US appears to be applying that policy in Yemen and the Gulf region, which may account for the fact that Saudi and the Gulf states have committed their own boots on the ground to counter the Houthis' growing insurgency threat. In Syria, the situation is much more complicated and calls for strategic calibration of US military and diplomatic engagement.

In Iraq and Syria US strategies and policies for defeating ISIS have not been working and clearly are insufficient. Counterterrorism strategies that rely on surgical airstrikes cannot counter the spread and escalation of disorder and destabilization of these countries. A new counterinsurgency strategy is required that commits a highly specialized US ground force to control ground conditions and airstrikes, and prevents ISIS from taking over these countries. Declarations of war against ISIS in response to terrorist attacks in France and elsewhere reflect political conviction but offer no guidance on how to contain or destroy ISIS and America's strategy and leadership role.

* * * *

The chaos and disorder in Iraq is not of the US's making, but misguided US interventions to bring democracy to Iraq, at great cost in bloodshed and finance, have not made any difference in the nation's fundamental problems of corruption and incompetency. As Iraqis on the streets of Baghdad say in response to the chaos: "We used to have one Saddam Hussein, now we have a thousand." US interventions did nothing to stop or deter Iraqi public officials from stealing money in every way possible. Few people if any in the country believe that leadership exists with sufficient vision and competence to create a brighter future for Iraq. Thousands of Iraqis are leaving the country, heading for Germany and Europe, buying fake Syrian passports to get them to their destination as "asylum seekers" rather than face rejection as merely economic immigrants.

For a great many Iraqis, Prime Minister Haider al-Abadi's announcement of a bold set of political reforms and attacks on fraud and waste in Iraq's government aren't persuasive. A cynical Iraqi response, based on ample past history, is that this is just one more leader's effort to remove rivals, grab and consolidate power. Does the US have any conceivable role in this next labyrinthine phase of Iraqi governmental reform? Perhaps not since Iraqis blame the US government for funding and supporting their corrupt and ineffectual government, and for being instrumental in structuring the government in ways that have allowed and facilitated the rise of corrupt, ineffectual leaders. But perhaps the US does have a role in the future of Iraq that the Obama administration or a future occupant of the Oval Office could embrace that combines defeating ISIS with strengthening Iraqi governance at all levels.

A significant note of hope for Iraq in an Abadi administration, that easily could get lost amidst reactions to other components of his reform plan, was Abadi's openness to a "limitless" decentralization of power and privatization of public services. He did not use the word federalism, but his decentralization plan could include federalism, which is not a new idea. In fact, as a Senator, Biden proposed a plan to create three separate regions in the country: Shia, Sunni, and Kurdish that, although it amounted to partitioning, could be framed as power-sharing within federalism.

When Abadi met with Obama at the White House, he discussed decentralization of Iraq's government and power sharing. And Abadi also said at the Center for Strategic and International Studies (CSIS) in Washington: "In a major government reform, we are decentralizing decision-making from Baghdad to the local administration and local governments." In response to a question at the CSIS Forum, Abadi said, "If you do not decentralize, the country will disintegrate."

His plan includes security and defense decentralization including a controversial transfer of jurisdiction over security from Baghdad to local governments. "The National Guard will take the responsibility to defend the provinces from any threat, and they will be accountable to the governors," he said. Even the "Great Awakening" in a sense was revived with, for example, the formation of the National Mobilization Forces in Nineveh, arming Sunni tribesmen in Anbar. At the same time, Abadi arranged for the release of thousands of Sunnis who were in custody for years under Maliki's government. Also quite positive, Abadi's administration last year already struck an oil-revenue sharing deal with the Kurdistan Regional Government (KRG) to resolve a yearlong budget crisis and create a $1 billion fund to support the Peshmerga in 2015. Consequently, the Kurds postponed their call for a referendum to declare independence.

A strong case can be made for US reengagement in Iraq to assist, in whatever ways possible, with the complex tasks involved in planning and implementation of the removal of layers of Iraqi bureaucracy, the decentralization of government and dealing with about 3 million displaced persons. In the process the US would help Iraq to build its capability to stand up to ISIS through a combination of effective decentralization of security and improved support from Baghdad. This would provide an excellent way for the US to strategically restore its role and positive status in Iraq and the Middle East.

CHAPTER 13

Kurdish Wild Cards

Predominantly Sunni Muslims, with a distinct culture and their own Indo-European language, an estimated thirty million Kurds with a variety of tribal identities and political interests reside primarily in mountainous regions of present-day Iran, Iraq, Syria, and Turkey. About 16 million Kurds live in Turkey, 8 million in Iran and about 6 million in Iraq. The Iraqi Kurdish fighting force, known as Peshmerga (Kurdish for "those who face death"), played an important role in defeating Saddam Hussein and, in both Syria and Iraq, has been fighting ISIS.

In the process the Kurds have solidified control of large territories in both Syria and Iraq. In Turkey, Turkish guerrilla fighters of the Kurdistan Workers' Party (PKK) also have fought ISIS. Unsuccessfully thus far, the Turkish government and the PKK have been attempting to resolve a thirty-year conflict which would give the Kurds increased rights and recognition. The PKK, with affiliates in Syria, Iran and Iraq, envisions itself as a movement that doesn't need or want national or state boundaries.

In Iraq, Kurds primarily reside in three provinces that make up the Kurdistan Regional Government (KRG), a semiautonomous region since 2005. The Kurds also have laid claims to the oil-rich Kirkuk region which has been a focal point of dispute with Baghdad. Kurdish control over Kirkuk and its oil would be a key factor if one day the Kurds decide to seek an independent Kurdistan. In northern and northeastern Syria, Kurds occupy and have declared self-rule in areas near the border with Turkey and Iraq that also have large oil deposits. Kurds in Syria are more than 10% of the population, about 2.5 million people, not accounting for many Kurds that have fled Syria.

The Kurds have a long history in Syria, dating back to the 11th century. Over the centuries, under Ottoman, French, Turkish and Syrian rule, the much persecuted and repressed Kurds have sought political autonomy and independence, similar to Iraqi Kurdistan, leading to the formation of People's Protection Units (YGP) to control Kurdish inhabited areas in Syria (Syrian Kurdistan). Syrian government forces have abandoned many Kurdish-populated areas, leaving the Kurds to fill the power vacuum and govern these areas autonomously.

Anyone who thinks that the rift between Turkey, the U.S. and other Western allies is closing or perhaps narrowing, think again. For Turkey, the dominant view is that the U.S.-backed Kurdish militia in northern Syria is intent on creating a de facto zone of control in the region. The Turks say that the Syrian Kurdish YPG militia and its political wing, the PYD, has been forcibly removing Arab and Turkmen civilians from areas liberated from Islamic State control. At present there is no way of confirming this accusation. Turkey's view has led to cancellation of their involvement in creation of a safe zone in northern Syria for civilians, obviously a very unfortunate shift. Turkey contends that this initiative has been shelved due to, as they often repeat, 'the lack of western political will'.

Turkey's very deep antipathy towards Bashar al-Assad has not diminished at all. Turkey finds it impossible to imagine Assad as part of a legitimate transition government. In other words, the senior leadership of Turkey's ruling party remains at odds with the U.S, and its allies on how to deal with the crisis in Syria. Here again, they see weakness in the way that the international community has been dealing with Syria. These concerns are intensified by what they see as the response of the U.S. and its allies to the PYD in Syria. The only "moderate opposition" to Assad that Turkey backs is represented by the exiled Syrian National Coalition and the Free Syrian Army.

The latest blow against any reconciliation with the Kurdish militias in Syria came when recently Turkey struck Kurdish positions in Tal Abyad. The strike against the Kurdish militias, U.S. allies in the battle against ISIS, to say the least adds complexity to the U.S.'s effort to put together a unified effort in northern Syria to fight ISIS and counter Russia's military moves. Turkey continues to be an unpredictable ally of the U.S. in Syria, time and again proving that the interests of the Turks and the U.S. in Syria diverge on key issues.

Tal Abyad, a largely Arab border town in Rojava, was captured by the Kurds from ISIS during the summer. The Turks did not do more than fire machine guns across the border at YPG (People's Protection Units) positions in Tal Abyad and also in the village of Buban. Turkey has long considered the Syrian Kurdish group known as the Democratic Union Party (PYD) as an enemy because it is the Syrian offshoot of the Kurdistan Workers' Party (PKK) which has long fought an insurgency against the Turkish state.

The limited Turkish strikes, however, came after the PYD recently declared that Tal Abyad now was part of an autonomous region in northern Syria that the Kurds call Rojava. Turkey views this development as a national security threat because it fuels separatist sentiments among both Turkish and Syrian Kurds. The U.S. has argued that Turkey should view the PYD as separate from the PKK even though they share past history and a socialist ideology. Turkey is adamant about viewing both groups as one.

Complicating the situation even more, the Russians have ties to both the PKK and the PYD that go all the way back to the days of the Soviet Union. True or not, the Turks believe that Russia also is offering support to the Syrian Kurds and have raised this issue with the ambassador of Russia. In addition to the fact that the U.S. and the PYD have been allies against ISIS in northern Syria, the U.S. recently supplied Kurdish militia in Kobani with over 100 tons of weapons and ammunition. The Turkish response to this kind military support to the PYD from the U.S. is that "No one can guarantee that arms given to the PYD today, won't tomorrow fall in the hands of the PKK and be used against Turkey," For Turkey the PKK and the PYD remain "… terror organizations that have declared war against Turkey."

Syrian Kurds in the region known as Rojava have been engaged in a remarkable, and totally surprising, democratic experiment in governance. Rojava is an autonomous region in Syrian Kurdistan to the east of the Kurdistan Regional Republic, and north of ISIS-occupied Mosul. Rojava has a population of about 3 million. To the west of Rojava is the proposed Turkish-U.S. ISIS-free zone. Just before that, on the Turkish border, is Kobani where, in January 2015, Kurdish forces ended a five month siege of the city, leaving the city mostly destroyed and many residents joining the flow of refugees to Europe. Southwest of Kobani is the ISIS frontline and further west is Raqqa, the ISIS headquarters in Syria. In other words, Rojava is in the midst of and surrounded by a violent war zone that makes its experiment in democracy all the more remarkable.

The political philosophy behind this Kurdish experiment in "communalism" came from a relatively obscure Jewish New York City radical and political writer, Murray Bookchin (January 14, 1921 – July 30, 2006). How did it happen that the writings of an American anarchist, a pioneer in the ecology movement before Rachel Carson's Silent Spring, who founded his own libertarian socialist ideology, shaped political and civic life in Kurdish Rojava? Bookchin's writings on what he called "libertarian municipalism," a theory of face-to-face assembly democracy, probably has had its purest manifestation in the "democratic confederalism of Rojava."

Credit for bringing face-to-face, assembly democracy to Rojava goes to Abdullah Öcalan, one of the founding members of the militant Kurdistan Workers' Party (PKK) in 1978 in Turkey. Arrested in 1999 by the Turks (with assistance from the CIA), and taken to Turkey where he was sentenced to death, Ocalan has remained in prison ever since. Reading Bookchin while in prison, Öcalan wrote about his ideal society of "Democratic Confederalism" in which land, enterprises, and all goods are placed in the custody of citizens in free assemblies that manage and make decisions about their distribution in ways that protect the environment. The needs and interests of the community, and not the state, are paramount.

The Kurds are the only fighting force in Middle East countries that, even with occasional battle loses to ISIS, consistently has proven its ability to contain and even win against ISIS. In the process of reclaiming territory from ISIS, the Kurds have provided sanctuary for nearly two million refugees and internally displaced persons.

The Kurds have been prepared over the years to make politically expedient alliances to protect their interests and territory. They have fought alongside US forces to remove extremist Ansar al-Islam from their territory.

In recent years, the Kurdistan Regional Government (KRG) has negotiated an impressive series of security and intelligence pacts with Ankara, Tehran, Baghdad, and local leaders mainly focused on securing KRG's borders. The KRG appears to be prepared to join and form alliances in anti-ISIS campaigns if it makes sense for their own interests. Pacts that the Kurds have made with insurgents, militias, Iranians and other groups in various Iraqi territories to fight ISIS are impressive.

In northern Iraq's Nineveh Province, for example, Masoud Barzani, president of the KRG, and Abdullah al-Yawar, head of the Saudi Arabian–influenced Shammar tribe joined forces in an attempt to reclaim territories from ISIS along the Iraqi-Syrian border. In Kirkuk and Diyala, the Patriotic Union of Kurdistan (PUK) is fighting alongside Iranian forces to counter ISIS. Thanks to the Kurds, Diyala is now the only province in northern Iraq with no ISIS presence. Likewise, at least for the moment, Kobani and surrounding Syrian villages also are ISIS-free. Around Aleppo, Kurdish–Sunni Arabs have pushed ISIS all the way back to Raqqa and the surrounding countryside.

Kurdish successes against ISIS, however, come with a variety of political problems. The Peshmerga claim former ISIS-controlled lands as part of the Kurdistan Region. Consequently many Sunni Arabs have been unable to return to their communities and homes. Kurdish officials state that the disputed lands belong to the KRG. Negotiations on this issue are likely to go on for a long time, with growing tensions between Arab Iraqis and Kurds. Mosul will continue to be a special political problem for the Kurds. Sunni Arabs regard Mosul as the heartland of Sunni Arab nationalism. Kirkuk, viewed by Sunni Arabs as the "milk of the mother of Iraq," is regarded by Kurds as the "bleeding heart of Kurdistan." After taking control of Kirkuk last year, KRG officials stated that they would never allow Arabs to control it again. Part of the Kurdish passion obviously comes from oil reserves in Mosul's Nineveh Province.

The ethnic issues for Kurds in Iraq have their counterparts in Syria. The PYD has used its military successes in Syria to extend the borders it controls to displace Sunni Arabs, reinforcing support for ISIS among Sunni Arab tribes. Empowerment of Kurds and expansion and protection of Kurdish territories has created serious concerns in Ankara that another autonomous Kurdish region is emerging in Syria. For Turkey, the rising influence of the PYD and PKK appears to be even more of a concern than defeating ISIS.

Iran has supported the Kurds during the ISIS onslaught in Syria. In combination with the growing presence of Iranian-backed Shiite militias in Iraq's disputed northern territories, the fragmented Kurdistan region becomes increasingly volatile, which makes it more difficult for policymakers and military planners in the United States to rely on Kurdish partners to degrade and destroy ISIS. The US balancing act in Iraq has to support both the KRG and Sunni Arab groups that oppose ISIS in ways that don't fuel deep-rooted conflicts over disputed territories and resources.

Without a doubt the Kurds will continue their quest for independence within and across Iraq, Syria and Turkey. This quest will take different forms in different countries, probably including legitimate political parties. No matter what happens in Kurdish struggles for autonomy or independence, the Kurds in both Iraq and Syria will continue to fight ISIS. In the past the United States has trained Iraqi Kurds and backed Syrian Kurds with airpower and they are likely to continue this support while navigating risks of backlash from both the Iraqi and Turkish governments which are resisting further empowerment of an autonomous Kurdish region.

The Middle East today is filled with conflicts, chaos and disorder within and between states driven by sectarian, religious, ideological, political and other dynamics. Making matters continuously worse, there has been no strategic meeting of the minds among Middle East leadership about dealing with the threat of ISIS. Each initiative to resolve conflicts seems to have a double agenda: the publically-stated goal and the underlying real goal.

A good example was the Turkish announcement that it is joining the US-led international coalition against ISIS. But since making that announcement, Turkish warplanes have bombed Kurdish strongholds in Turkey and Iraq. In other words, Turkey focused its initial military effort as part of the anti-ISIS coalition not on Islamic extremists but on the secular Kurdistan Workers Party (PKK) and its Kurdish affiliate in Syria, the PYD, that has been in the vanguard of fighting ISIS. Turkish officials accuse the PKK and the People's Protection Unit (PYD) of terrorism.

When Turkey joined with the US to create a "safe zone" in northern Syria, critics said that the "safe-zone" actually was aimed at preventing Kurdish militia fighters from increasing their control of the Syrian side of Turkey's border. Critics also said that Turkey is using the ISIS fight to ensure that Kurds in northern Syria are not able to establish an independent territory. Some critics have even suggested that Turkey has been an accomplice in empowering ISIS in Syria to strengthen their battles with the PYD. The PYD says that they have no quarrel with Turkey.

Turkey claims that the PYD is worse than ISIS. Turkey seems to think that, by bringing down Assad, the ISIS problem will be more or less resolved. Realistically, however, after Assad the killing and bloodletting in Syria probably will increase, followed by chaos and precisely those chaotic conditions that are conducive to ISIS and other Islamic terrorists thriving. Bottomline, Turkey has fundamentally different priorities than the US in northern Syria. The Turks want to make sure that Kurdish nationalism is suppressed. Turkey will not accept or tolerate an independent Kurdish state in northern Syria.

For the US, Turkey attacking the PYD is a special issue since the U.S has made a tactical alliance with the PYD, which is the only non-extremist insurgent group that has beaten ISIS in northern Syria, and has done so with the US acting as its air force. Between mid-2014 and mid-2015, the US made more than 6000 air strikes in the Euphrates River area between Syria and Iraq, without support from any "moderate opposition forces" other than PYD. With all of the talk by the US and its allies, including Turkey, that the anti-ISIS campaign will rely on "moderate opposition forces," realistically as yet there are only a few "moderate insurgents" in northern Syria that have volunteered to be trained for the fight against ISIS. They're all too busy battling Assad's forces.

As the YPG Kurdish militia captures territory from ISIS, with the critical help of coalition air strikes, it has expanded its territory in northern Syria by more than a third, now controlling more than 11,000 square miles. For the YPG, the PKK unquestionably is a vital militia partner against ISIS. Increasing numbers of PKK members have streamed from Turkey into northern Syria to aid the YPG. The YPG now controls a great deal of Syria's border with Turkey. Its fighting force consists of about 50,000 fighters. That should be good news for the US that currently has only one strong, reliable ally in the fight against ISIS in Syria, namely the YPG. However, inciting Turkish opposition, the PYD is determined to unite Kurdish areas in much of northern Syria and move on to take the ISIS stronghold of Raqqa.

ISIS and the YPG have been in intense battles on the Syrian border of Turkey, for example, in Tal Abyad, where control of the city has changed hands several times. Tal Abyad was a crucial ISIS supply hub and stronghold for around a year before the YGP expelled them, backed by air strikes from the US-led coalition. The battle for Tal Abyad prompted tens of thousands of refugees to flee across the border into Turkey. In this battle the YPG learned the hard way that it has to be very mindful of reactions from Islamic insurgent groups to what they perceive, whether it is warranted or not, as violence or even ethnic cleansing aimed at Arabs. Counterinsurgency, with the best of intentions and best laid plans, can backfire, causing internecine warfare, if the "good guys" are not sufficiently controlled when they capture territory, and indiscriminately abuse and terrorize people suspected of being "bad guys," which happened in Tal Abyad.

The YPG strategy involves ISIS containment in concert with local Arab partners, other affiliated partners, and remnants of the Free Syrian Army (FSA), while guiding the targeting of US airstrikes. (The FSA consists of officers and soldiers, mostly Sunni Muslims, that defected from Assad's Syrian Army.) YPG fighting units may not include exact counterparts of the full-blown "frontline advisors" but they do have their own versions of "CyberWarriors." Armed with tablet computers and digital maps, YPG fighters send GPS coordinates showing the location of ISIS targets to American operations staff guiding Coalition aircraft strikes against ISIS forces.

The YPG's connection to the PKK -- a US - EU - Turkey-designated terror group – no doubt is problematic for US relations with Ankara, but the US also, hopefully, realizes that, although it's a risky bet, the YPG probably offers the best foreseeable option for establishing a post-Assad governance model, for territory outside of Syrian Kurdistan, that is functional, ethnically and multi-culturally inclusive. Although the YPG's Kurdish identity will continue to be a liability in non-Kurdish territory, the YPG offers the best wild card option for providing trusted leadership in the next phase of Syria's resurrection.

CHAPTER 14

Lessons Learned in Yemen

The historical context for counterterrorism strategy in the Middle East and Muslim countries is the resurgence of ancient struggles between Sunni and Shia forces. Not only have they violently fed the Syrian civil war, sectarian warfare has transformed the Middle East in recent times and spurred transnational jihadi networks within and beyond the region. At the center of Islam's schisms and geopolitical forces in the Middle East is the competition for leadership and dominance of Sunni Saudi Arabia and Shia Iran. Both of these nations have been using well-financed proxy battles between complex arrays of organized, armed sectarian militants throughout the region who have proven resistant to any efforts to curb their escalating violence. Presumably the US and its allies are well aware that this historic sectarian divide between Sunnis and Shias, and their proxy wars throughout the region, and not the intervention of the UN or the US, are most likely to shape the future of the Middle East and North Africa and every one of their countries.

The main foreign policy focus of the White House and lawmakers in much of the last year has been the Iran nuclear agreement and Iran's threat to US national security. Well under the radar has been Saudi Arabia that spawned the 9/11 hijackers and that for decades has been sending billions of dollars to its sundry "proxies" around the world to promote a Wahhabi Salafist brand of Islam that has fed global terrorism. Thousands of Saudis have joined ISIS and Al-Qaeda because these Sunni Jihadist groups actually are offspring of Wahhabism. Iran and its proxies like Hezbollah are proven terrorism threats, but the most dangerous terrorism threats in the modern world can be linked to Saudi Arabia and also the government in Pakistan, a Saudi ally, also driven by Wahhabi Islam that, unlike Iran today, possesses more than a hundred nuclear bombs.

Although Sunni and Shia Muslims have lived peacefully together in many countries for centuries, Shia also have a long history of domination by Sunnis which constitute roughly 85 percent of the world's 1.6 billion Muslims. Shia have been viewed and treated by Sunnis as heretics. The complex history of Sunnis and Shia helps in part to explain the significance and ramifications of Iran's Islamic Revolution in 1979 that gave Shia cleric Ayatollah Ruhollah Khomeini the opportunity to implement his vision for an Islamic government ruled by Shia and providing leadership to Shia in Lebanon, Iraq, Afghanistan, Bahrain, and Pakistan. The sudden rise of Khomeni's Shia Iran spurred Saudi Arabia, with its millions of adherents to puritanical Sunni Wahhabism, to revive a centuries-old sectarian rivalry with Iran over the true interpretation of Islam. Saudi Arabia backed Iraq in the 1980–1988 war with Iran.

The conflict and rivalry between Saudi Arabia, the leader of the Sunni Muslim world, and Iran, leader of the Shia Muslim world is being played out in Yemen. Years of violent conflicts in Yemen, the poorest country in the Middle East, have been going on between whoever ruled the country and the Houthis in the north and separatists in the south, intermixed with terrorist attacks by AQAP. These conflicts reflect power struggles between tribal groups and corrupt Yemen leadership, between northerners and southerners fighting against unification and, most important, between Saudi Arabia and Iran. Yemen's strategic importance is based on its long border with Saudi and the fact that it sits on the Bab al-Mandab Strait, a narrow waterway linking the Red Sea with the Gulf of Aden through which much of the world's oil shipments pass. Realistic or not, Saudi Arabia, Egypt and other countries fear that a Houthi takeover of Yemen would threaten free passage of oil and other shipping through the Strait.

Houthis are a branch of Shia Islam known as Zaidism that make up about one-third of the population of North Yemen where they have ruled for about 1000 years. The Houthis take their name from Hussein Badr al-Din al-Houthi who led the group's first uprising in 2004 in an effort to win greater autonomy for their heartland of Saada province and to protect their Zaidi religious and cultural traditions from encroachment by Sunni Islamists. The Houthis battled the government of Ali Abdullah Saleh, also a Zaydi, between 2004 and 2010. Then, in 2014, the Houthis captured Sanaa, Yemen's capital, with ousted president Saleh's supporters. Today the main fight in Yemen is between forces loyal to President Abdrabbuh Mansour Hadi and those allied to the Houthis who forced Hadi to flee Sanaa to seek political refuge in Riyadh.

Yemen's security forces have split loyalties, with some units backing Hadi and others the Houthis and Saleh. Hadi is supported in the predominantly Sunni south of the country by local tribesmen and yet another militia known as the Popular Resistance Committees (PRC). Both Hadi and the Houthis are opposed by Al-Qaeda in the Arabian Peninsula (AQAP). Since the US and the West consider Yemen's AQAP the most dangerous branch of Al-Qaeda, the US has been carrying out drone strikes against AQAP's leadership.

The more serious problem in Yemen is the conflict between the Houthis and Hadi's government which really is part of a regional power struggle between Iran and Saudi Arabia. Iran denies backing the Houthis financially or militarily. Although Saudi leaders have portrayed the Houthis as an Iranian proxy force, Iran's connection to the Houthis was pure speculation until Saudi made its accusation. For months since March 25, 2015, Saudi Arabia and its allies have bombed Yemen without much success in forcing Houthis to retreat from seized major cities. The Houthis actually have gained ground and thousands of people have been killed. Cease-fire talks have failed. Clearly Saudi had no strategy when they started the war and no idea how to end it. Fighting the Houthis with air power alone could never win. Nor was destruction of the Houthis homeland in Saada province likely to win hearts and minds.

The Republic of Yemen rarely gets into geography lessons and has not been a hotspot in Congressional or presidential debates. But Yemen has considerable geopolitical importance that most of the American public does not understand or appreciate. Located at the southwestern tip of the Arabian Peninsula, Yemen has a very long border with Saudi Arabia and is located at the entrance to the Bab-el-Mandeb Strait, which links the Red Sea to the Indian Ocean (via the Gulf of Aden), one of the most active and strategic shipping lanes in the world.

For Saudi, Gulf States (GCC) and the US, concerns about Yemen have focused on broad and deep internal political conflicts and insurgencies, including insurgent groups like the Houthi, and especially the rise of Al-Qaeda in the Arabian Peninsula (AQAP). For years, without any success, the GCC has made efforts to enable Yemen to achieve nonviolent resolution to its many challenges.

Since Mansour Hadi was sworn in as president in February 2012, Yemen has been immersed in a civil war between forces loyal to Hadi, predominantly in the Sunni south of the country, and Houthis who forced Hadi to flee the capital, Sanaa, in February 2015, and head for refuge in Saudi Arabia. Hadi's predecessor, Ali Abdullah Saleh, has remained politically influential. Both Hadi and the Houthis are opposed by Al-Qaeda in the Arabian Peninsula (AQAP).

Citing a request by Yemen's deposed President Hadi, the governments of Saudi Arabia, the United Arab Emirates, Bahrain, Qatar, Kuwait and Jordan launched "Operation Decisive Storm" and bombing attacks against the Houthis in Yemen. Egypt sent warships to Aden in southern Yemen and expressed willingness to send in ground troops. Saudi's other allies (Turkey, Pakistan and the Sudan) committed to joining the operation. The United Arab

Emirates (UAE) sent a brigade to Yemen to battle the Houthis. The justification for GCC action was that the Houthis are fighting on behalf of Iran. The Houthis deny that they are operating as an Iranian proxy.

The Houthis, also known as *Ansar Allah* in Arabic, or God's Partisans, are a Shia movement that began as a rebellion in northern Yemen on Saudi's southern border in 2003 and 2004. When the Arab Spring led to the removal of Yemen's long-serving ruler, Ali Abdullah Saleh, in 2012, with Iranian support the Houthis sought to undermine the Saudi-backed Hadi government by linking up with allies of the Saleh family and pushing southward to Yemen's capital, Sanaa, which they captured, and then moved on to the port city of Aden. The story of the Yemen "revolution" and the Houthis role in it is further complicated by a separate Salafi-Sunni insurgency led by AQAP that has raged in the south and east of the country. In addition, the Islamic State recently emerged in Yemen and committed a series of highly publicized massacres.

When Yemeni nationals were brought back to Yemen from Afghanistan by the Saleh regime, he sent them to fight the Soviet-backed Marxist government of South Yemen and to crush southern secessionists. Among those who returned were Arab veterans of the Afghan war, including Osama bin Laden. Bin Laden advocated a central role for Yemen in global jihad. Returning jihadists formed the Islamic Jihad in Yemen (1990–94) and several other militant AQAP predecessors in the 1990s. AQAP's aims have been to: purge Muslim countries of Western presence and influence; replace secular "apostate" governments with fundamentalist Islamic regimes; assassinate Western nationals and their allies, including members of the Saudi royal family; and attack the US homeland. Ironically, even though the Saudi royal family has been on AQAP's hit list, in the past the Kingdom has been AQAP's most significant source of funding.

AQAP has been responsible for countless bombings and other acts of terrorism in Yemen and elsewhere, including the October 2000 detonation of explosives on the hull of the USS *Cole* in the

Aden harbor. More than half of the prisoners in Guantanamo Bay were Yemenis. Controversial US drone strikes in Yemen have killed more than a thousand suspected militants as well as civilians, including AQAP leaders and members. The US has withdrawn its special operations force that was training Yemeni troops and supposedly the Saudi air force destroyed the military installations where these counterterrorism units previously had been trained.

One has to wonder whether any cost-benefit analysis of the US engaging in warfare in Middle East states, even just airstrikes, includes the large numbers of innocent civilians likely to be killed or turned into refugees in the process of bombing insurgents or recapturing territory. Yemen certainly is a good example. More than 1.3 million Yemenis have become refugees. Destruction of Yemen's infrastructure has left millions of people without clean water, electricity or medical care. US warships have enforced a blockage in the Gulf of Aden to prevent weapons shipments that also blocks food and fuel supplies needed by desperate Yemenites.

Saudi Arabia has become a wild card in the Middle East at least as much as Iran. Saudi's political and military actions in Yemen show that the Kingdom is prepared to take ruthless direct action to implement Saudi foreign policy. Saudi counts on support from Egypt and Pakistan in a regional Sunni coalition to counter Iran. Pakistan, which is estimated to have 120 nuclear weapons and can produce as many as 20 nuclear warheads annually, has ominously indicated that it stands behind the Kingdom. The extent to which Egypt will get involved with the interventions of Saudi and Gulf States in Yemen remains to be seen. Egypt has its own terrorism issues and concerns.

For many years, Saudi has supported the military, security apparatus, education and social services, transportation projects, health care and a wide array of other government services in Yemen. With perpetual tribal conflict, one of the most heavily armed civilian populations in the world and a growing Al-Qaeda presence, understandably Saudi Arabia's priority has been to have a stable neighbor to the south, protect its southernmost cities of Najran, Jizan and Khamis Mushayt, and prevent Yemen's complete collapse. Saudi was not successful even after providing billions in aid, with additional billions from the Gulf Cooperation Council (GCC) and more than $4 billion in remittances from almost 1 million Yemeni expatriates in Saudi Arabia.

The Houthis are a Shia sect that makes up roughly one-third of Yemen's 25 million people. The Houthi founder, Hussein al-Houthi, was killed by the Yemeni government in 2004. Ten years later, in September 2014, Houthi militias ransacked Sanaa, Yemen's capital, and Saudi Arabia assumed that it was left with only one choice in Yemen: military intervention. Until recently Saudi military forces have not engaged in any ground warfare in Yemen, but GCC troops have been very engaged in Yemen. Saudi has changed its position about fighting a ground war in Yemen. Saudi expects that, with funds from sanctions relief, Iran will most likely increase its military and other support to the Houthis, but Iran is unlikely to replace Saudi Arabia as Yemen's big aid benefactor.

Yemen's southern port city of Aden has been the scene of a civil war since March 19, 2015, when Houthis, along with insurgents loyal to the country's former president (for 33 years) Ali Abdullah Saleh, launched an assault on the city. That's the same deposed Saleh that for decades was supported by the Saudis. The insurgents loyal to Saleh joined forces with Saudi's enemy, the Houthis. Another renegade group, the Southern Resistance, loyal to the Saudis, has been battling the Houthis. Key anti-Houthi factions in the south either oppose former president Hadi or don't support his return. Months of Saudi airstrikes against the Houthis have done little to stop them.

What did work for the Southern Resistance in the battle with the Houthis for the port city of Aden and its airport was the arrival in mid-July 2015 of a large delivery of modern armored vehicles from Saudi Arabia or the United Arab Emirates. These protected mobility vehicles were used extensively in operations in Aden. In addition to improving the Southern Resistance's overall mobility, the RPG-protected vehicles can deliver personnel close to the fighting and provide fire support from onboard heavy weapons.

At about the same time, Republican Guard forces loyal to former President Saleh removed their support for the Houthis in Aden, leaving them to deal with the Southern Resistance offensive alone. More than 10,000 personnel in Saudi's coalition from the UAE, Morocco, Egypt, Sudan, Kuwait and Qatar have attacked the Houthis in the capital of Sanaa which already has been the target of devastating airstrikes.

The historic background of Yemen's chaotic militancy obviously is very complex. The fact that Yemen also serves as the home base for AQAP complicates counterinsurgency. After a decade-long insurgency fought against Houthi rebels, assuming that the Houthis somehow can be shutdown or contained (whatever that means), the question remains as to how the country can be governed in the future and by whom. What we do know is that it's highly unlikely that Saudi Arabia and Iran will bury the hatchet in their decades-long strategic rivalry for power and influence in the Middle East. Bad blood runs too deep between Saudi Arabia, as the leader of the Sunni Muslim world, and Iran as the leader of the Shia Muslim world. No doubt Yemen, which shares a 1,770km border with Saudi, will be an important piece for Iran in its Middle East chess game. As for Iran, the question is one of strategic intent. What does Iran want in Yemen? A base of operations? Easier access to Saudi Arabia?

Iran's intent in Yemen may not be clear but for the Saudis what happens along and south of its border with Yemen is of the highest national security concern. Ever since Saudi's ally, Ali Abdullah Saleh, was forced to step down as Yemen's president in 2011, and the Houthis emerged, from the Saudi's perspective Yemen has been an increasingly unstable threat. Iran gaining a strong foothold in Yemen is an even graver threat, especially since AQAP in Yemen also is a serious Saudi security threat.

The Saudi-led coalition of Arab states began its bombing campaign in March 2015 that resulted in more than a thousand civilian deaths and other casualties. Along with airstrikes the Saudis engaged tribal fighters in Yemen with longstanding ties to Saudi Arabia and sent them arms shipments and other gear. Now soldiers trained in Saudi and Gulf states have joined the battle.

The Obama administration has given Saudi Arabia and its Gulf Cooperation Council allies more or less free reign in Yemen based on the president's determination, expressed at his May 13-14, 2015 summit at Camp David, that the US should stay in the background of efforts by the Gulf States to crush Houthis. US policy in the Gulf is complicated by the fact that GCC members have committed to purchasing as much as $200 billion worth of US arms. The US has provided advice on Yemen bombing targets that led to large numbers of civilian casualties. Expanding violence has worsened both the military and humanitarian situation in Yemen and made it easier for ISIS to expand its terrorist operations there. ISIS shows no regard for human life. For example, ISIS bombed two mosques in Sanaa which killed close to 140 people and injured 350.

Supposedly Yemen's president Hadi is building a government in exile from his new home in Saudi, but there's no real evidence of it. The mix of fighters involved with the Houthis makes any negotiated settlement unlikely. The Yemeni Army loyal to the previous president, Saleh, has joined the Houthis in order to regain power. Even different groups within the Houthis hold different views on their goals. Some envision destroying both Jerusalem and Mecca. All of the Houthis' supporters see their opponents as terrorists to be destroyed and America as the devil. Their opponents include a variety of armed tribes, others who want their own independent regimes, Al-Qaeda, and sundry other Islamic groups. Hadi in exile has virtually no support among any of these groups.

About a year ago, President Obama touted Yemen as a counterterrorism success story and said it would be the model for the US's strategy against ISIS. "This counterterrorism campaign will be waged through a steady, relentless effort to take out ISIL wherever they exist, using our air power and our support for partner forces on the ground. This strategy of taking out terrorists who threaten us, while supporting partners on the front lines, is one that we have successfully pursued in Yemen and Somalia for years. And it is consistent with the approach I outlined earlier this year: to use force against anyone who threatens America's core interests, but to mobilize partners wherever possible to address broader challenges to international order," he stated.

Besides massively lethal airstrikes supported by the US, coalition actions to control maritime traffic and block imports have succeeded in increasing widespread deprivation in Yemen. Food prices are soaring. Malnutrition is spreading. Increasing fuel shortages have shut down hospitals. Diseases like malaria are spreading. The coalition's strategy for pressuring the Houthis has only managed to intensify Yemen's humanitarian crisis and turn Yemenis against Saudi and the US

A year later, as President Obama hosted Saudi Arabia's King Salman in their first White House summit, as expected he reaffirmed US support for the effort to oust Iranian-backed rebels in Yemen, and repeated warnings that the fighting is having very serious impact on civilians. Saudi had intensified its bombing since Obama's previous warnings. In late August 2015 the White House expressed concern about Saudi-led air strikes on the port city of Hodeida, a "crucial lifeline used to provide medicine, food and fuel to Yemen's population." Obama stressed the need for ports to reopen and for infrastructure not to be damaged. "We have been urging all the parties involved, including the Yemen government, coalition members and others to take steps to allow for unfettered humanitarian access to all parts of Yemen," he said. "There is no military solution to the crisis in Yemen." There is no evidence that the White House has followed up to change the strategy or tactics used in Yemen or significantly increase humanitarian support for Yemenis.

In the port city of Aden, the United Nations' top humanitarian relief official has made an emotional plea to let aid get to civilians caught in the crossfire. Only a fraction of the $1.6 billion emergency relief fund for Yemen has been filled by international donors, including $274 million pledged by Riyadh. Oxfam has reported that 16 million Yemenis -- about two-thirds of the population -- lack clean water and sanitation, in part because they do not have fuel to operate water pumps. The Saudi blockade of Yemen's ports allows only 20 percent of the fuel that is needed into the country. Oxfam long has been critical of Saudi Arabia's war strategy and has had to pull most, if not all, of its international staff from Yemen as the violence escalated.

In 2014 the UN brokered a peace deal in Yemen which did not last. Another one in the foreseeable future is unlikely. The Houthis view compromise as the pathway to destruction. Without political and financial support from Saudi and the GCC, Yemen faces financial collapse and a continued humanitarian crisis. The UN's human rights chief has called for an independent inquiry into violations in Yemen by the Saudi-led coalition and by the Houthi rebels. In addition to thousands of civilians killed and many thousands more wounded and injured in the Yemen conflict, Zeid Ra'ad al-Hussein told the UN's Human Rights Council that the fighting has left 21 million people or 80 percent of the population in dire need of humanitarian aid.

Mr. al-Hussein's statement opened a month-long session of the Council which will hear a slew of reports on human rights violations in Syria, the Ukraine, Sri Lanka, and more. The UN has its hands full with humanitarian crises in the Middle East and elsewhere. Besides the White House's periodic admonitions from the sidelines, and whatever else may be going on behind the scenes, the US's role continues to be support for military action in Yemen by the Saudis and the GCC.

For too long the devastating humanitarian situation in war-torn Yemen has been overshadowed by the severe humanitarian crisis in Syria, including a vast number of refugees and displaced people in both countries. It is reassuring to hear from a top State Department diplomat that the situation in Yemen has become so awful that Saudi Arabia finally is becoming serious about finding a political resolution. Anne Patterson, the assistant secretary for Near Eastern Affairs, told the Senate Foreign Relations Committee recently that "there are some hopeful signs" that Riyadh is intent on bringing the conflict to a close.

Talks aimed at ending the months of fighting in Yemen took place in Geneva at the end of October under the auspices of the United Nations. All sides agreed to attend these talks. This is not the first time that U.N.-sponsored talks have attempted to end the civil war in Yemen and Saudi's military engagement in it. In June UN-sponsored talks failed due to disagreements about the implementation of a U.N. Security Council resolution that called on the Houthis to withdraw from the cities they hold, including Sanaa.

The Saudis are realizing, belatedly, that the Yemeni population is turning against them. In addition, at some future time, hopefully sooner rather than later, Saudi Arabia, its Gulf allies and the U.S. will have to take responsibility for rebuilding the country. This likelihood has not been discussed by either the White House or Congress, neither of which has taken any responsibility for aiding in the destruction in Yemen and the escalating human cost.

The United Nations estimates that at least 5,600 Yemeni civilians have been killed since fighting began between a Saudi-led coalition that supports exiled President Abed Rabbo Mansour Hadi and the Iranian-backed Houthi rebels who control a number of Yemeni cities. In addition, more than 535,000 children face malnutrition, imminent famine, and death, according to UNICEF. The World Food Program estimates that 13 million people do not have adequate access to food. The U.N. says 1.3 million are moderately malnourished.

For the United States, which has assisted Saudi's deadly airstrike campaign with logistical and intelligence support, the war in Yemen is another dark stain on its frequent statements of lofty principles and denials. Guided by the U.S., hospitals in Yemen have been hit by Saudi air strikes, including a Doctors Without Borders (MSF) hospital. Unlike the MSF hospital in Kunduz, Afghanistan, no one was killed in the Yemen strikes on hospitals, but their destruction will leave hundreds of thousands of Yemenis without health care services.

Saudi Arabia's U.N. envoy, Abdallah Al-Mouallimi, at first confirmed, and then denied that he had confirmed, the coalition's responsibility for the strike, saying that the bombing was a "mistake" caused by the failure of MSF to provide the coalition with their hospital's accurate GPS coordinates. Again, like in Kunduz, MSF quickly challenged that account, issuing a statement asserting that the correct GPS coordinates for the hospital were shared with coalition forces. Here again, like the U.S. senior military leadership on the Kunduz hospital bombing, Mouallimi said at a news conference, "How was the hospital hit or damaged? We do not know and we will have a full and transparent investigation carried out by the Yemeni authorities."

CHAPTER 15

Lessons Learned in Libya & Benghazi

Muammar Qaddafi, his pursuit of WMD and terrorist actions, especially the bombing of Pan Am 103, were a focus of the CIA for a long time. Brokering the deal to remove WMD from Libya resulted in a resumption of diplomatic relations with the US after a hiatus of almost 30 years. The CIA knew that Qaddafi and Libya definitely were targets of Al-Qaeda. Then, in 2011, apparently much to the surprise of the CIA, rebellion (or call it revolution) broke out across Libya, including in Benghazi. Other than the conviction in Washington that, some day, Qaddafi had to go, for reasons that were never made clear by the White House or the CIA, the US supported the rebels, eventually providing military support through NATO. No mention ever was made or cautions issued about the possibility of unintended consequences.

After considerable bloodshed, Qaddafi's regime finally collapsed, about six months after the rebellion started. Libya quickly turned even more chaotic. Militias filled the void. The CIA, that had spent a vast amount of time and money monitoring Libya and Qaddafi for years, looked on as a vast amount of unsecured military weapons in Libya poured out of the country into the region. Al-Qaeda in the Islam Maghreb (AQIM) loaded up on these weapons. The CIA warned Libya's interim Prime Minister about the imminent threat of AQIM, but did nothing to enable Libya to prepare for what was happening or likely to happen.

When Qaddafi was killed in 2011, the country already was full of armed militias. NATO watched as the county inevitably fell apart. Leaders like the UK's David Cameron acknowledged that the US and other Western countries shared some responsibility for Libya's collapse and "prematurely" leaving Libya to the Libyan Islamists. The West also watched for the next few years as Islamist extremists returned home from fighting in Iraq and Syria and seized Libyan territory. ISIS took over Derna and later Al-Qaeda brutally removed ISIS from the city. ISIS moved on to take over Sirte, Qaddafi's home town in Libya's "Oil Crescent." Without question, Libya had become a victim of brutal civil war. Benghazi became the scene of jihadists doing battle daily with much of the city in ruins and countless civilians dead.

What happened in Libya, which the CIA should have anticipated, was a failed state that provided fertile ground for Al-Qaeda. Libya's interim government had no ability to govern or provide security anywhere in the country. Extremism was exploding across Libya. CIA reports on the worsening situation in Libya were pouring into the White House, Congress and the rest of the intelligence community. Everyone in Washington with the right security clearances knew more or less exactly what was happening in Libya. Most of the recipients of these intelligence reports had supported the overthrow of Qaddafi. Although sometimes acrimonious debate raged, none of the recipients of this intelligence, including the White House, the NSC, the Pentagon and the State Department had any idea of what would happen afterwards or the role that the US should play.

The State Department had a mission in Benghazi. The CIA had a unit located in a nearby annex in Benghazi to collect intelligence. The city was a hotbed of extremism, including Al-Qaeda. US and allied facilities in Benghazi frequently were attacked in 2012. The CIA duly reported all of these incidents and recommended security enhancements, including at the State Department facility. On September 11, 2012, the anniversary of 9/11, much to the amazement of CIA staff, US ambassador Chris Stevens was allowed to visit Benghazi. He should not have been allowed anywhere in Libya, and especially in the heart of violent extremism.

During three separate attacks on the State Department's facility in Benghazi, none that appeared to be well-planned or organized, fires set to the buildings killed Ambassador Stevens and one other person. After multiple attacks on the CIA annex, two staff members were killed and others injured. These CIA personnel previously had responded to the attacks on the State Department's building and heroically saved lives. The security provided to all of these US facilities was much too small.

The tragedy of Benghazi was 9/11 all over again on September 11, 2012, just on a much smaller scale. In the 2015-16 presidential election year, Benghazi has become politicized, which it should be, but for the right reasons. In light of what the CIA knew about Libya and their warnings about the terrorism threat in the Middle East and Libya on the anniversary of 9/11, no US State Department employee, ambassador or even a janitor, and no CIA official, should have been in Benghazi on September 11, 2012.

In the aftermath of Benghazi, there was much controversy in Congressional hearings about whether the attack was planned in advance by Islamic extremists or was a spontaneous assault by an agitated local populace that morphed into violence. No matter what caused the attack or whether Al-Qaeda or other terrorists were involved, the State Department and CIA staff should have been evacuated before the anniversary of 9/11, and Ambassador Stevens should never have been allowed to show up in Benghazi. Like before 9/11, when no one in the CIA had ever thought about airplanes as WMD, with all of the warnings based on volumes of intelligence, no one in the U.S intelligence or diplomatic establishments was thinking about a worst-case scenario in Benghazi connected to the anniversary of 9/11.

Benghazi is a classic example of the disconnect between US intelligence gathered, analyzed and communicated to everyone in the Washington information and decision-making loop, at a huge Federal cost over time, and the inexplicable failure to act on it in a timely manner to protect national security. If the US system for gathering intelligence and converting it into actionable plans has not improved significantly in the few years since Benghazi, national security in the homeland is at serious risk of another 9/11 or much worse.

Benghazi became a major political issue in the 2012 presidential campaign and, for the right reasons, should be an issue again in 2016. The issue is NOT whether the Obama administration and Hillary Clinton tried to downplay the terrorism aspect of the attack in Benghazi. It is why, with every sign pointing to either the strong possibility or likelihood of a terrorist attack on US facilities in Libya on September 11, 2012, especially highly visible ones in Benghazi, Ambassador Stevens and any other US personnel were allowed to go there, especially, as everyone connected with Libya knew, the US had provided only minimal security.

The other issue that no doubt should get considerable attention leading up to the election in 2016 is whether the White House tried to cover-up the fact that they knew about the CIA's terrorism warnings prior to September 11, 2012 and, for whatever reasons, did not act on them. Secretary Clinton and her State Department unquestionably were responsible along with the White House and the intelligence community for the situation in Benghazi that resulted in Stevens' death. They blamed the YouTube video defaming Prophet Muhammad that happened in Cairo earlier in the day as the motivation and trigger for the Benghazi attacks. Even if that was true, and no one in the intelligence community believed the video to be the cause of the attacks, Stevens and the rest of the State Department and CIA staffs should not have been in their Benghazi offices on 9/11/12.

Technically no one in the Obama Administration's leadership was lying in their public statements and communications about Benghazi to Congress. However, as a matter of record, the State Department and the White House did want to remove language in any report to Congress or to the public indicating that they had *prior warning* about what had happened in Benghazi on September 11, 2012. The White House and its minions did not have a specific *prior warning* of the Benghazi attack, but for months, weeks and days prior to the attack the CIA had issued warnings about the deteriorating security situation in Eastern Libya and the potential for terrorist attacks. In fact, US installations in the entire Arab world had received dire warnings about possible attacks before the anniversary of 9/11. Nothing was done in Benghazi by the State Department in response to those warnings.

The most striking, and surprising, outcome of the Congressional hearing on Benghazi, that became an 11-hour endurance contest, was that, in order to make their case, Republicans attacking Hillary Clinton's credibility did not simply state the facts about dire reports from staff at the U.S. Mission Benghazi about their security concerns and the incomprehensible lack of any response to them from the either the U.S. State Department or the Defense Department. Hopefully the truth of what actually went wrong in Benghazi can be found somewhere in the nine government reports already published, providing hundreds of pages of findings on what went wrong in Benghazi.

At the Benghazi hearing, there was frequent reference to the Accountability Review Board (ARB) convened by Secretary Clinton under Federal law to impartially examine the facts and circumstances surrounding the September 11-12, 2012, killings of four U.S. government personnel and severe wounding of several others in Benghazi's Special Mission Compound (SMC), including Ambassador Chris Stevens. The ARB study was supposed to examine, among other things, whether the security systems and procedures for the SMC were adequate and whether relevant intelligence or other information was available to mitigate risk for the SMC.

The findings of the ARB report state, without qualification, that "systemic failures and leadership and management deficiencies at senior levels within two bureaus of the State Department resulted in a special mission security posture that was inadequate for Benghazi and grossly inadequate to deal with the attack that took place. Security in Benghazi was not implemented as a "shared responsibility" by the bureaus in Washington charged with supporting the post."

These statements are indicative of the kind of language used throughout the ARB report which tends to state it findings and conclusions in a manner that diplomatically soften the blows to people in the State Department (none of whom are named). More important, the actual leadership and management dysfunction and failures by State Department employees in Washington, including Secretary Clinton, are not discussed. The failure of State Department and DOD communication and coordination on SMC security is not discussed at all. The reasons why Ambassador Stevens' repeated, and increasingly urgent, calls for security enhancements for SMC were not answered by the State Department in Washington, and Tripoli Embassy's responsibility, also are not at all discussed in the ARB report. None of these omissions in the ARB report on Benghazi were discussed at the recent Congressional interrogation of Sec. Clinton. But they may have been discussed in previous testimony before House and Senate committees.

According to the ARB report, in Washington, and between Washington and Benghazi, there was confusion over who was empowered to make decisions about security and other matters. Communication and coordination with respect to SMC at the senior State Department leadership level was poor. It was known that the Libyan government had no control or influence over what was happening in Benghazi. Given the deteriorating security situation, the lack of any security protection, the total lack of any host government protection, it is noteworthy that the only reference in the ARB report to intervention by "U.S. military assets," and probably the most significant omission in the report, is "there simply was not enough time for armed U.S. military assets to have made a difference."

Embassy Tripoli was singled out for failure to advocate sufficiently for increased security for SMC. As a consequence of all of these failings and shortcomings, the number of Bureau of Diplomatic Security (DS) staff in Benghazi before and during the day of attack were inadequate, in spite of repeated requests from SMC staff (and Embassy Tripoli) for additional security. In addition, the SMC facility itself totally lacked sufficient security measures and equipment, including, for example, as basic as security cameras, safety grills on windows, and lighting.

The ARB report also confirms that, in the weeks and months leading up to the attack on the SMC, the security situation was deteriorating and Washington failed to respond to SMC security reports, including that their security was dependent on unskilled, untrained, unreliable and unarmed local militia. Although not stated in the ARB report, clearly the DS failed the SMC, Ambassador Stevens and his staff. The ARB report's response is to recommend "reexamination" of the DS organization and management.

U.S. intelligence failed to adequately assess the high-risk, high-threat situation of the SMC. Specifically the DS Office of Office and Threat Analysis failed to provide adequate threat analyses to senior State Department officials in Washington and the SMC itself, especially in light of dozens of violent "security incidents" in Benghazi in 2012 involving the SMC, NGOs, diplomats and others, and in generally and unquestionably a seriously deteriorating security situation in Benghazi

On Sunday, September 9, 2012, the U.S. mission wrote a letter requesting "additional police support at our compound for the duration of U.S. ambassador Chris Stevens' visit. We requested daily, twenty-four hour police protection at the front and rear of the U.S. mission as well as a roving patrol. In addition we requested the services of a police explosive detection dog," the letter reads. "We were given assurances from the highest authorities in the Ministry of Foreign Affairs that all due support would be provided for Ambassador Stevens' visit to Benghazi. However, we are saddened to report that we have only received an occasional police presence at our main gate. Many hours pass when we have no police support at all."

Stevens wrote two letters on his final day alive addressed to Mohamed Obeidi, the head of the Libyan Ministry of Foreign Affairs' office in Benghazi:

"Finally, early this morning at 0643, September 11, 2012, one of our diligent guards made a troubling report. Near our main gate, a member of the police force was seen in the upper level of a building across from our compound. It is reported that this person was photographing the inside of the U.S. special mission and furthermore that this person was part of the police unit sent to protect the mission. The police car stationed where this event occurred was number 322."

Numerous warnings were flowing into the State Department from SMC staff about security disintegrating in Benghazi in the month of the assault. Stevens himself sent a cable to State on August 8 about a "security vacuum" in the city that enabled jihadists to attack western targets like the Red Cross "with impunity." On September 11, the day he was killed, he sent a separate message describing "growing problems with security" due to the weakness of Libyan government forces:

"RSO (Regional Security Officer) expressed concerns with the ability to defend Post in the event of a coordinated attack due to limited manpower, security measures, weapons capabilities, host nation support, and the overall size of the compound," Steven's cable said. In addition to describing the security situation in Benghazi as "trending negatively," the cable said explicitly that the mission would ask for more help. "In light of the uncertain security environment, US Mission Benghazi will submit specific requests to US Embassy Tripoli for additional physical security upgrades and staffing needs by separate cover.."

Hillary Clinton's Emergency Action Committee focused on the SMC also was briefed "on the location of approximately ten Islamist militias and AQ training camps within Benghazi … these groups ran the spectrum from Islamist militias, such as the QRF Brigade and Ansar al-Sharia, to other nameless ones." Extremist militias inside and outside of Benghazi were gaining strength. Benghazi was becoming an increasingly lawless city run by a diverse group of Islamist militias. The police presence was completely ineffectual. All of this could and should have been known to the State Department and DS.

The Obama Administration and State Department's public statements that the attack on the SMC came without warning clearly were preposterous. SMC staff unquestionably knew that they were in grave danger before the attack. They did not receive security support before or during the attack even as the event was being watched live on TV in the White House.

The ARB report does not discuss why the U.S. Military's Africa Command (AFRICOM) was not requested to supply security support to the SMC via the Benghazi airport before or during the attack, when the SMC was going up in smoke or when the Annex with CIA staff was under attack by mortar fire. DOD did supply an unnamed aircraft for surveillance of evacuation of SMC and Annex personnel that were not killed, which was accomplished by a chartered jet and a Libyan Air Force plane arranged for by Embassy Tripoli.

Virtually overlooked in the politically charged Congressional hearings on Benghazi was the fact that Libya's radical Islamist groups, which Qaddafi had suppressed, including Ansar al-Sharia, a terrorist organization affiliated with Al-Qaeda, and including factions aligned with ISIS, now were fighting for control of the entire country. ISIS moved to capitalize on the chaos and fill the void in Libya, fighting two rival factions, Tobruk and Tripoli, for control of the country.

The interim Libyan government appealed to the Arab League for help as ISIS spread rapidly across Libya, extending across much of the Sirte basin oil fields on the northern coast. In spite of an embargo, black market weapons had been flooding into Libya from Egypt, the UAE and Qatar, supplying rival factions with everything from jets to ammunition. Post-Qaddafi Libya was in the midst of a proxy war with its eastern government backed by Egypt's military regime, Saudi Arabia, and the United Arab Emirates, and the Tripoli coalition was backed by Turkey and Qatar.

Was there any way of predicting that ISIS would push into Libya in the last two years? Was it not apparent that a deepening political crisis and collapse of state institutions in Libya would attract and feed the growth of terrorist groups like ISIS? Given ISIS's financial strategy in Iraq and Syria, was it not predictable that Libya's oil and gas infrastructure and revenues would be an extremely attractive target for ISIS? As the CIA had known for more than a year, ISIS was urging foreign fighters from various countries to travel to Libya to help build its forces there.

When ISIS conquered Derna in Libya's northeast and then announced three other ISIS provinces (Barqa in the east, Tripoli in the west, and Fezzan in the south), was that not sufficient to indicate ISIS's intentions in Libya? And if not ISIS, then what about the intentions of other rival militant groups (mostly Sunni) suppressed by Qaddafi? What, if anything, can be done by the US and the international community to enable Libya's highly fragmented, increasingly armed, competing and politically divided insurgent groups to resist ISIS without further promoting chaotic civil war?

Libya's civil war is more than a year-old. UN Support Mission in Libya (UNSMIL)-led peace negotiations continue with little progress or any optimism. Negotiations involve the "exiled" and anti-Islamist House of Representatives, ruled from the eastern city of Tobruk, recognized by the UN, and the Islamist-aligned governing body based in Tripoli. The only "good news" has been that Libya's two rival governments actually were willing to sit down at the same negotiating table in Morocco. What will be the ultimate value for Libya and North Africa of a mediated solution between these two rival governments?

About a year ago, Libya Dawn, a collection of militias from Tripoli, the Berber areas of western Libya, and the port city of Misrata took over the capital and reinstated the defunct General National Congress (GNC). Dominated by Islamist militias, Libya Dawn lacks international support. Libya Dawn and the GNC expect to lose out in any UNSMIL-led "peace" settlement, giving the House of Representatives the upper hand in an international treaty and empowering their military campaign against whomever they define as jihadists (mainly political rivals).

Who in NATO and the US's NSC had anticipated that secular parties would decide to form a new legislature, the House of

Representatives, and that Islamists would form another one? Where did the Islamist's Libya Dawn coalition come from? Did anyone making the decision to invade Libya and depose Qaddafi think that one result might be competing and warring governments, neither of which controls more than a fraction of the country? A prospective "peace agreement" virtually guarantees a political stalemate in Libya that further empowers militias, jihadists and ISIS, and feeds continuing instability in Libya and the region. Any agreement that explicitly or implicitly conveys sovereignty to either competing government in Libya probably will backfire. Realistically, neither rival "government" can act on Libya's behalf.

A UNSMIL-brokered "peace settlement" also will have to define the future roles of the Central Bank and the National Oil Corporation and somehow reconcile the conflicting interests of the US, UK and Italy, Saudi, Turkey, Qatari, the Emirates and, not least of all, Egypt. Realistically is there any hope for creating a stable civil society in Libya, disarming and delegitimizing militias and bringing them into a national military structure or is Libya likely to become its own version of chaotic Afghanistan, Iraq or Somalia?

Although still being vigorously debated by academics, national security analysts and others today, and no doubt also within the CIA and NSC, the US intervention in Libya to remove Qaddafi probably was based on false premises and failed intelligence, for which the Obama administration and the US intelligence community are largely responsible. Former Secretary of State Hillary Clinton claimed credit on behalf of the Obama administration for the "successful" outcome in Libya. The fact that she and her NSC colleagues believed that the intervention in Libya was a success probably will come up many times in the 2016 presidential campaign, in addition to what happened in Washington and Benghazi that led to the deaths of US diplomats and CIA staff.

Seven months after the UN Security Council passed Resolution 1973, in March 2011, militias and extremists had taken over Libya. When President Obama authorized military intervention in Libya, the goal was to save lives: "We knew that if we waited one more day, Benghazi—a city nearly the size of Charlotte—could suffer a massacre that would have reverberated across the region and stained the conscience of the world," In 2012, the US and NATO both declared that NATO's operation in Libya was a model intervention." In the Rose Garden, Obama declared: "Without putting a single US service member on the ground, we achieved our objectives." Obama's intervention in Libya, however, proved to be a failure that produced death, destruction and a failed state, and created a safe haven for vicious militias affiliated with Al-Qaeda and ISIS.

The intervention in Libya by the US and its allies was another classic illustration of failed intelligence and strategic misjudgment. Most important, neither the US nor NATO had a post-Qaddafi plan for regime change in Libya in 2011. Congress and the American public still have not seen one to this day. In retrospect the conviction that intervention in Libya would provide the underpinnings of and lead to some form of "democracy" seems absurd. Likewise, that intervention by the US and its allies would stop or prevent large-scale killings and other human rights abuses or would combat terrorism in Libya.

Was there any way of predicting that Islamists would dominate the first post-war parliament, the General National Congress? Was there a US/NATO plan for disarming Islamist and many other militias that had arisen during NATO's seven-month intervention? Was there any expectation in planning the Libya intervention that rival tribes would engage in violent turf wars? What were expectations for the outcome of Islamist rivalries in eastern Libya where most of the country's oil is located? Did anyone in the NSC or NATO make a persuasive case in 2011, on humanitarian grounds, for not intervening in Libya at all in order to prevent even more chaos and bloodshed?

Hard to imagine but it was only three years ago that more or less democratic elections in Libya brought to power a moderate, secular coalition government. At the time, advocates for removing Qaddafi, after four decades of dictatorship, prematurely celebrated. Who in NATO and NSC planning for Qaddafi's overthrow anticipated the possibility that Libya's first elected prime minister might not last in office (Mustafa Abu Shagour lasted less than one month in office)? That's an important question because, among other reasons, the answer might reveal some insights into why, in spite of the US/NATO's good intentions, Libya has had seven prime ministers in less than four years.

Was there any discussion in the NSC about the possibility that Islamist influence was likely to grow strong within Libya's government? Was there a backup plan in the event that the US/NATO could not or should not train Libyan troops (which was decided in the spring of 2014)? Was there any contingency plan to deal with the possibility of violent reprisals by rebels against Qaddafi's supporters? Was there any consideration of the possibility of such violence resulting in large numbers of displaced persons and refugees trying to escape the country (conservatively estimated thus far at roughly 400,000 Libyans)? What has been the NATO/US response to the economic and humanitarian impact on Libyans of their intervention decision?

In addition to all of these questions, the overarching question for the US/NATO and lessons learned from the 2011 intervention in Libya is: did the US intelligence community speculate about the potential for unintended consequences of the US/NATO intervention in Libya in terms of a significant escalation of violence and death toll, national and local political and economic disruption, population dislocation, and Libya providing a terrorist haven?

Another question for US/NATO decision-makers should have been the potential impact on future nuclear disarmament negotiations of taking out Qaddafi, in 2003, who had voluntarily halted his nuclear and chemical weapons programs and surrendered his arsenals to the United States. Seeing that Qaddafi's reward for disarmament cooperation was a US-led regime change, how might the leadership of Iran and North Korea respond to US efforts to negotiate with them for nuclear disarmament?

Did US/NATO decision-makers think about the potential impact of removing Qaddafi on Assad's government and Syrian rebels in terms of their expectations for a similar invention in Syria and their respective responses? What did the US/NATO have in mind when they obtained a no-fly zone in Libya, with UN Security Council approval (including Russia), and then bombing Libya afterwards, virtually guaranteeing Russian antagonism to UN intervention in Syria?

What have the Obama administration and its NSC learned from the failed intervention in Libya? What lessons learned in Libya apply to, for example, Syria, other than that intervention to quash a dictator can backfire and pave the way for an even more violent civil war and deadly consequences for the population?

Libya's recent past exemplifies the messy situation in the Middle East in which corrupt, dictatorial governments of questionable legitimacy, often financed by an abundance of energy resources, afflicted by sectarian religious conflicts and secular rivalries, implode under the stress of interventions and release all of their latent religious and secular antagonisms, empowering either Sunnis or Shiite Muslims and, in the process, further empowering and triggering Iranian or Saudi interventions.

Regime change in Libya, Iraq and Egypt produced these kinds of results. None of these countries were anywhere near ready for transitions to "democracy." In retrospect it's amazing that anyone in Washington could dream up scenarios in which the removal of Egypt's President Hosni Mubarak or Libya's Muammar al-Qaddafi, especially without effective followup plans, would create situations beneficial to their countries and would not lead to increasing domination by military forces, militias, ISIS or other terrorists or governments operating without any pretentions of democracy.

The civil war in Libya understandably is not near the top of US foreign policy issues in the 2016 presidential campaign. It probably will not make it into presidential debates except perhaps for a trick question, for example, who are Libya's two competing governments (answer: Libya Dawn and The House of Representatives) or perhaps what is UNSMIL (answer: United

Nations Support Mission in Libya). Part of the reason for Libya's undeserved low foreign policy priority is that negotiations for any peace deal under UNSMIL auspices between Libya Dawn and the House of Representative are continuously on the verge of collapse and, more important, no one involved really is sure of what a Plan A or Plan B consist of as mediated solutions. With current negotiations between opposing parties in a stalemate, it's time to get the international community, and especially Saudi, Egypt, Qatar, Turkey, the United Arab Emirates and, of course, the US to the negotiating table for as long as it takes.

Lessons learned in Libya are highly relevant today because they highlight the complexity of decisions about the fate of dictators in countries involved in civil wars. After the United States supported the ouster of President Bashar al-Assad, nothing was done to bring it about, which demoralized potential Syrian allies and helped ISIS to flourish. In Afghanistan, Iraq, Syria and Libya, the gap between US rhetoric and consistent followup action has reinforced America's reputation for unpredictability and unreliability among local leaders and most citizens.

This is especially problematic in Middle East countries where sticking one's neck out frequently results in getting one's head cut off. US strategic and tactical policy choices in the Middle East have raised doubts about the judgment of US military and national security policy makers. The persistent gap between US promises, commitments, threats and actions raises significant doubts about US reliability as a partner against the Taliban, ISIS, and other threats to "nation-building" and stability in the Middle East.

Turbulence and disorder in Libya, Syria, Afghanistan, Yemen and elsewhere in the Middle East is likely to increase rather than diminish. Realistically, bad situations in the Middle East will become worse before they get better. It should be assumed that the struggle against ISIS and other extremist groups is likely to be difficult, expensive, and very long. Announcement of dates for accomplishing military and civil changes should be jettisoned, like the dates when US forces are due to exit any country. American presidents, and presidential candidates, should inform and educate the American people about the nation's aims for the Middle East and discuss reasonable and restrained interventions that are based on what this nation has learned from interventions in countries like Libya. A vastly better job needs to be done on planning humanitarian aid, especially when it can be predicted that intervention is likely to fuel violent civil war. The price for overthrowing an awful dictator should not be the death and displacement of countless innocent civilians.

CHAPTER 16

Terrorism Threats from Central America & Mexico

In the fall of 2015 the number of families illegally crossing the US border more than doubled over the same period in 2014, including more unaccompanied children. More than 5,000 families were caught. The number of families and unaccompanied children not caught of course is unknown. Smugglers apparently have figured out alternative routes in more remote US-Mexico border areas patrolled by fewer border patrol agents. The surge in illegal crossings is especially driven by violence and transnational criminal groups in El Salvador, and elsewhere in Central America and parts of Mexico. The homicide rate in El Salvador is the highest of any country in the world not engaged in war. At the same time, asylum-seekers in Mexico are at all time highs according to a recent UN report.

The US and Turkey have established an "ISIS-free zone" along the Turkey-Syria border. The US-Mexico border has no comparable "ISIS-free zone." In fact, although verification is difficult, ISIS recruits are flowing through the porous Mexico-US-Texas border with the help of Mexican cartels such as the Sinaloa Cartel and the recently established Jaslisco New Generation Drug Cartel (CJNG). Most of the recent publicity about the Sinaloa Cartel has focused on the escape from prison of Chapo Guzman, the Sinaloa Cartel's leader. What we don't see is news about collaboration between Mexican cartels and ISIS to penetrate the US border.

We hear a great deal about ISIS in the Middle East but not enough about the continuous penetration of the Texas-Mexico border by would-be terrorists, including ISIS, drug cartels, organized crime and transnational criminals, which has been documented by the US Intelligence Community, the Texas Department of Public Safety, the US Department of Homeland Security, and other law enforcement sources. Mexico's cartels operate throughout Texas in human smuggling and drug (heroin, meth and marijuana) trafficking. Human trafficking of children and women from Central America and Mexico is highly profitable. Violent transnational criminal gangs such as MS-13 have a stronghold in Texas.

Mexican drug cartels smuggling foreigners from countries with terrorist links into small Texas towns is not new. It has been going on for years. In 2011, as part of a study prepared for the Texas Department of Agriculture, my colleagues and I in the San Antonio-based Colgen consulting company documented that large numbers of foreigners, classified as Special Interest Aliens (SIA), had been entering the US along the Texas-Mexico border for years, including members of known Islamist terrorist organizations. What is new, however, are unsubstantiated reports that cartels have been moving ISIS members into rural border areas of Texas and New Mexico to conduct reconnaissance of military, energy, educational and other facilities.

In May 2015, Gen. John Kelly, commander of the US Southern Command (Southcom), warned US lawmakers that Sunni extremists are radicalizing Muslims in Latin America and that ISIS may be exploiting drug and human trafficking networks in the region to infiltrate the United States. Gen. Kelly's observations corresponded with findings and conclusions of the Colgen study that included interviews with dozens of sheriffs along the Mexico-Texas border and Texas Rangers engaged in special operations in the border region.

In addition to documented evidence of the presence of the Lebanese terror group Hezbollah among SIAs, the Southcom commander told the Senate Armed Services Committee that Iran had established more than 80 "cultural centers" in the Latin American region in an effort to promote Shiite Islam. Among the thousands of Central Americans fleeing poverty and violence crossing the border, according to Gen. Kelley "foreign nationals from countries like Somalia, Bangladesh, Lebanon, and Pakistan are using the region's human smuggling networks to enter the United States." Gen. Kelly added that in addition to Sunni jihadists in Latin America radicalizing converts and other Muslims in the region, they are "providing financial and logistical support to designated terrorist organizations within and outside Latin America."

Iran has been seeking closer ties with governments in Latin America in an effort to circumvent sanctions. When sanctions are lifted, those Iranian outreach efforts can be expected to increase significantly. Gen. Kelly stated that the high level of trafficking and sophistication of the smuggling networks makes it easy for drug cartels in Latin America to smuggle terrorists and weapons of mass destruction into the US. "While there is not yet any indication that the criminal networks involved in human and drug trafficking are interested in supporting the efforts of terrorist groups, these networks could unwittingly, or even wittingly, facilitate the movement of terrorist operatives or weapons of mass destruction toward America's border with Mexico, potentially undetected and almost completely unrestricted."

Very few analysts of the Middle East talk much about the connection between Lebanon, Hezbollah and drug cartels in Mexico, Central America and South America. Hezbollah usually is discussed, as in this book, as a proxy of Iran supporting Assad's regime and also as a presence in the Gulf and other countries around the globe. The Lebanon- money laundering – Hezbollah - drug cartel – Zeta connection story could be of more importance for US national security than the US government and media has recognized. The US intelligence community has not revealed much about Hezbollah-drug cartel connections but what little has been revealed by the Department of Homeland Security (DHS) suggests that, in the future, it is a potentially serious national security issue.

Lebanon is an important financial hub for banking activities in the Middle East and eastern Mediterranean. As one of the more sophisticated banking sectors in the region, according to a report by the US State Department's Bureau of International Narcotics and Law Enforcement Affairs, "Lebanon faces significant money laundering and terrorism financing challenges." The report discusses Lebanon's substantial influx of remittances from expatriate workers and family members, estimated by the World Bank at approximately $7.3 billion annually over the last four years. However, the report, without citing sources, suggests that a number of the Lebanese working abroad are involved in "underground finance and trade-based money laundering (TBML) activities."

Neither the World Bank nor US intelligence and law enforcement agencies have any idea about the amount of money from international criminal activities that is laundered through Lebanon, including from Mexican and Central American drug cartels, but they estimate that it far exceeds remittances from expatriates. They also know that Lebanon's banks are connected to an international cybercrime network of money laundering operations in which Hezbollah is a hub. Although the United States has designated Hezbollah as a terrorist organization, the Government of Lebanon does not recognize this designation.

Over a period of decades, Lebanese expatriates in South America and also Africa have established financial systems outside of formal financial sectors in order to facilitate money laundering. Hezbollah started its infiltration of Latin America already in the mid-1980s in the Tri-Border Area along the lawless frontiers of Argentina, Brazil and Paraguay. From this base deep in the heart of South America, Hezbollah launched money-laundering, counterfeiting, piracy and drug trafficking. According to a 2009 Rand Corporation report, Hezbollah was netting around $20 million a year in the area. Hezbollah wanted to create revenue sources independent of Iran that at the time was giving Hezbollah as much as $200 million a year. Iran wanted more control in return for financing than Hezbollah was prepared to accept.

The flood of drugs and money and the crime waves and violence in Central American countries have intensified with the arrival of the Zetas cartel in 2008. Invited to Guatemala by local cartels to provide protection, the Zetas soon began taking over the territory for themselves. At that time, Mexican cartels also started to pay their collaborators on the ground in drugs instead of cash – creating a boom in local drug sales and violent street crime. Any cartel that wants to do business in Guatemala has to pay an extortion fee to the Zetas. Guatemala is a failed state. Over the last three decades, organized crime and drug cartels have infiltrated politics through money and violence. A mix of corrupt politicians, businesses and organized crime work together on various interests in ad hoc networks. Election campaigns are bought and sold. The availability of dirty money, the lack of regulations and transparency allows corruption to dominate in Guatemala.

Hezbollah wanted to recruit Lebanese expatriates and other Muslim populations. Brazil and Argentina had the largest Muslim populations in South America, with more than 1 million members each. Venezuela had more than 100,000 Muslims, mostly of Lebanese and Syrian descent. During this time, Hezbollah became involved in the drug trade through the Revolutionary Armed Forces (FARC) of Colombia. US intelligence sources indicated that, with help from drug cartels and Hezbollah's involvement, many Lebanese and Syrians from South America entered Mexico illegally. In Mexico and Central America after 2008, Hezbollah formed a strong connection with the Zetas cartel and facilitated money laundering, not just in Lebanon but also other countries where it had a footprint. For both Iran, during its sanctions, and Hezbollah, the entire region south of the US border has been ideal for expanding sources of funding and recruits.

South of the US border, the scale of atrocities committed by Mexican drug cartels dwarfs those of ISIS in the Middle East. A recent United Nations report estimated nearly 9,000 civilians were killed and 17,386 wounded in Iraq in 2014. Assuming that ISIS was responsible for a large number of these deaths and wounded people, and another several thousand deaths in Syria, these numbers are far surpassed by drug cartel murders in Mexico, the way that people were brutally murdered, and the tens of thousands of kidnapped children used as assassins or on suicide missions, as drug mules, prostitutes and other forms of depravity. And the atrocities committed in Central America are much worse than in Mexico.

With 677 murders, June 2015 posted El Salvador's highest monthly number of homicides since the civil war ended in 1992. Murders in July dropped to "only" 350, but that still means someone is murdered every two hours in El Salvador rather than every hour. Brutality and savagery in El Salvador is comparable to Islamic terrorism in the Middle East, arguably much worse. Criminals in El Salvador hang, decapitate, burn, chop up, and play soccer with the heads of victims. Like ISIS, gangs in El Salvador use terrorism to intimidate communities and maintain their control and authority. Honduras is even worse than El Salvador, with the highest homicide rate in the hemisphere.

The main criminal rings in El Salvador, Mara Salvatrucha and Barrio 18, were born on the streets of Los Angeles, formed by thousands of young people who fled to the United States to escape the violent civil war in El Salvador that began in 1979. When that civil war abated in the early 1990s, the United States deported thousands of the LA gangsters who simply regrouped in El Salvador to fight one another for control of drug markets and territory in their homeland.

El Salvador's President Salvador Sanchez Ceren moved some gang leaders out of maximum-security prisons to lock-ups closer to their families and extended more privileges to them as part of a cease-fire agreement. Recently he moved them back and launched a crackdown against an estimated 60,000 gang members terrorizing the nation of 6 million. The latest body count in El Salvador is the result of not just gang-on-gang violence but a mounting "small scale war" between the government and the gangs. Gangs are trying to force the government to let up on its crackdown, and President Ceren has not been cooperating.

Consequently, gangs in El Salvador have been sending a violent message to the government by targeting the capital's public transportation system. In July 2015 the media was full of stories about gangs in El Salvador attacking and killing public transportation workers. Around El Salvador, government forces are outnumbered by gang members and gangs control some parts of the country. People are fleeing El Salvador to the United States to escape the violence. Last year, there was a surge of unaccompanied minors arriving at the US border from Mexico, many of them from Central America trying to escape gang warfare. The outflow to the US also included members of Mara Salvatrucha (MS-13) and Barrio 18 that today can be found in every part of the US.

In addition to ramping up relationships with powerful political, criminal and economic players, Sinaloa and Los Zetas cartels have established relationships with countless Central American street gangs. The two biggest gangs in the region, MS-13 and Calle 18, are loosely organized around local cliques. Mexican cartels have relationships at varying levels of closeness with different cliques. These gangs have multiplied and migrated within the region. Many have also returned to the United States. US authorities estimate that MS-13 and Calle 18 have a presence in as many as 42 states.

The gang phenomenon in the El Salvador-Guatemala-Honduras triangle, and proposed US interventions, need to be viewed and understood in its historical perspective. In June 2011, Secretary of State Hillary Rodham Clinton promised that the US government would spend nearly $300 million helping governments in Central America confront the mafias that smuggle cocaine to American consumers. "The United States will back you," she said at a regional summit held in Guatemala City. "We know demand for drugs rests mostly in my own country."

On a visit to El Salvador in March 2011, President Obama said the United States would provide $200 million to fight the street gangs and drug traffickers that left the region with the highest homicide rates in the world. Clinton acknowledged that the murder rates in Central America surpass even the incredibly violent civil war levels in Guatemala, Nicaragua and El Salvador in the 1980s and 1990s. Even more importantly, Clinton said: "We know the wave of violence also threatens our own country."

The announcements by President Obama and Sec. Clinton represented a repackaging of money dedicated to other programs, reflecting heightened concern among US officials that the extremely fragile so-called "democracies" of Central America were struggling unsuccessfully with surging criminality fueled by the movement of drugs north and weapons south. The former Department of Homeland Security (DHS) Sec. Napolitano, however, denied that "spillover violence" was occurring along the US Mexico border. She never discussed the potential threat of violence in Mexico and Central America for national security in the United States, even as the US Department of Justice documented, and made public in great detail, the threat of transnational criminal organizations and drug-financed gangs in virtually every city in America and their suburbs.

The United States has long played an important, complex role in Latin America. In the early 20th century, US policy in the Western Hemisphere was characterized by the extension of US economic and military control over the region. The United States used the first several decades of the 20th century to ensure that Central America -- and by extension the Caribbean -- was under US control. After World War II, Central America became a proxy battleground between the United States and the Soviet Union. On a strategic level, Central America is far enough away from the United States (thanks to being buffered by Mexico) and made up of small enough countries that it does not pose a direct threat to the United States.

The majority of money spent combating drug trafficking from South America to the United States over the past decade has been spent in Colombia on monitoring air and naval traffic in the Caribbean and off the Pacific coasts, though the US focus has now shifted to Mexico. Central America, by contrast, has languished since the Reagan years, when the United States allocated more than $1 billion per year to Central America. It's possible that endemic narco-fed corruption and violence in Central America gets less attention than Islamic extremism in the Middle East because neither religion nor ideology are drivers in the Triangle states.

When the United States attends "summit" events with leaders of Mexico or Central America to discuss their conflicted relationships, the pattern of rhetoric at each event is familiar. The US, as the world's largest consumer of drugs, most of which are shipped from Mexico and Central America, joins these Latin American "transit countries" in announcing plans, projects and funding for professionalizing their police forces, training judges, reforming corrupt prison systems, sharing intelligence and equipment, and trying to divert poor young people away from lives of crime.

Another summit resulted in another plan – the "Alliance for Prosperity." President Obama and leaders from Central and Latin American nations met in Panama City for the Summit of the Americas on April 10th, 2015. The US already had stated in 2014 that it intended to fund social and economic projects in Guatemala, Honduras, and El Salvador through an "Alliance for Prosperity in the Northern Triangle" Program, and it was part of the 2016 US fiscal budget. The program includes a $1 billion fund primarily focused on promoting human rights, assisting the 40,000 unaccompanied children that crossed into the US in 2014, and a variety of other measures to improve Central American governments. The Alliance for Prosperity, however, was most likely to provide opportunities for large businesses, including American-owned corporations, to benefit from the $1 billion plan.

At a recent summit event in Guatemala, the seven countries of Central America proposed 22 projects costing about $900 million. "For us, it is the difference between life and death," said Guatemalan President Alvaro Colom. He said the United States and other "consumer countries" in Europe owe support to "transit countries." Colom said that Central America spends $4 billion in security-related costs but that last year, despite pledges of almost $1 billion from the United States, Europe, the World Bank and other donors, only $140 million in aid actually was delivered. Another familiar pattern associated with hemispheric leadership summits is that commitments for financial support are made to "transit countries" that later usually are not fulfilled.

Luis Alberto Moreno, president of the Inter-American Development Bank, said the fund would spend $500 million over the next two years supporting the Central American plan. "They are working together, in a serious way — this is an important part of the story," Moreno said. Mexican President Felipe Calderon made one of the most revealing statements: "What would happen if Mexico or Central America were to the north of the United States? We would not be sitting here today." Calderon's obvious reference was to the fact that the main source of cocaine for US consumption was from South America. Instead of the more benign term "transit route," Calderon referred to the trafficking route for cocaine from South America through Central America and Mexico to the US border as "a highway of death." Today the "highway of death" conveys a great deal more heroin northward to the United States.

Calderon went on to say that the US and other "consumer countries" should give the same amount of money to "transit countries" that the drug cartels make from their illegal trade -- roughly and conservatively about $35 billion a year. Sec. Clinton countered by saying that the private sector in Central America should contribute more. "The businesses and the rich in each ["transit"] country must pay their fair share of taxes," she said. In part Clinton was referring to the fact that the region has some of the lowest rates of tax payments in the world.

President Mauricio Funes of El Salvador said that the Zetas crime mafia was trying to bribe elite police units in his country with $5,000 monthly payments to steal guns and grenades from the armed forces. Honduran President Porfirio Lobo said, "Our democracies have never been so vulnerable," and reiterated that gang members in his country far outnumber police officers and soldiers.

Leaders at the Central American summit were well aware of the fact that, whether measured by increased public safety, reduction of the supply of illegal drugs on the US market, or the dismantling of drug trafficking organizations, the war on drugs in their countries and in the US was failing. Arrests of drug kingpins and lesser cartel figures set off violent turf wars, with no discernible effect on illicit drug flows northward. The murder of politicians, threats to civilians and disruption of daily life have furthered the downward spiral in Mexico and in Central America.

Central America has been experiencing not only increasing levels of crime but the prospect of heightened competition from Mexican drug cartels in the region. From the 1970s to 2011, the shifting geography of drug transit has doomed Central America to become the route of necessity for drug cartels. The US military shut down of Caribbean drug transit routes empowered Mexico's cartels, leading to the Mexican government's crackdown that forced Mexican drug trafficking organizations (DTOs) to diversify transit routes to Central America as the middleman for South American suppliers and Mexican buyers.

When Colombian President Santos told his Central American counterparts not to lose heart and Secretary of State Hillary Clinton held up Plan Colombia as a model for Mexico, every leader present at the Summit knew that, at least up to that point, the drug war didn't work in Columbia either. After a full decade and $7 billion dollars invested in Plan Colombia, regional drug production remained stable and smaller paramilitary groups have replaced the large cartels as traffickers. Some violent crimes, such as kidnappings, went down but corruption deepened. Furthermore, militarization left Colombia with one of the worst human rights records in the hemisphere. And not unlike Mexico, US military involvement in Colombia's drug war was viewed within the country and among its neighbors as a threat to regional self-determination.

The problem facing US policy-makers, drug production and "transit countries" has been that the regional drug war has proven to be unwinnable. As long as an incredibly lucrative market for drugs exists in the US, the cartels will find ways to serve it. Cocaine? Heroin? Meth? Doesn't matter. Eliminating drug cartel leaders and operatives has merely diversified and redistributed the business within flexible cartel structures with new leaders and expanding criminal gang networks that draw from a virtually inexhaustible pool of young men and women who would rather "die young and rich than old and poor."

In the meantime, US taxpayers are asked to spend billions to deal with transnational organized crime problems outside of US borders when, based on US Department of Justice data, cartel-related transnational crime proliferates inside US borders. Rarely do we hear anything about Washington rethinking its drug war or border security strategy. For example, shifting the drug war to an all-out effort to "follow the money" -- attacking the financial structures of transnational criminal organizations that launder billions of illicit dollars through mainstream US and international financial institutions and businesses. London is the money-laundering capital of the world and its international banks, like HSBC, have been the preferred conduit for hundreds of billions in dirty money from Mexican cartels.

Tens of billions in illicit cash in bulk and electronic forms flowing from Mexico to the international banking system and southward from the US to Mexico, Central and South America have fueled further empowerment of cartels as they take over these countries and establish "dual sovereignty" primarily for the purpose of increasing profits and not for political or ideological reasons. If drug cartels were proclaimed "Communists" or "Islamists," the US government would be rapidly mobilizing for defense of national security. The enemy, however, is just well- organized and highly successful transnational criminal capitalists exploiting their political, financial and paramilitary advantages.

One of the main differences between cartels and traditional multinationals is that the business activities of cartels generate enormous numbers of displaced persons in their business territories in addition to profits from narcotics and other illicit manufacturing and trade. Hundreds of thousands of people have been displaced in Mexico alone because of drug violence. According to a recent study, about half of them may have taken refuge in the United States. Call these people *narco-refugees*.

Neither Mexican nor Central American governments compile statistics on people who have had to leave their homes because of turf battles between drug gangs or because they are driven off their land by cartels that want to use it for drug production, storage or distribution purposes. An estimated 5 million people were displaced by decades of drug- and guerrilla-war violence in Colombia. A comparable exodus probably has occurred in Mexico and Central American countries. A great many of these *narco-refugees* are part of human trafficking or other illegal immigration along the US border.

Many of these *narco-refugees* didn't have to travel far to escape drug war mayhem. For example, a 2010 census reported as uninhabited 61 percent of the 3,616 homes in Praxedis G. Guerrero, a border township in the Rio Grande Valley east of Ciudad Juarez, adjoining El Paso. Violent turf battles between the Juarez and Sinaloa cartels forced them to leave in order to save their lives. This census also found that 111,103 of the 488,785 homes in violence-wracked Ciudad Juarez were abandoned or about 23 percent, and almost one-third of the 160,171 houses in Reynosa were unoccupied. The startling census figure for Mexico as a whole was 14 percent of homes uninhabited! These kinds of statistics don't create headlines in the US media but may be more significant than most other cartel news.

Mexican drug cartels now operate virtually uninhibited in Central America. US-supported crackdowns in Mexico and Colombia have only pushed traffickers into a region where corruption is rampant, borders lack even minimal immigration controls and local gangs provide a ready-made infrastructure for organized crime. Drugs and other illicit goods moving through Central America from the coca-growing countries of Colombia, Peru and Bolivia require aircraft and watercraft transport since overland travel is virtually impossible through the swampy jungle region along the Panamanian-Colombian area known as the Darien Gap. This accounts for Honduras becoming a major destination for planes from Venezuela laden with cocaine heading for the Honduran-Guatemalan border and then through the largely unpopulated Peten department to Mexico.

The northern province of Peten has long been a strategic drug-trafficking zone with jungle landing strips used by several cartels. It has one of the highest murder rates in Guatemala. Both the Zetas and Mexico's Sinaloa cartel have interests in the Peten. Their competition for territory is accompanied by murder, extortion, kidnapping and other violent crimes. By comparison with the Middle East, media in the US and the rest of the world does not seem to be paying much attention to the violence associated with drug trafficking occurring in Central American countries, especially in the "Northern Triangle" of Guatemala, El Salvador and Honduras. El Salvador's homicide rate has increased to 66 per 100,000 inhabitants; Guatemala's homicide rate is estimated at 50 per 100,000 inhabitants; and Honduras is 77 per 100,000 inhabitants. By comparison, Mexico's murder rate, that gets most media attention, is "only" 18 per 100,000.

The governments in each triangle country know what needs to be done to confront violence and criminality. For example, on July 16, 2015, El Salvador's National Council on Citizen Security (CNSCC) officially launched "Secure El Salvador": the government's new security strategy that on paper looks comprehensive and impressive but, in addition to lacking provisions for dealing with corruption, the question remains whether political leaders have the will to implement it. As for the United States and international groups, they have been spending hundreds of millions working with Central American countries to build national and regional programs to deal with cartels, organized crime and corruption, without much success.

The bloody eruption of Mexican-led cartels in Guatemala and other Central American countries is only the latest chapter in a vicious cycle of violence and institutional failure. The misfortune of geography has placed these countries midway between Colombia and the US-- the world's biggest consumer of drugs and one of the world's biggest producers, Columbia. Cocaine and now increasingly ingredients for synthetic drugs flow into this Central American intersection by air, land and sea and from there into Mexico en route to the US. The curse and blessing of vast acreages in cool highlands provide an ideal climate for massive poppy cultivation. Weapons are plentiful thanks to a long history of lenient gun laws and arms smuggling. An impoverished, underemployed population provides a ready source of recruits.

What more could Mexican cartels ask for? Still recovering from decades of political violence and military rule, Central America provides fertile territory for cartel rule by force, extortion, and bribery. Cartels thrive on endemic social and economic inequities, without advocating any political philosophy to exploit them, just unlimited cash, violence and corruption associated with drug trafficking. An indecisive and politically conflicted US government and an international community preoccupied with fiscal and monetary crises and terrorism in the Middle East provide the perfect context for cartels to establish dual sovereignties in Central American nations without much focused attention and opposition.

Local gangs and common criminals can operate with brazen impunity and flourish under these conditions along with drug traffickers. Their opposition consists of demoralized police forces, intimidated or corrupted judicial systems and a fearful population that over the past decade has seen the homicide rate double, youth gangs terrorize their neighborhoods, and politicians who have neither the strategy nor the means to establish the rule of law.

Citizens in Central American countries also have countless reasons and personal histories to cause them to be cynical about their governments fostering the rule of law. For decades they have experienced the state itself being the most prolific violator of human and democratic rights. During the 36-year conflict that ended with the peace accords of 1996, the armed forces murdered dissidents in urban areas and razed villages suspected of harboring guerrilla forces. In recent years, after barely starting to recover from years of political violence, Guatemalans see control of the South American drug trade shifting from Colombia to Mexico and its cartels, thereby multiplying local illegal activities and violence, especially in coastal and border departments, where traffickers and gangs have diversified into other activities, such as prostitution, extortion, kidnapping, human trafficking and countless licit and illicit businesses.

With little opposition from under-resourced and often corrupt local police and judicial authorities, these drug trafficking entrepreneurs of every description finance opium poppy cultivation that provides impoverished indigenous communities with greater monetary income than they have ever known, but at a terrible price in Guatemala and other Central American states. Increased involvement by Mexican cartels in Central America inevitably has affected the region's politico-economic structures, a process most visible in Guatemala. Its territory spans Central America, making it one of several choke points in the supply chain of illicit goods coming north from El Salvador and Honduras bound for Mexico.

Guatemala has a complex and competitive set of criminal organizations, many of which are organized around tight-knit family units. First rising to prominence in trade and agriculture, these families control significant businesses in Guatemala and transportation routes for shipping both legal and illicit goods. The relationship of these criminal organizations to Mexican drug cartels is murky at best. The Sinaloa and Los Zetas cartels are both known to have relationships with Guatemalan organized criminal groups.

Though Mexican and Central American gangs are truly transnational, their emphasis is on controlling localized urban turfs. They effectively control large portions of Guatemala City, Guatemala; Tegucigalpa, Honduras; and San Salvador, El Salvador. Competition within and among these gangs is responsible for a great deal of the violence in these three countries. Though limited in their ties to the Mexican cartels, the prevalence of MS-13 and Calle 18 in the Northern Triangle states

225

and their extreme violence makes them a force to be reckoned with, for both the cartels and Central American governments.

In the future, dealing effectively with political, military and economic corruption in Central America is central to its transformation, not just change. The challenge is somehow rolling-back decades of US- and Western-backed dictatorships in Central America, that included the overthrow of democratically elected heads of state that were replaced by corrupt US-compliant regimes. How will the Alliance for Prosperity, for example, contribute to undoing the mutually beneficial relationships among cartels, corporations and national politicians?

House and Senate versions of the Alliance for Prosperity (also named the "US Strategy for Central American Engagement") do more than promote foreign investment in El Salvador, Honduras and Guatemala with the help from the Inter-American Development Bank (IDB). The bills significantly increase funding for the Central America Regional Security Initiative (CARSI) to improve border security, counter the activities of criminal gangs, drug traffickers, and organized crime, and also include anti-migrant conditions, including the militarization of regional borders to stop migrants and asylum-seekers from leaving their countries of origin. In the Senate version, funds would be withheld until Central American governments sufficiently combat corruption.

At the risk of perhaps sounding too cynical, it is likely that dirty money and corruption of politicians and law enforcement that have plagued Central American countries will continue to do so regardless of the party in power and legislation passed by Congress. The US cannot depend on either Mexico or Central America for dealing effectively with political and corporate corruption, narco-traffickers, human rights abuses and other problems in order to prevent ISIS or other Islamic terrorists from entering the United States through the Mexican border. The few ISIS fighters that have been caught crossing the Mexican border into Texas, as reported by the US Customs and Border Protection (CBP) agency, are a sufficient warning that the 1,933-mile southern border has to be secured. Terrorism infiltrating into the US, however, may not be the most concerning aspect of a porous southern border, but it's all a matter of how terrorism is defined.

For the American public the number of criminal aliens in the US from Mexico, Central America and dozens of other countries that are committing felony and violent crimes in "sanctuary cities" (i.e., have policies and practices designed to shelter illegal immigrants) and other US political jurisdictions amounts to de facto being terrorized and subjected to terrorism. There are more than 276 sanctuary cities in 43 states and the District of Columbia. These cities released more than 9,000 illegal immigrants with criminal records in the past year, more than 2000 of whom were rearrested for criminal activities. The threat of ISIS infiltration into the US across the border with Mexico is not to be underestimated. But the inundation of American cities by criminal aliens and penetration by Mexican drug cartels is perceived as even a greater threat. As another profitable business, and for no other apparent reason, drug cartels are creating pathways for terrorists into American society

The US Customs and Border Protection (CBP) agency frequently reports that its agents along the Rio Grande border have arrested "special interest aliens" -- Afghans, Iranians, Iraqis, Syrians, Libyans and Pakistanis -- from 35 countries in Asia and the Middle East that have come to the US-Mexico border knowing that it is porous and to take advantage of its security gaps. CBP and Texas law enforcement officials say seven of the eight major Mexican drug cartels operate throughout Texas and these cartels have sent assassins as far north as the Dallas-Fort Worth area to commit murders, and their drug trade is thriving. The cartels also operate sex trafficking rings in Texas, Georgia, Mississippi, Alabama, Louisiana, Tennessee and several east coast cities. These human smuggling rings with ties to Mexican drug cartels also serve as pathways for SIAs through the nation, as another source of revenue.

The terrorist threat from cartels and international terrorists, including ISIS, is hidden within data on border security from the US Department of Homeland Security (DHS). Based on FY 2014 data from the Office of Immigration Statistics, US Customs and Border Protection (CBP), and US Immigration and Customs Enforcement (ICE), the numbers of apprehensions nationwide of illegal immigrants (486,651) mostly occurred along the southwest border. DHS conducted a total of 577,295 "removals and returns" (414,481 removals and 162,814 returns) that included the removal of convicted criminals. 85 percent of all interior ICE removals and returns in FY 2014 involved individuals who had been previously convicted of a crime, up significantly from FY 2011 when it was just 67 percent. DHS's FY 2014 statistics showed a 68 percent increase in migration from countries "other than Mexico" (OTM), predominately from Central America, and a 14 percent drop in Mexican migration since FY 2013.

Enforcement actions at ports of entry included arrests of 8,013 people wanted for serious crimes, including murder, rape, assault, and robbery. Officers also stopped 223,712 "inadmissible aliens" from entering the United States through ports of entry, an increase of more than 9 percent from FY 2013, including immigration violations, and criminal and national security-related reasons. In addition, CBP officers and agents seized more than 3.8 million pounds of narcotics across the country. Of the 44,905 illegal immigrants apprehended in California, 41,983, or 93 percent, were deemed inadmissible.

Another significant FY 2014 ICE statistic was the increase in the number of state and local law enforcement jurisdictions limiting or declining cooperation with ICE "detainers," which is now more than 275 jurisdictions nationwide. ICE detainers, requested to ensure that dangerous criminals and other "priority individuals" are not released from prisons or jails into US communities, and instead are transferred into ICE custody, show that cities across the nation are refusing to comply with ICE "detainers" issued for illegal immigrants facing robbery and drug-related charges.

For clarification, a "detainer" is the primary tool used by ICE to take custody of criminal aliens for deportation. It is a notice to another law enforcement agency that ICE intends to assume custody of an alien. It includes information on the alien's previous criminal history, immigration violations, and potential risk to public safety or security. Local police in sanctuary cities have the option of not complying with ICE detainers. As of June 2015, the total number of detainers rejected by local sanctuary jurisdictions reportedly had grown to more than 17,000.

When detainers are not honored, ICE must expend additional resources to develop and execute operations to locate and arrest at-large criminal aliens. The point here is that identifying, locating, apprehending, and removing convicted criminal aliens who are at-large in the US has become more difficult for ICE, requiring significantly more officers, time, money, and other resources, and overall removals of criminal aliens have declined, even as national security threats have increased.

Questions can be raised about the accuracy and reliability of statistical reporting by DHS agencies, including ICE, which require tracking individuals from the point of encounter through removal. Currently both ICE and CBP use multiple tracking systems that need to be integrated and significantly upgraded. DHS Secretary Johnson is well aware of the importance of improving the system used to identify, track, and report immigration data accurately across DHS and to share such information with stakeholders and the public. This is especially crucial since cartels in Mexico and throughout Central America are continuously in flux and their involvement with transnational criminals and terrorists appears to be increasing in ways that are not understood by DHS.

The spiking murder (and shooting) rates in sanctuary cities like Chicago, New Orleans, Houston, Baltimore, Milwaukee, St. Louis, Detroit, and others have become one of the most serious domestic US problems in recent years. The more than 200 homicides (and almost 400 nonfatal shootings) in Baltimore, for example, in the first half of 2015 cannot be blamed primarily on cartels, illegal immigrants, or even drugs, but the number of criminal aliens in Baltimore, competition among dealers of illegal drugs and drug-related turf wars are big parts of the city's problems. In Baltimore, about 30-40 people are being murdered each month (more than 200 homicides in 2015 as of August). Baltimore, like many other US cities, is a candidate for a counterinsurgency program focused, as COIN advocates, on dealing with the root causes of the community's problems. Everyone in Baltimore, especially West Baltimore, has known this for at least 50 years, ever since the inception of OEO's "War on Poverty" in 1964.

Much of Metropolitan America is experiencing serious gang activity and crime. At least 35 of the nation's cities have reported increased violent crime, murders or both. While the White House, Congress and the American people focus on the threat of terrorism in the Middle East and spillover to the homeland, the shocking increase in murder rates and violent crime in US cities in 2015 should be a wakeup call to the fact that, whether it's termed "terrorism," "insurgency" or just "street violence," dozens of cities in America are experiencing an unprecedented spike in violence. The number of gangs involved in drug and human trafficking in America has been increasing along with gang-related homicides and access to drugs. Gangs in America are responsible for at least 25 percent of homicides in the nation's larger cities.

In sanctuary cities, most criminal alien offenders released from prisons and jails had prior arrests. One out of four already was a felon. The majority (63 percent) of aliens freed by local law enforcement agencies had serious prior criminal records, many that included violence, assault, weapons, drug distribution or trafficking. Several thousand of these released alien offenders were later arrested multiple times. ICE's controversial Secure Communities Program, that guided ICE and local law enforcement, and that has generated community hostility and many court cases (detainer-based detention that may have violated the 4th Amendment), was replaced in November 2014 by the "Priority Enforcement Program" which targets aliens who pose a threat to national security.

There is simply not enough data to conclude that criminal aliens are contributing significantly to the uptick in murders and other violent crime in the nation's cities. The bottomline, statisticians say, is that there is not enough data to conclude that a new crime wave is upon us or, if in fact there is one, what factors are behind it. The data that we do have indicates that criminal aliens and non-Muslim extremists probably are more of a threat in post-9/11 America than radical Muslims. Twice as many people have been killed by white supremacists and non-Muslim extremists as by radical Muslims, according to *New America*, a Washington research center. According to researchers at the University of North Carolina and Duke University, police and sheriff's departments nationwide agree that, at least for the present time, anti-government and revenge homicides are much greater threats than "Al Qaeda-inspired" violence.

In the meantime, continuing a much publicized trend over the past 18 months, migrants from Central America, including tens of thousands of unaccompanied minors and tens of thousands of adults accompanied by children, have been streaming into the United States along the Southwest boarder, fleeing gang violence, sexual abuse, poverty, and other problems. A growing number, with strong support from the US, are being turned back at Mexico's southern border. Mexican officials stopped nearly 93,000 Central American migrants at their southern border between October 2014 and April of 2015, far exceeding the 49,800 detained in the same period 12 months earlier.

The United States has been investing heavily in security along its southwestern border over the past decade. The Border Patrol has more than 20,000 agents. Its parent agency, Customs and Border Protection (CBP), has seen its budget balloon from $5.9 billion in 2004 to more than $12 billion in 2015. Judging from hearings and reports of the US House Committee on Homeland Security, however, efforts by the US to secure the US-Mexico border have been doing very little to lower the terror threat level in the US, which remains high. None of these US Congressional hearings have projected the longer-term threat to US national security of failed states in Central America that have been attracting terrorists and criminals and arguably have turned the Northern Triangle into a more dangerous region than any Middle East country.

The challenge of preventing criminal aliens and terrorists from entering the US through any of its borders has to be counterbalanced with the challenge of reforming the US immigration system to enable undocumented immigrants to remain legally in the US, provided that they meet certain requirements. The overwhelming majority of Americans believe that it's time for illegal immigrants to come out of the shadows and have a pathway to apply for US citizenship. Although at least half of this country sees immigrants as strengthening the country because of their hard work and talents, that could quickly change if there are any terrorist attacks on American soil committed by illegal immigrants.

PART III

NEXGEN COIN

CHAPTER 17

Next Generation Counterinsurgency (NexGen COIN)

Public opinion polls are what the eye of the beholder makes of them. But they do have some value, especially over time, as benchmarks of perceived changes about where people think life, politics and the world are going. It's only been a year since the media was focused on the Al-Qaeda jihadist group in the Middle East. Since then the US military campaign against ISIS in Iraq and Syria has captured attention from the American public. And now in the aftermath of horrific ISIS terrorist attacks in Paris, polls soon will show that defeating the Islamic State in the Middle East and protecting the US homeland are at the top of the public's concerns.

Based on the latest CNN/ORC poll, the American public is very disturbed and disillusioned, moreso than any time in the past year, by how things have been going in military action against ISIS. The public's worst impression, however, flows from concerns about President Barack Obama's failure to develop a clear and effective plan to deal with ISIS. Just 31% say that military action against ISIS is going well for the US, down from 38% in May and 48% a year ago. More telling, the poll numbers say that opinions about military action against ISIS compare closely with the low point reached in the public's assessment of the military action in Iraq in 2007, when just 28% said that mission was going well.

These public opinion poll numbers, derived from a survey of registered American voters, should send a very clear message to presidential candidates in both parties. Nine in 10 consider ISIS a serious threat to the US. By a wide margin, American voters are more concerned about ISIS than about Iran, China, North Korea or Russia. ISIS is not only viewed as a threat to America, 70% describe ISIS as a "very serious threat," way more than the threat of Iran which was viewed as a "very serious threat" by 44% of those polled.

Reflecting their perceptions and concerns about the growing ISIS threat, the American public appears to be paying close attention to what the White House and its military and national security arms are doing about it. Very few American voters in both parties see Obama as having a clear plan for dealing with ISIS: just 27% think that the White House has a clear plan, while 71% say he does not. The opinion has been worsening over the past year. A year ago, 66% of those polled said Obama lacked a plan for ISIS. Even among Democrats, just 49% say they think Obama has a clear plan for ISIS, down from 56% a year ago. In future polls, after the ISIS attack on Paris, the Obama administration's poll numbers are likely to worsen.

Of course views on the fight against ISIS are sharply divided based on partisanship. Republicans are far more likely than Democrats to see ISIS as a very serious threat (84% among Republicans, 61% among Democrats). Many more Republicans say things are going poorly in the fight against ISIS (80% among Republicans, 50% among Democrats) and overwhelmingly doubt that Obama has a clear plan for dealing with jihadists (96% among Republicans, 48% among Democrats). But the core message about the ISIS threat for presidential candidates in both parties is that basically it crosses party lines and transcends partisan politics.

The partisan gap on how the fight against ISIS is going has closed slightly in the past six months. But not trust for President Obama as commander-in-chief. Half of those polled have distrusted him as commander-in-chief for the entire past year. By a very small margin they agree with Obama on the question of sending ground troops into combat operations against ISIS forces in Iraq and Syria (51% opposed and 46% in favor). There is significant partisan difference on this issue with 62% of Republicans in favor of sending ground troops and 61% of Democrats opposed.

On the matter of Russian military intervention in Syria, Americans are divided on whether it is a problem for the US. Fifty percent call it a crisis or major problem and 50% say it's a minor problem or no problem at all. However, of more concern to American voters than Russian intervention, about three-quarters are worried that US military action against ISIS will develop into a larger war that could spread.

The international terrorism threat from Islamic extremists has grown significantly since the last book that I wrote on the subject at the end of 2003 in the aftermath of 9/11, *Regime Change: National Security in the Age of Terrorism*. Written just before the 2004 presidential election, it consisted of a series of faux speeches and position papers supposedly written and delivered by Sen. John Kerry and his advisors, who was soon to be a presidential candidate. The book definitely was not a partisan pitch for Kerry. Hastily written, the primary motivation for writing the book was fear of another 9/11 catastrophe stemming from my complete lack of confidence in the effectiveness of US intelligence, which has only deepened in the last ten years. The book's main aim was to enable American voters to better understand the most serious national security issues preparatory to Election Day 2004.

As the presidential election of 2016 fast approaches, and faced with a Parisian counterpart of 9/11, the author's aim is basically the same as in 2004, propelled by an even greater sense of urgency. Civil war rages in Syria, supported and inflamed by Iran, Hezbollah, and Russia. Iraq, Yemen, Afghanistan and Libya face escalating insurgencies and turmoil. Al-Qaeda still remains a serious terrorism threat in the Middle East, North Africa and Europe, but in recent years the emergence of the ISIS has taken center stage from Al-Qaeda as the main global terrorism threat. Since 2004, US border security has become a serious national security issue. Infiltration by ISIS, transnational narco-terrorists and criminal aliens crossing the porous US-Mexico border justifiably has become a controversial election issue in 2016.

Regime Change was dedicated to World Trade Center widows, especially four of them, the "Jersey girls," as they came to be known, that with no political background, no axes to grind and no political agenda formed an ad hoc Family Steering Committee for the 9/11 Commission because they "simply wanted to know why our husbands were killed." The "Jersey girls" battling with the 9/11 Commission was only the beginning of a long, contentious, politically-charged war of words, reactions and counter-reactions in Washington and elsewhere in the world struggling, without much success thus far, to cope with increasing terrorism threats.

The main focus of *Regime Change* was decisions made, and mainly not made, by the White House and the US intelligence community pertaining to terrorism threats overseas and to the homeland, Al-Qaeda in Afghanistan, Pakistan's nuclear black market, nuclear threats from Iran and North Korea, and other serious national security issues. Ten years later, all of these national security threats and urgent policy issues have become even more complicated and challenging, and still await effective strategies for resolution. In the meantime, terrorism threats in the Middle East, North Africa, and elsewhere have escalated and morphed into the Islamic State, affiliates of Al-Qaeda and many other dangerous extremist groups.

Development of counterinsurgency strategies continues to be at the forefront of US military and foreign policy planning, much as it was in March 2001 when the National Security Agency (NSA) learned that Osama bin Laden's operatives were planning an "imminent" attack on the US. By the summer of 2001, warnings indicated that terrorists were planning to hijack airplanes. All of these dire warnings about terrorist threats to the homeland in July 2001 immediately went to the Bush White House. No one knows what Commander-in-Chief Bush or his national security staff did with these warnings. Previously, however, for eight months, a classic Washington bureaucratic struggle had been going on to decide who was going to produce a US "counterterrorism" plan.

During this time, $10 billion of the US budget already was being spent on items classified as "counterterrorism." No one in Washington had any idea about what this money was being spent for and the potential short- or long-term benefits. None of these funds was being spent on initiatives to undermine Al-Qaeda in Afghanistan or anywhere else in the world. In 2016, as in 2004, a central issue for voters in the presidential election will be confidence in the judgment of the next president, the nation's Commander-in-Chief, to make the right national security decisions at the right time.

The Commander-in-Chief in the Oval Office, relying heavily on the National Security Council (NSC), is the key strategist and decision-maker in US counterterrorism (COIN) planning. The story of how that counterinsurgency planning actually happens in the military is fascinating, but not at all reassuring. Spurred by Al-Qaeda in Iraq (AQI) and the Taliban in Afghanistan, a series of counterinsurgency manuals were written by Gen. David Petraeus, and significantly influenced by the French officer, David Galula, Lieut. Colonel John Nagle, a protégé of Petraeus at West Point, David Kilcullen, an Aussie who became an assistant to Petraeus, and others that became part of a remarkable inner circle of military, academic and other experts who, for years, strenuously lobbied the Army's bureaucracy, a plethora of agencies, institutes and commands, for a revamped COIN strategy and military culture.

The focus of their frustrating campaign was to persuade a bureaucratic maze, intent on protecting its turf, what the strategic focus of COIN should be: Soldiers and Marines should live among the people and insurgents; they should do their best to keep these people secure and to build trust; and as a result, these presumably grateful locals will supply US forces with vital intelligence needed to find, capture or kill the "enemy." The heart of Petraeus's revised COIN manual, reflecting the sum of his learning and experiences in Iraq and Afghanistan and that of his scholar-soldier colleagues, was that the purpose of all counterinsurgency operations should be Soldiers and Marines collecting intelligence that is combined with a myriad of other US and foreign sources of intelligence for the purpose of analysis and bottom-up decision-making at the frontlines.

So what was so controversial and outrageous about this COIN concept? Simply, it violated core Army doctrine. It placed intelligence (HUMINT or "human intelligence") collection and even analysis in the hands of Soldiers in the frontlines. These Soldiers at the frontlines also had to become "experts" on all key cultural, social, political and other elements at the roots of insurgencies so that US forces could reach out to tribes, clans, ethnic groups, and across sectarian lines to bring insurgents into the US mission, thereby making it their own mission and making it possible to leverage local assets to support COIN. That's the essence of lessons learned in Anbar Province's Great Awakening. The primary "revolutionary" goal of counterinsurgency, therefore, was not to kill all insurgents – the "enemy."

The entire story about writing what became *FM 3-24, Counterinsurgency*, published in 2006, and its aftermath, is told brilliantly by Fred Kaplan in *The Insurgents*. Read it! The author's NexGen COIN in effect adds chapters to the COIN strategy formulated by David Petraeus and his colleagues and supporters. NexGen COIN provides:

- an ISIS update and amplification focused on the Middle East, Libya and Yemen, and also the US border with Mexico;
- more historical reinforcement and analysis of COIN strategy that puts intelligence collection and analysis in the hands of frontline advisors-CyberWarriors who reach out from safe havens, protected by no-fly zones, in order to find, train, protect and partner with local insurgents and also to provide protected environments for displaced persons and refugees;
- the justification for frontline advisors-CyberWarriors who create and manage protected safe havens for insurgents in training and displaced people, and are armed with the latest

cognitive computing, analytics, and Big Data to enhance their capability to collect and analyze US and foreign intelligence for the purpose of bottom-up decision-making.

NexGen COIN proposes that networked safe havens for counterinsurgents fighting ISIS and sheltering displaced persons be planned and managed by frontline advisors in Syria and elsewhere in the Middle East using a cloud-enabled cognitive computing technology platform. These safe havens have to be protected by no-fly zones. NexGen COIN represents a new era in counterinsurgency whereby bottom-up decision-making by frontline advisors utilizes a cloud-based cognitive system that, in real-time, integrates all intelligence and other data from any and every structured and unstructured source of any value for fighting ISIS and that over time continuously learns from all previous activity and interactions. Just as "artificial intelligence" or "AI" is being commercialized across a variety of industries, NexGen COIN will include "AI" that serves the gamut of battlefield intelligence needs, provides a humanitarian crisis intervention system, and can be used to manage every aspect of local governance, planning, infrastructure and service delivery.

Central to NexGen COIN strategy is providing safe havens for displaced people in the Middle East who otherwise would decide to join the flow of refugees to Turkey and Europe. Years of violence and chaos in Syria have displaced 22 million Syrians, more than 4 million of whom have fled to Turkey, Jordan and Lebanon, and now to Europe. They are part of the 60 million people displaced by conflicts worldwide. The massive migration from the Middle East to Europe has just begun. The next phase of the migration crisis will involve a great many more people from chaotic Afghanistan and Iraq. After decades of violence and unmet promises, suffering corrupt, sectarian political elites, Iraqis are leaving their country in droves as brutal domination by ISIS expands.

Afghanis resent and have no faith in their government and are joining the flood of refugees heading for Europe. The number of refugees from Afghanistan to Europe in 2014-2015 has been second only to those from Syria. Thousands are lining up every day at the passport office in Afghanistan's Kabul to pay officials thousands of dollars in "brokerage fees" for passports or Turkish visas to leave the country, and travel at great risk to reach Turkey, Iran, Greece, the Baltic countries, Hungary, and Austria in transit, hopefully, to Germany or Scandinavia. Not unlike refugees from Iraq, the reasons also are endless war, poor job prospects and no confidence in the future of their homeland.

When the US and its coalition partners were formulating a strategy for warfare in Syria, without US boots-on-the ground and without removing Assad, there was little visible discussion of the profound humanitarian impact of the Syrian civil war on the country's population. No one in the EU or Washington had any plan for absorbing millions of people fleeing the war in Syria. There was no discussion of a unified and effective humanitarian border security policy in Europe in anticipation of refugees pouring out of Syria, the Middle East and Africa. US COIN doctrine, which talks a great deal about "stabilization," "legitimization" of and "nation-building" for collapsing regimes and failed states had no provisions for COIN campaigns that resulted in very large numbers of refugees and displaced people in any country.

Fortunately for millions of displaced people and refugees, Germany appears to be willing to take in at least 800,000 asylum seekers in 2015 and as many as half-a-million a year for several years afterwards. As a fortuitous accident of history, Germany needs a great many young people, especially those with skills. At least a half-million jobs in Germany are unfilled. Many Syrians are from middle-class households and are educated and skilled. With the lowest birthrate in the world, Germany is faced with a huge population drop within the next 15 years and needs large numbers of working age asylum-seekers that still will only amount to about 1% of the German population.

In Iraq, as in Syria, a major challenge for NexGen COIN will include figuring out realistic ways to persuade Iraqis that, in the midst of severe disorder, there's sufficient hope for the future in their own country for them to remain and work for it. Iraqis arriving in the Balkans, many with their families, struggling to reach Germany or Sweden, all say that they are looking for a future and have given up on the past. In Iraq that future will have to include the transformation of national governance, currently the goal of protestors demonstrating in Baghdad's Tahrir Square. The future also will have to include sufficient security for Iraqis and their families to remain in their homeland.

NexGen COIN advocates a national decentralization strategy in Iraq that builds on lessons learned in Anbar Province's Great Awakening for resolving sectarian conflict, provides security and confidence in local governance and law enforcement, and endorses a national form of Iraqi "federalism" that creatively accommodates the goals of Iraqi Kurdistan. Obviously that's asking a great deal, but it's not at all a strategic departure from the stabilization and reconciliation goals that Petraeus and his colleagues fought for so bravely in order to reshape 21st century warfare and its aftermath.

Former CIA Director Petraeus, the driving force for revamping US counterinsurgency (COIN), appeared before the Senate Armed Services Committee in September 2015 and, in his first public testimony since resigning in 2012, asserted that the US should establish safe havens (that he called "enclaves") in Syria to protect moderate rebel forces and displaced Syrians. He also urged that the US strengthen its military effort against the Islamic State in Iraq and Syria by using small American teams to call in airstrikes. As Director of the CIA, Petraeus had proposed to the Obama Administration a covert program to train and arm moderate Syrian rebels.

As the US military leader who most influenced the writing of this book, Petraeus's statement to the Senate Committee was a very welcome omen because it also was the first time that he publically expressed the idea of creating safe havens for training insurgents and sheltering displaced persons in Syria, which is one of the central strategies of the next generation of counterinsurgency -- NexGen COIN. Without explicitly addressing the failure of US efforts in Syria to combat ISIS, Petraeus said that Syrian rebels would not agree to be trained by the US if they and the Syrian civilian population could not be protected against all extremists in Syria, not just ISIS.

"Without building up its military leverage against the Assad regime," he said, "there can't be any political solution to the bloody conflict in Syria. It is frequently said that there is no military solution to Syria or the other conflicts roiling the Middle East," Petraeus said to the Senate Committee. "This may be true, but it is also misleading. For, in every case, if there is to be any hope of a political settlement, a certain military and security context is required, and that context will not materialize on its own. We and our partners need to facilitate it – and over the past four years, we have not done so."

Petraeus also addressed the White House's response to Russia's military buildup at the base near Latakia, Syria. Secretary of State John Kerry had expressed hope that Russia would cooperate with the Obama Administration in combating the Islamic State. Expressing his skepticism, Petraeus said, "Russia's recent military escalation in Syria is a further reminder that when the US does not take the initiative, others will fill the vacuum – often in ways that are harmful to our interests."

President Obama has accepted Vladimir Putin's proposal for US-Russian discussions on Syria. Russia has been one of brutal President Assad's strongest supporters. The idea that dialogue with Putin would yield a joint strategy that contains the Islamic State while pressuring Assad to step down might seem preposterous. But let's remember that even as the US opposed Russia's aggression in the Ukraine, it worked with Russia on the Iran nuclear agreement. Especially since another American military intervention in Syria or the Middle East is very unlikely, even with a new president in 2016, finding a way to constructively engage Russia in working out a solution to the ISIS, humanitarian crisis and Assad problems in Syria should not be rejected for partisan political reasons.

The US-Russian dialogue on the future of Syria and "political transition" of Assad has been broadened to include Iran, Saudi Arabia and its allies among other Persian Gulf states. Presidential candidates in 2016 all will have to have strong positions on the US posture towards Assad, Iran, and its proxy wars, and Russia, and also the issue of Saudi Arabia and the Gulf States and their war in Yemen. The relationships between Saudi Arabia and all Gulf countries have been in flux for many years largely based on the personal relationships of their respective leaders.

A recent meeting between Saudi's King Salman and Qatar's emir Tamim bin Hamad al-Thani and other meetings between King Salman and leaders of Jordan (King Abdullah) and Egypt (Abdel Fatah al Sisi) in Riyadh suggest that Saudi and its allies are preparing to collaborate more closely on critical Middle East and Gulf issues. All of them and also Jordan are sworn enemies of Iran, ISIS and Al-Qaeda. They all are concerned about the possible consequences of new financial resources pouring into Iran from removal of sanctions and escalation of Iran's proxy wars.

Turkey also is an essential partner in the proposed Syrian peace process. A Saudi-Turkish alliance has been moving forward since Turkish President Recep Tayyip Erdogan visited Saudi King Salman in March 2015. In all of these evolving political relationships in the Middle East and the Gulf, Iran is on everyone's mind since it has been involved in wars that have spiraled out of control in four Arab countries – Iraq, Afghanistan, Syria and Yemen. As all of the potential participants in the Syrian peace process know, the nuclear deal with Iran includes nothing about what Iran needs to do to end the Syrian civil war and cease meddling in Yemen and Iraq. For discussion purposes, Vladimir Putin probably has his own plan for combating ISIS and for Syria that involves bringing together Western and Arab countries to form an anti-Islamic State coalition that would include Assad's forces, Iran and its proxy, Hezbollah, Syrian and Iraqi Kurdish troops, and Russia.

In the US homeland, one of the perversely valuable aspects of the current partisan controversy pertaining to immigration reform in the 2016 presidential election campaign has been bringing controversial US-southern border security issues to the attention of the American public. The problem, however, is that even with all of the hyperbole about terrorists and criminals infiltrating the US across its southern border, the real strategic and operational story of warfare along the US southern border has not been presented to the American public as a US priority for counterinsurgency action on a par, for example, with Syria.

In 2011, at the request of the Texas Department of Agriculture, several retired military colleagues (MG Robert H. Scales, PhD, Ret., Gen. Barry R. McCaffrey, and Ret., Col. Jack H. Pryor, Ret.) and I conducted a study of *Texas Border Security* from a military perspective that revealed America was being invaded from Mexico and Central America by crime, violence, narco-terrorism, drug cartel members and terrorists. Exploiting porous borders, drug cartels were attacking the 2,000 miles of Mexico's borders with four states, with the most success along the 1,000-mile Texas border. Cartel terrorists were organizing transit for transnational gang members and terrorists, including members of ISIS and Hezbollah, from the Middle East and Southeast Asia that had moved to chaotic countries in South and Central America. Tens of billions of dollars in illicit smuggling also was moving north annually through southern US borders.

The well-documented violent narcotics-related crisis in Central America and Mexico has driven hundreds of thousands of refugees to and through the southern US-Mexico border, comparable to the impact of civil war in and the collapse of Syria. Criminality spawned in Mexico and Central America, fed by past US "export" of the worst Mexican gangs, has enabled Mexican cartels to fuel and control the drug trade and narco-crime in hundreds of American cities and towns. Federal and state authorities are aware of the fact that terrorists from the Middle East and elsewhere have accompanied this flow of criminality into the US from south of the border. Some of these terrorists, such as Hezbollah, have been supported by Iran as part of its proxy wars. When sanctions are removed, Iran intends to expand its influence and proxy network into Latin America. Hezbollah is likely to be a beneficiary in the Middle East, Latin America and elsewhere as a ubiquitous arm of terrorism.

The refugee crisis in the Middle East and Europe resembles the refugee crisis between Central America-Mexico and the US in that organized transnational crime is one of the main beneficiaries in both regions. The *Texas Border Security* study confirmed that, with the help of Mexican drug cartels, transnational criminal groups were emerging as the greatest threat to US national security. International criminal organizations operating transnational narcotics business empires had begun to establish links to insurgents and terrorists in the Middle East, Africa and Asia. Three years later, those transnational crime connections probably include ISIS.

Rather than view ISIS as just an apocalyptic religious organization promoting a transnational caliphate, ISIS also should be viewed as a transnational criminal organization. Even Moscow has voiced strong concerns about ISIS broadening its activities into Afghanistan and from there into countries bordering Russia and Central Asian states. Vladimir Safronkov, Russia's deputy UN ambassador, has called on the UN Security Council to take action to prevent further expansion of ISIS.

Russia's concerns were reflected in a news report in early 2015, attributed to Viktor Ivanov, head of the Russian Federal Drug Control Service (FSKN), that ISIS has been trafficking as much as $1 billion annually in heroin from Afghanistan through territory it controls in Iraq into Russia and Europe. For Russia, which has been coping with a major heroin addiction problem undermining its national economic growth, the growing role of ISIS in heroin transport through the Middle East to Russia and Europe is a very serious matter.

In the US national security concerns usually are equated with terrorism and a repetition of an even worse version of 9/11. A strong case can be made, however, that the greatest threat to national security in America is drug abuse in every demographic that has been skyrocketing in recent years. The US Center for Disease Control (CDC) reports that more than a half million people in the US use heroin each year and more than 8,000 people die of heroin-related overdoses annually. The use of prescription opioid painkillers, that fuel heroin use because heroin is cheaper, is at epidemic levels. Virtually all of the people using heroin also use at least one other drug regularly and more than half at least three other drugs. No wonder that drug smuggling from Mexico into the US, eclipsing the flow from Columbia, has become a multi-billion dollar business. Creation of a barrier to ISIS infiltration at the US border also would serve as a barrier to the even more dangerous and deadly flow of heroin from Mexico, controlled by cartels, and corrupting Mexican law enforcement and government officials.

Turkey joined the US to create an *ISIS-free zone* along part of the Turkish-Syrian border. This protected zone was created because Turkey was under assault from ISIS and to control the movements of Syrian Kurds. Based on information and analysis in the hands of the Department of Home Security (DHS) and Texas criminal justice agencies, the author proposes that the US should create a 30-50-mile wide terrorist and narco-terrorism free zone along both sides of the US-Mexico border. This will require US and Mexican army boots-on-the-ground irrespective of which party or candidate occupies the Oval Office. This narco-terrorism free zone would be supported by advanced intelligence, surveillance and reconnaissance technology (ISR) and cognitive computing and analytics in the hands of frontline advisors – CyberWarriors.

CHAPTER 18

ISIS Containment Strategy & Protected Safe Havens

Almost 7,000 Americans have died in Iraq and Afghanistan wars. Over 900,000 Americans were injured. The financial costs of these wars have been in the trillions, including a substantial percentage of the VA budget that for 2016 will be about $170 billion. The lasting beneficial results of Coalition counterinsurgencies have been meager and chaos still reigns from Afghanistan and Iraq.

In addition, according to the United Nations refugee agency, tens of millions in the Middle East are internally displaced people (IDPs) or refugees. Tens of thousands of people have been forced to leave their homes every day to seek some unknown and uncertain form of protection elsewhere. More than half of the people involved in this massive exodus have been children. Refugees have been arriving in Greece at the rate of thousands a day. It's amazing that the Greek government, which is bankrupt, and the Greeks themselves, can provide food, shelter and medical care for this huge refugee population.

In this context, counterinsurgency doctrine has to be redefined for both Iraq and Syria. ISIS is conducting all-out civil wars in Iraq and Syria and instigating civil warfare elsewhere in the region while, at the same time, plotting terrorist attacks in Europe and elsewhere. In Iraq, Sunni extremists from ISIS and Shiite extremists committed to Iran more or less divide the non-Kurdish parts of Iraq between them. In Syria, the US and its coalition allies are fighting a proxy war with Iran that is providing Assad with arms, financing, and training support. At the same time, the US and Iran share a common foe in Syria, ISIS, that has more than 30,000 fighters, as many as half of whom are foreign fighters.

Political pressure has been building in Congress to get answers about strategies and programs aimed at stopping ISIS from expanding. With the recent ISIS terrorism in Lebanon, France, and over Egypt's Sinai, the presidential election debates will add fuel to rhetorical fires. Pressures on the Obama administration for more aggressive attacks on ISIS will grow in 2015-16, especially after Defense Secretary Ash Carter was forced to publicly acknowledge that only about 60 anti-ISIS rebel fighters -- well below the thousands projected -- are participating in training at US bases in Iraq and the number in Jordan and Turkey had dropped below 100. Carter claimed that involvement of "moderate rebels" in training had yielded valuable intelligence, which satisfied no one on both sides of the aisle.

"Our means and our current level of effort are not aligned with our ends," Senator McCain told Carter at a July 7, 2015 Capitol Hill hearing. "That suggests we are not winning, and when you are not winning in war, you are losing," McCain said, correctly. There is no reliable ground force in either Iraq or Syria that can seize territory from ISIS, with slim prospects for success from the US-led coalition's current training efforts of "moderate insurgent" ground forces. Air campaigns against ISIS continue to be limited significantly by a lack of ground intelligence. For Sec. Carter and Gen. Martin Dempsey, chairman of the Joint Chiefs of Staff, recapture of Iraq's Ramadi will test the competence of Iraqi security forces (ISF). Carter said, "It is a test that they must pass."

Since politically, in President Obama's presidency, US military engagement in Iraq and Syria only will be limited, the military goal can be nothing more than effective ISIS containment. Neither Carter nor Dempsey nor the President publicly have made that admission. Within these constraints, the US has provided assistance in Syria for the Kurdish Peshmerga while maximizing diplomatic efforts to engage other major powers and regional players in efforts to weaken ISIS and also provide humanitarian assistance to Jordan, Turkey and Lebanon struggling to deal with huge influxes of refugees from Syria.

Given current political limitations on the US increasing "boots on the ground," a strong case can be made for the US and Coalition forces to maintain flexibility and ambiguity in Middle East military strategies and policies. Within that framework, the US can pursue a strategy of ISIS containment in each fracturing and increasingly chaotic country in the Middle East. Such an ISIS containment strategy would aim to prevent ISIS from expanding control of territory, pushing ISIS back where they already have control and, in the vicinity of these containment zones, providing protected safe havens for both civilians and local insurgent forces in training that are managed by frontline US special ops advisors and linked by satellite-based cybernetworks.

These networked protected safe havens would be high-tech counterinsurgency bases in which frontline advisors would be supported 7x24 via satellite by cognitive computing and Big Data analytics. Frontline special ops advisors would use, learn from and contribute to the development of predictive analytics tools and data feeds that over time increasingly have value for ISIS containment and counterinsurgency applications. The development of protected safe havens for local insurgent forces and displaced persons would avoid making costly, dangerous promises, conserve, focus and leverage US resources, and serve very specific strategic and tactical purposes that reflect geopolitical realities in each region, state and locality.

Counterinsurgency strategies for protected safe havens and ISIS containment have had an abortive beginning in a counteroffensive to reclaim Ramadi from seizure by ISIS in May 2015. The Ramadi counteroffensive was planned by American advisers sent to Al Taqqadum, an Iraqi base east of Ramadi. Along with an announcement by President Obama, an additional 450 American forces were sent to Al Taqqadum recently. More than 5,000 Sunni "volunteers" in Iraq were supposed to have been trained by the US to fight ISIS and retake Ramadi. Only a fraction of that number actually was recruited.

These Iraqi "volunteers" were supposed to serve as a new kind of assault force led by Iraq's counterterrorism service that would include Iraqi federal police and soldiers. Also, according to US-Iraqi plans, Iraqi Shiite militia (Popular Mobilization Force) would not join in the assault on Ramadi in order to avoid inflaming sectarian tensions in the largely Sunni city. The Shiite militia would have a specific role in the plan – setting up blocking positions south and west of Ramadi to prevent ISIS fighters from escaping. American-led air power and aerial surveillance, including armed drones, would support this Iraqi push to seize Ramadi. The plan made sense, but did not happen as planned. Iraqi military and police, backed by Shiite militias, Sunni tribal fighters and US-led coalition air strikes, are only making very slow progress in trying to retake Ramadi

The Army's COIN strategy states, "Using violence to achieve political goals is known as insurgency … Most of the work involves discovering and solving the population's underlying issues, that is, the root causes of their dissatisfaction with the current arrangement of political power." According to the *US Government Counterinsurgency Guide* (2009), counterinsurgency is defined as 'comprehensive civilian and military efforts taken to simultaneously defeat and contain insurgency and address its root causes". Faced with escalating terrorism threats in Europe and the Middle East, and the urgent need to combat and contain ISIS expansion and its global terrorism reach, US and Western leaders have to decide whether aggressive new ISIS counterterrorism policies should include efforts to address the "root causes" of jihadist terrorism.

General David Petraeus described counterinsurgency in *The US Army–Marine Corps Counterinsurgency Field Manual* in 2006 as a three-legged approach known as "clear, hold, and build": push insurgents out of a designated area; prevent them from returning;

and build local institutions, resources and services that help the population move forward. In other words, COIN according to Petraeus is a mix of military, political, and economic goals and activities. The military mission part of COIN operations always is bloody and brutal. It lasts longer and costs more lives than anyone wants or expects. The main challenge in COIN, however, is implementing programs, activities and actions after the military conflict is over that address the "root causes" of the conflict, retain and build local support and governance credibility, and contain the spread of insurgency. That's the "build" part of Petraeus's COIN prescription and the real long-term political and investment challenge for US and Western leadership.

The wars in Iraq, Syria, Yemen, Afghanistan, and Libya are wars within states. These internal wars can be as deadly as, or even deadlier, than wars between countries. The death toll in Syria, for example, is more than 225,000. Internal wars require at least as much post-war planning as wars between countries. A counterinsurgency strategy for civil wars has to address even more complexities than in the aftermath of a Country A vs. Country B war. US counterinsurgency strategy for a country struggling with ISIS or the Taliban has to take into account every aspect of rebuilding the political, economic and social fabric of each country, including development of legitimate political authority.

ISIS consists of Islamic extremists engaged in sectarian violence. At the risk of oversimplification, the central issue in counterinsurgency strategy in the Middle East is that Iraq, Syria, Libya, Yemen and other countries are embroiled in religious and sectarian conflicts. In Iraq, it's Sunni vs. Shiite vs. Kurd (most Kurds are Sunnis). In Syria (70% Sunni Islam), the Sunni opposition, dominated by ISIS and the Al-Qaeda franchise, Jabhat al-Nusra, are fighting a government dominated by an Alawite minority (about 12% of the population). In Iraq and in Syria, the only effective fighting forces -- on either side -- are based on sect or ethnicity.

Another key factor in Iraq is that the US has spent huge amounts of money to equip, train and support an Iraqi army that simply vaporized in battle when faced by only minimal opposition. New recruits for the Iraqi army are way below the numbers projected. The US strategic commitment in Iraq is primarily shaped by President Obama's ambivalence about further military engagement in the Middle East. He doesn't want to be in Iraq, but also doesn't want to be responsible for the total collapse of Iraq. Hence half of the new commitment of several hundred US "advisors" will work in what is euphemistically referred to as "tribal engagement."

At some point Iraqis will have to retake Ramadi. In Baghdad, faced with losing all of Anbar Province to ISIS, Prime Minister Abadi almost has no choice other than to unleash Shiite militias, backed by Iran, to reconquer the city. One sure result, even if that counterinsurgency strategy is successful, will be alienation of the local Sunni population. Iraqi security elements dominated by Shiites have to work at the local level, but the question is how to do it? And that's just Iraq. Coalition forces might agree on what needs to be done in Iraq to contain ISIS, but they hold widely divergent views on what needs to be done to contain ISIS in Syria, Libya, Yemen and Afghanistan.

With a few notable exceptions (Petraeus in 2007, and McChrystal after 2003), publicly and privately we are always hearing from the White House and US military commanders at all levels that, slowly but surely, coalition forces are making progress in Iraq, and even Syria, and all challenges gradually are being overcome. This may be an admirable expression by military officers and civilian leaders of unwillingness to accept failure or excuses for it, but the beginning of successful strategic counterinsurgency thinking usually has to involve confronting uncomfortable truths. However, when that "uncomfortable truth" resembles the rationale for Petraeus's "Surge" decision, requiring tens of thousands more US troops, the White House and Congress both predictably reacted by putting on the brakes. As General Stanley McChrystal and his staff learned too late, it is imprudent to openly criticize White House decisions to the media, especially when the criticism is blatantly demeaning.

Understandably, for the American public and even members of Congress who are not familiar with the battlefields of Iraq, Syria, and elsewhere in the Middle East, it is extremely difficult, if not impossible, to understand and appreciate their complexity. Not only are insurgencies and terrorism complex, but also the context of social, economic and political problems and the prevalence of sectarian violence. The first thing that military leaders in the field need to realize and followup on is acquiring as much understanding as possible about all of these contextual factors. This dictum should seem quite obvious, but it is much easier said than done, especially when the system of military intelligence is not designed to answer questions about contextual factors impinging on tactical military decisions.

In addition, every individual in a battlefield needs to learn and operate as part of a secure intelligence network so that everything that happens, across all parts of the battlefield, and in every corner of the communities within and around the battlefield, provides relevant intelligence and information that instantly flows to and can be questioned by each soldier and civilian participant in the battlefield network. The intelligence network not only needs to cover battlefield terrain and its vicinity but what is going on in any part of the country or elsewhere that is experiencing similar problems so that every participant in the network can learn, analyze and think about everything potentially relevant to their situation no matter where it is happening. Modern information technology, Big Data and cognitive computing bring that intelligence acquisition and analysis capability to bottomup military decision-making.

In 2004, back in the comparative dark ages of such information technology, the technology advances included use of global positioning systems, night-vision goggles and unmanned aerial vehicles (UAVs) that enabled a bird's eye view of battlefields. As Col MacFarland realized in Ramadi, using this technology enabled his men in the 1st Brigade, 1st Armored Division (the "ready First Brigade") to hit multiple enemy locations simultaneously in order to have decisive effects. At the same time, Gen. McChrystal learned in Iraq that his forces could conduct more than a dozen high precision raids on insurgents in a day or night, but that it did little to deter insurgency. Two years later, improved information technology enabled his forces to conduct 20 times that number of raids using intelligence captured from the experiences of each military encounter.

In addition to improved technology that enabled more precise raids at amazing speeds, McChrystal realized that the key to success was decentralized, bottom-up decision-making. His forces became a "learning organization." His "learning organization" operating as a network became the key to military success. McChrystal also learned that, in addition, the perspectives and cultures that individual soldiers brought to battlefields had to be changed. Soldiers had to get comfortable with constant communication connections with one another, which for some or perhaps many of his soldiers was threatening. Soldiers also had to learn to deal with constant information flows. But once those mental changes happened, soldiers could see the positive results.

Counterinsurgency amplified by more advanced information and communication technology still had its limitations. McChrystal concluded in Afghanistan that it would take a great many more troops to successfully conduct a successful nationwide counterinsurgency campaign. McChrystal's math said it would require as many as 500,000 boots on the ground. Of course President Obama wouldn't buy that plan or any number of troops even close to that figure. Instead, for McChrystal that meant focusing on key districts in Afghanistan. McChrystal selected 80 out of a possible 364. McChrystal advocated a completely revamped Afghanistan strategy: changing the primary mission of international forces from conducting raids against Taliban strongholds to protecting civilians; moving troops out of remote mountain valleys where Taliban fighters have traditionally sought sanctuary and concentrating more forces around key population centers, here again to protect local populations and to work, live and train with Afghan security forces; and to fight government corruption wherever possible.

McChrystal had realized that to succeed in a counterinsurgency, and defeat the very unpopular Taliban, the US had to be able to offer a viable alternative to the Afghanistan government that itself had no legitimacy among the people and, most important, was unable to provide security from retaliation for Afghanis that backed opposition to the Taliban. McChrystal's proposal to Obama for additional troops was to provide sufficient security to Afghanis to persuade them that joining a counterinsurgency was not committing suicide or jeopardizing their families. That was exactly the same challenge faced by US forces under Col. MacFarland in Iraq's Ramadi. In addition, the other critical ingredient of US counterinsurgency, in Afghanistan, Iraq or anywhere, was a commitment to staying engaged for a long-time. How long? No time limits set: "Until hell freezes over!"

The most important counterinsurgency lesson that McChrystal learned in Iraq and Afghanistan was the critical importance of figuring out why the "enemy" is fighting an insurgency and why the rest of the local population is not fighting with or against them. Then the challenge became, illustrated most clearly and effectively during the Great Awakening in Ramadi, figuring out strategies and adaptable local-US team operations that provided effective actions based on answers to those questions. COIN strategy has to focus on enabling Afghanis, Iraqis, Syrians, and the people themselves of any Middle East country and locality to solve their own problems, with US help to protect and care for people in the conflicted and unpredictable process.

In theory a key component of counterinsurgency strategy is "nation-building." A vast amount of research and thinking by some of the brightest, most informed minds in America has been invested in studying past nation-building efforts in Germany, Japan, Bosnia, Kosovo, and elsewhere. The lessons learned, however, provide little basis for optimism regarding post-conflict nation-building in Iraq, Afghanistan, Syria, Libya and Yemen where national governments either have collapsed or are in various stages of failing. Realistically the American public has no commitment to or even interest in these countries except for their role in breeding international terrorists. The American people would prefer that their nation and their president to do less, rather than more, in these countries.

The American public may not know or understand the dynamics and details, but they understand that the US has less and less influence over what happens in Afghanistan, Iraq, Middle East and North African countries. When they read about or watch television reports on massacres of innocent citizens or tourists, for example in Paris or at a beach resort in Tunisia, understandably they think about possible ramifications, sooner or later, for their own cities, beaches, resorts and vacation havens.

Part of this fearful post-9/11 reaction by the American public to international terrorism is based on the fact that they no longer have a great deal of confidence in the judgment of their nation's commander-in-chief, national security and other leaders. This negative opinion would be even stronger had they read what Gates, Panetta, McChrystal and others among these former military and national security leaders have to say about their nation's national security and military decision-makers and their decision-making. They would know that the nation's leadership invariably overestimates its ability to develop effective strategic military thinking and accomplish its military and foreign policy agendas.

From Afghanistan to Syria and Yemen to Libya, the term "nations" probably has become a misnomer. There is no foreign policy doctrine that the US can devise and advocate around "nation-building" in these fragmented countries that makes sense any longer. ISIS containment, including protective safe havens, on the other hand, at least represents a realistic organizing principal for action to prevent expansion of ISIS control of territory, provide protection and humanitarian support for civilians, and bases for training insurgents into effective fighting forces.

An Iraqi national identity does not exist and communal identity rules, especially Shiite and Kurdish. In the aftermath of prolonged totalitarian rule, national Iraqi politics is completely fragmented. The military, security services and bureaucracies need to be radically reformed. Corruption is rampant in every corner of the Iraqi government and its military hierarchy. The Iraqi economy requires a total overhaul. Iraq's Prime Minister Haider al-Abadi pushed a program of reforms through Parliament that included a crackdown on corruption. There is no precedent for nation-building in Iraq in terms of overcoming entrenched sectarian and ethnic divides that feed an unstable, broken state. Iraqi policing cannot ensure law and order in any Iraqi nation-building scenario. Neighboring states (Iran, Syria) are fundamentally opposed to democratization and will provide no support for democratization in Iraq.

Turkey under Recep Tayyip Erdogan and the Justice and Development Party (AKP) government recently attempted to move the country more towards authoritarianism and voters at first rejected the move and then embraced it in the next election. The liberal People's Democratic Party (HDP) made the difference in the initial vote by winning more than 13 percent of the vote to become the first Kurdish-oriented parliamentary party in Turkey's history. This Kurdish rejection of Erdogan's executive-power grab, however, resulted in an Erdogan military backlash against Kurds in Turkey, Syria and Iraq. The Turkish city of Cizre, near the intersection of the Syrian and Iraq border, provides a good example of why the Turks are cracking down on Kurds. Battered by a Turkish government crackdown, Cizre is one of the cities in Turkey where the Kurdish HDP got huge support in the last election.

The difficulties of putting together a stabile Iraq or Syria are increased significantly if nations in the vicinity, like Turkey, are not supporting the process, and actually are trying to prevent or subvert it. All of the principal multilateral participants in Iraq and Syria would have to share a common vision for nation-building and containment of ISIS. The level of effort across all resources would have to remain high throughout the entire process. International involvement in maintaining security would have to remain long after attainment of some semblance of democratization goals. There would not be much room for serious trial and error. The challenges facing democratization efforts in a post-Assad Syria or in Abadi's Iraq are formidable.

What then would be a meaningful, workable and sustainable strategy for dealing with ISIS and terrorism in Iraq and Syria that also serves the basic political, economic and social purposes of nation-building, and also might be acceptable to the White House and members of Congress, the nation's military leaders, Coalition partners, the American people, and Iraqis and Syrians themselves? Thus far the nation's military leaders have not expressed much optimism about the prospects for nation-building or even stabilization in either Iraq or Syria.

Early in June 2015, America's two top defense officials presented a dismal outlook on the situation in Iraq during testimony before the House Armed Services Committee. Defense Secretary Ashton Carter conceded that the US did not move quickly enough to arm Iraqi Security Forces (ISF) in their struggle against ISIS, and disclosed that the US will train just 7,000 of the 24,000 Iraqi troops it had expected to by the fall of 2015 due to a lack of recruits. Meanwhile, Gen. Martin E. Dempsey, chairman of the Joint Chiefs of Staff, cautioned House committee members that there are limits to what America can do to stabilize a country torn by sectarian strife and the advances of ISIS.

Both Carter and Dempsey know what needs to be done in Iraq in terms of the goals: vastly improved governance; denying ISIS a safe haven and support; enhanced training, expedited equipping, and frontline advisors assisting Iraqi security forces; stopping the flow of foreign fighters to and from extremists; recruiting Sunnis into the fight; and more. But it is of crucial importance to make distinctions between military "goals" and "strategies." For example, building more effective, inclusive, multi-sectarian governance in Iraq, a goal enunciated by Secretary Carter and affirmed by defense Chief Dempsey, needs a set of clearly defined actions to make it a strategy.

Looking back to 2007 in Iraq for lessons learned, after four years of insurgent activity, the US was forced to change it strategy to subordinate military activities to political aims, adopt COIN's clear-hold-build strategy, and establish advisory teams and provincial reconstruction teams. Still, even with an understanding of the critical role played in preceding years by Iraq's sectarian divide, military strategists failed to address this issue and initiated a "democratization process" that inevitably elected a government with a Shia majority. This sent a very clear message to Sunnis that the Maliki government was not interested in reconciliation and the US was not going to make a difference. The Iraqi army also was afflicted by the sectarian divide, which still is a fundamental problem in Iraq, exacerbated by Iran's support for Shia militias.

By 2007 the Sunnis had learned one of the most important lessons of counterinsurgency: if the host government is not effective and legitimate and does not have the capacity to introduce basic reforms in governance, neither local governments nor insurgents will join foreign interventions in a counterinsurgency. The critical question for the US, therefore, is: does the US have to engage in regime change in Middle East countries before committing to counterinsurgency or is there a COIN strategy that can work even though the government in power needs top-to-bottom reform? The rapid territorial expansion of ISIS, including Afghan insurgent factions pledging their allegiance to ISIS, has made answering this question even more urgent for the US

Any next-generation US counterinsurgency strategy focused on ISIS and Islamic extremism in the Middle East region has to answer some very tough questions, all of which point to governance issues: How to get Arab Sunnis back to support Shia-dominated governments? How to reduce divisive tensions between Kurdish forces and Shiite militias? How to reduce Iraqi government dependence on Shiite militias and Kurdish forces? What is the role of Shiite militias connected to Iran? How to deal with Iranian influence in Iraq, Syria and Yemen? What supporting civil and civil-military activities by the United States are needed? How to deal with humanitarian crises and the destabilizing impact of refugees and displaced persons?

Looking back to the emergence of the Taliban in Pashtun tribal areas of Pakistan and in Afghanistan after the withdrawal of the Soviet Union in 1989, and the coup in 1992 that led to the country's disintegration into warlord controlled fiefdoms, there are parallels to the sources, power and influence of ISIS in recent years. For the beaten-down, war-weary Pashtuns, the Taliban were potential saviors and peacemakers. From the outset, more than a political movement, the Taliban aimed to enforce Sharia law and defend Afghanistan's Islamic character. To achieve these goals, they imposed brutal punishments for violating their strict interpretation of Islam. Pashtuns accepted Taliban repression in return for stability and security. In addition, the Pashtuns had their own political motivation -- to unseat the Tajiks and Uzbeks that humiliated them in the 1992 coup, after 300 years during which the Pashtuns had been the politically dominant ethnic group in Afghanistan.

The success of the Taliban, much like that of ISIS, has been its ability to establish reliable governance in the midst of conflict and disorder. ISIS has mastered Islamic governance. Across sectarian divides and in the midst of lawlessness, communities in territories conquered by ISIS setup and administer self-rule that allows no exceptions, starts with disarmament and includes dispute mediation. Once ISIS controls any area, order is imposed and reigns. Residents become ISIS fighters and enforce law and order, while ISIS maintains total military, religious and political control.

One of the key factors undermining non-ISIS Islamist insurgencies in Syria, Iraq and elsewhere has been financial backers that want a say in how the money is spent, which feeds divisiveness. Not so with ISIS that owns, controls and dispenses all financial and other resources. ISIS uses hard and soft power to attract people to work with it in every aspect of making communities function efficiently. ISIS eliminates corruption. Bandits and looters do not survive long. Moving within or between communities becomes safe – no bribes at checkpoints, no extortion, kidnappings or random killings. A seeming contradiction, brutal ISIS does not allow human rights abuses. The same laws and rules that apply to people in communities apply to all ISIS members at all levels.

People in the community may not support ISIS, but they do not oppose it, and not just because of fear. Effective governance means that the local population has little motivation to rebel. What's the alternative? For formerly disillusioned and alienated insurgents, ISIS plays an unprecedented role, and seeks to avoid the mistakes of its insurgent predecessors. Having established control over any city or town, and making it a hub, ISIS moves outwards to surrounding towns and villages that already have heard about what they do and how they do it.

The combination of effective governance and force is the ISIS strategy for making it hard for the "crusaders" or any other counterinsurgency force to retake areas it controls.

In other words, ISIS has its own ruthless version of a "safe haven" and "containment" strategy that enables it to stabilize, manage and control large swathes of captured territory and fend off various enemies. The challenge for the US and its allies is to create comparably effective protected safe havens.

A NexGen COIN strategy that includes creating protected safe havens for supporting loyal insurgents and civilians initially should target areas and communities that ISIS has not occupied. Otherwise the NexGen COIN challenge immediately becomes creating comparably reliable governance while, at the same time, filling the void left by removal of ISIS governance and, in the process, assessing and figuring out how to (re)structure myriad relationships with local political and other leaders. The US and its allies may not have a choice, however, as they succeed in removing ISIS from territory in Iraq, Syria and elsewhere.

NexGen COIN intelligence will be crucial for planning protected safe havens in order to know as much as possible about and understand every aspect of the ISIS governance structure and its operations in provinces (*wilayat*) and their communities as well as ISIS military and security operations. ISIS governance in its provinces and communities is ubiquitous, covering every component of the infrastructure, communications, food supplies, services, and the like. Overlaying the development of US safehaven governance and operations on former ISIS governance will require unprecedented computer modeling, planning, and intelligence, with continuous data input from frontline advisors and aerial reconnaissance.

CHAPTER 19

COIN Revisited and Revamped

The United States and its military and academic experts don't need to spend another dime or minute researching and writing counterinsurgency field manuals to guide combat forces and civil-military (CMO) operations in the Middle East or elsewhere. Going backed to Vietnam, and to "small wars" before that, and thoroughly revisiting counterinsurgencies in Iraq and Afghanistan, the US military establishment has documented what we have known for some time: every insurgency is different and, in every instance, the US did not really know what it was getting into and underestimated the scale, complexity and protracted nature of COIN operations.

As 2013 came to a close, the Joint Force Commanders (JFC) of the United States military services published a long-awaited revision to its counterinsurgency (COIN) manual, known as Joint Publication 3-24 when it was published in 2009. For anyone who wants to learn about the latest military and academic thinking on every aspect of counterinsurgency strategy and tactics, one that probably will last for many years, download and at least scan sections of JP 3-24.

(See http://www.dtic.mil/doctrine/new_pubs/jp3_24.pdf)

The new version of the field manual was supposed to incorporate and update lessons learned during six years of counterinsurgency warfare in Afghanistan. The counterinsurgency field manual developed by Gen. David Petraeus had served as the basis for operations in both Iraq and Afghanistan. The November 2013 revision was prepared with input from many experts (not named), including academics and active-duty and retired veterans of Iraq and Afghanistan. The revised manual was specifically aimed at affirming the necessity of varying strategies and tactics for COIN engagements depending on the operating environment (OE) and also focusing on tactical operations at Army brigade and Marine regiment levels.

Even if you don't read all 229 pages of the COIN manual, read Chap. IV, "The Operational Environment." The OE chapter stresses the possibility, indeed, likelihood of unintended consequences of tactical decisions that derive from and impact on countless sociocultural and other factors beyond the control or even influence (and, in more than a few instances, beyond the understanding) of decision-makers in COIN operations. Like many other sections of JP 3-24, the material stresses, as the central strategy of COIN, the critical importance of "addressing the root causes" of insurgency, and the "grievances" underlying it, and restoring or creating "durable stability" and "legitimacy" in the "host-government," in conjunction with militarily defeating insurgents.

In JP 3-24, COIN is defined as a "political struggle." Accordingly, depending on the OE, COIN should be lead by a civilian agency. Otherwise, as a unified civilian-military effort, COIN would be led by the JFC. These fundamental concepts underlying the redefinition of counterinsurgency and COIN goals commit the United States to an unprecedented role in rebuilding the governments in so-called "Host Nations" such as Iraq, Afghanistan, Syria, and Libya during and after battling Al-Qaeda, ISIS and other terrorist groups.

The civilian-military COIN role redefined in JP 3-24, which goes far beyond military defeat of extremists, becomes even more significant in connection with the Islamic State's determination to take over nation-states, eliminate their governments and borders, and merge them into a caliphate. ISIS proclaimed itself to be a caliphate in June 2014, just months before JP 3-24 was published. JP 3-24 makes very few references to Al-Qaeda but no doubt it was the model for the manual's approach to counterinsurgency. ISIS is not mentioned in JP 3-24. The authors of JP 3-24 had plenty of time to observe the emergence and spread of ISIS and the contrasts of its organization, aims and financing with those of Al-Qaeda.

The OE chapter and the rest of JP 3-24 provides an informative compendium of every aspect of the planning, execution and assessment of counterinsurgency operations that involve comprehensive, adaptive, sustained civilian and military efforts to defeat and contain insurgency and, as stressed in the manual, address its root causes. As a historical treatise, there's really not much more to be written on the subject of the dynamics of insurgency and the ingredients of COIN, except for the rise and spread of ISIS.

The inputs of social scientists, political scientists and other academic disciplines clearly have shaped JP 3-24 and its COIN concepts and strategies in ways that make it both more credible and incredible. See for example, the sub-section on "Focoism" in the section on "Insurgent Narrative, Strategy, and Organization." The problem illustrated by this section is that the sum of what military and civilian personnel at all operational levels, separately and together, need to know and do, in terms of strategic and tactical decision-making based on JP 3-24 probably exceeds most human capabilities, irrespective of education and training.

JP 3-24 as a print or digital manual absolutely and urgently calls for development by the JFC and one or more technology companies, perhaps in collaboration with the Defense Advanced Research Projects Agency (DARPA), of a cognitive computing version of JP 3-24 designed to integrate Big Data, answer natural language queries in real-time, and enable COIN planning, assessment and execution at the level of brigades and frontline advisors.

Effective counterinsurgency requires intelligent machines and predictive analytics fed by Big Data to augment and support inherently limited human brain capacities. Without Big Data and cognitive computing assistance, there is no way that military or civilian personnel at the frontline or in support roles will be able to (quotes are from JP 3-24):

- understand and adapt to the continuously changing COIN operating environment (OE);
- make decisions with a "continuous understanding of the dynamics of the insurgency, and its effects on the population, the insurgents, and counterinsurgents";
- "analyze not only how insurgents think, but also how the local population thinks";
- engage in continuous analysis, learning, assessment, dialogue and collaboration not only throughout the chain of command but with all interagency and multinational partners involved in COIN (all in real-time);
- utilize various tools and methodologies for understanding and making decisions in the COIN OE, including "traditional intelligence; intelligence, surveillance, and reconnaissance; sociocultural analysis; analytical frameworks; network analysis; social science; information management and information technology; and identity intelligence."

In sum, the operational requirements for COIN within and impacting on the OE are staggering. Assessment of the progress of COIN operations involves analyzing countless factors and types of information. The assessment process has to be conducted in real-time simultaneously with and as an integral part of frontline COIN operations. Satellite monitoring of the enemy (and its entire OE) has to be fed into a cognitive computer-based decision-making system to enable tracking, targeting and engaging the highly adaptive enemy.

There are several statements and assertions in JP 3-24 that we will leave to others to discuss and debate. For example, the manual says that COIN operations require a host government that is "capable and willing to counter the insurgency and address its root causes." This requirement cancels the possibility of COIN operations in today's Iraq, Afghanistan, Syria, Yemen, Libya and probably any other country under attack by ISIS and other Islamic extremists.

Another controversial statement is that the goal of insurgents is to force incumbent governments to the negotiating table and/or trigger their collapse, and then seize control. The only remotely relevant example is Pakistan's president recently attempting to host talks between the Kabul government and the Taliban. The Taliban did not "force" either Afghanistan or Pakistan to the negotiating table. The relationships among all of the parties are much too complex for that judgment. Since taking office in September 2014, Afghan President Ashraf Ghani has made it a priority to find a peace settlement with the Taliban for his war-battered country. He sought Pakistan's help in bringing the Taliban to the negotiations since Islamabad wields strong influence over the group and Pakistan has provided a safehaven for Taliban leadership for many years.

Of course no one can forecast where these talks will lead or whether they will lead to ending the Taliban's 13 year war against the Afghani government. The US government welcomed and, in some ill-defined manner, "supervised" the talks but there's no indication that the US has had any substantive role in them. With a new leader, the Taliban's bloody 2015 summer offensive continues. Recently one of the country's most important cities, Kunduz, fell to the Taliban. Apparently NATO-trained Afghan security forces made little effort to either dislodge insurgents from the city's outskirts or defend the city of 300,000 over a period of six months. A great many residents have left the city.

The Taliban today are as strong as they have been at any point since 2001. The Afghan state, largely built by Americans, and the Taliban both have unexpectedly seen the appearance of ISIS this year. Reports from Afghanistan say that many Taliban are joining the ranks of ISIS. In Afghanistan, as in Syria and Iraq, "peace talks" of any description are complicated by the multiplicity of factions and insurgent groups that will not have any place at negotiating tables.

Most governments hosting COIN operations need to significantly improve legitimacy and governance during and long after COIN military operations. As proven in Afghanistan, Iraq and Syria, US support for these extremely complex and challenging political efforts in the near- and long-term will be politically and financially untenable. President Obama, Congress and the American people have yet to face up to the financial obligations connected with civil and military COIN operations in the Middle East and North Africa.

The cost of counterinsurgency in the Middle East for the US, without any apparent results, has been huge. Syria provides a good example. About a year ago President Obama asked Congress for $500 million to train and equip 15,000 local fighters in Syria. As we've heard many times before and afterwards from the President and various NSC members, the battle against ISIL/ISIS "will not involve American combat troops fighting on foreign soil." About a year later, as reported to Congress in July 2015 by Defense Secretary Ashton, Syrian fighters trained numbered only 60, which Carter apologetically admitted was "not impressive." The cost? "Only" $36 million. The problem? The screening process designed to ensure that no Islamic extremists slipped into the training program was so extreme and slow that most "volunteers" could not qualify or simply melted back into their local groups or into ISIL. In addition, Syrian recruits had to pledge that they only would fight ISIL/ISIS and not Assad's forces, since the US was not officially at war with Assad's government.

With more than 30,000 ISIL/ISIS fighters in Syria, and the number growing daily, the Syrian civil war is likely to get much worse. The main question hovering over counterinsurgency efforts in Syria is survival of Assad's regime. As Gen. Dempsey recently told a US Senate hearing in mid-2015, the result of a collapse of Assad's regime probably would be "Islamic State and Al-Qaeda forces will be in a foot race converging on Damascus. I won't say here today," said Dempsey, "that I have an answer to that."

The civil war in Syria resembles the Sunni versus Shia civil war that been going on for years in Iraq, fueled by the Maliki regime and supported by Iran. When the last Americans departed from Iraq, Prime Minister Maliki attacked the country's Sunni minority, driving it into the arms of extremists like ISIS. When ISIS rolled into northwestern Iraq, the Iraqi Army built at great American expense disintegrated. Today, Iraq is a failed state that needs all of the help it can get to somehow, some day, reform its governance and achieve legitimacy.

Maliki's betrayal of and war against Iraq's Sunnis empowered ISIS. Ironically Iraq's Sunnis have been turning to ISIS to protect themselves from Iranian-supported Shia militias. It appears that no one in Washington wants to face these grim realities, especially because of their aversion to the possibility of more US boots on the ground for many years. As for Iraqis, why would they side with the US when they see no real, sustainable US conviction to take their side?

In many respects the 2014 COIN strategy could be entitled "Petraeus's COIN" based on his counterinsurgency "Surge" campaign in Iraq starting in 2007 that focused on protecting Iraqi civilians from insurgents and also from each other in violent sectarian warfare. Implicit in references running through JP 3-24 about the importance of improving Host Government's governance and legitimacy are acknowledgements that for many years Iraqis have needed to be protected from their own corrupt and deeply sectarian government.

JP 3-24 reflects what Americans have fundamentally learned in Iraq and Afghanistan which is that counterinsurgency as practiced in these two countries has been a failure in large part because COIN was not instrumental in political reform to bring about effective governance. Realistically, however, COIN's goal in Iraq, Afghanistan and the Middle East needs to stay focused on defeat and containment of ISIL/ISIS and preventing these and other extremist insurgencies from growing and spreading in any other country and globally.

JP 3-24 is extremely clear that COIN involves a very complex progression of civil-military interagency operations in which combat against insurgency often has to be secondary to nonmilitary activities. Interagency, intergovernmental and NGO coordination makes the OE even more challenging. Multinational corporations, including private security contractors, also are in the OE mix as well as various components of the Host-Nation's civil and military organizations. All of these entities have their own operating procedures and rules, which adds further complications to planning and management of OE actions.

Of course, there's no way of knowing whether the sum total of all COIN efforts in any country or local area, and the cost in human and financial terms, will result in enduring security or good governance. It should be reiterated here that publication of JP 3-24 occurred before ISIS emerged as a serious and growing transnational threat in the Middle East and elsewhere. COIN, as explicitly stated in JP 3-24, is nation-centric, whereas the highest priority of the US and "partner countries" has become containment and prevention of the spread of ISIL/ISIS whose OE is transnational rather than nation-centric.

In summary, a set of "rules" that could be derived from JP 3-24, that apply to any counterinsurgencies, including ISIL/ISIS, might include the following:

Rule #1: thoroughly understand every important aspect of the nature of the conflict, the parties involved and the context (operating environment or OE) in which the insurgency occurs.

Rule #2: make sure that both the strategic assumptions and the tactical decisions flowing from them consistently reflect Rule #1 and are continuously analyzed, assessed and incorporate learning experiences from both the bottomup and top-down.

Rule #3: COIN has to consistently empower even the lowest civil-military operational levels that are staffed by people who have received specialized pre-deployment training, for tactical planning and execution, including intelligence operations.

Rule #4: military sources can produce vast amounts of information from countless sources but establishing the operational relevance of such information in real-time (a real-time common operational picture/COP) is the key to successful COIN decision-making and operations.

Without indulging in too much military-related jargon, a COP serves as an invaluable common repository of information for all decision-makers at all levels engaged in COIN counterinsurgency. A COP leads to better synchronized COIN planning and execution decisions. In contrast to the now obsolete information warehousing paradigm, in which stored information is difficult to search, the next generation of COP, that incorporates BIG Data and utilizes cognitive computing systems, will enable civil-military stakeholders to deal with complex, often ambiguous problems, new types of emergent threats, and draw on a vast reservoir of empirical research that enables all levels of a command organization to know "what," "how" and even "why."

As JP 3-24 makes clear, emergent threats and opportunities in battlespaces, that are only a part of the OE, reflect a mixture of military, political and diplomatic issues. Understanding each of the ingredients in the mixture, extracting and applying actionable knowledge, avoiding being overwhelmed by too much irrelevant information, focusing on the most important information in any situation, sorting out multiple goals and constraints, checking against doctrine and experience, and more, all to meet specific decision-making needs at any moment, and to make tactical decisions that are consistent with civil-military strategies, requires that decision-makers have access to a combination of COP and cognitive decision-making tools that enable real-time collaboration among various stakeholders.

That's asking a great deal, especially in light of different decision-making responsibilities in each level of COIN civil-military organizations. Each decision-maker at each level needs to be able to adjust, improvise and synchronize decisions in real-time based on new inputs. Next-generation cognitive computing systems can enable frontline advisors and other military-civilian decision-makers to perform these functions while, at the same time, taking care of knowledge management, tracking key variables, events and situations, assessing progress and outcomes, and even using predictive analytics to wargame future scenarios and decision options. NexGen COIN will gather, integrate, organize and provide information to decision-makers in real-time, with a high level of security, in ways that enable them to continuously ask the system questions in their native languages and share the answers with all stakeholders and get their responses.

CHAPTER 20

NexGen COIN: Strategies

In the 2016 presidential election campaign, the two most important foreign policy and national security issues consist of the rise of the "Islamic State" or the "Islamic State of Iraq and the Levant" (ISIL/ISIS), and Iran as the "foremost state sponsor of terrorism" (according to the US Director of National Intelligence, James Clapper, in testimony before Congress). The US State Department, in its "Country Reports on Terrorism 2014," describes how Iran and Hezbollah actively pursued destabilizing terrorist, criminal, and militant activities throughout 2014. Closely connected to these top priority issues will be Russian combat operations in Syria, including dozens of fighter jets, especially the targeting of moderate insurgents that threaten the Assad regime, rather than targeting ISIS.

We have not heard anything substantive from the Obama Administration about whether the US is making any headway in the Middle East to restrain ISIS and other Islamic extremists in Syria, Iraq and elsewhere, progress on the civil war in Syria, and political reforms in Iraq that might provide future stability. What is the US doing in the Middle East, Gulf region and North Africa that is strategically correct, especially to bring stability to Syria and Iraq and at least to reduce civilian casualties in Yemen? What is the US doing to help remedy divisions and ease tensions between Sunnis, Shiites and Alawites, Kurds and Arabs, and Turks and Kurds?

After 14 years of war and billions of dollars invested in Afghanistan, clearly the US not only cannot remake the country but perhaps even influence its future. The Taliban and Al-Qaeda seem to have deepening ties. In the September 2015 edition of *Al Sumud*, the Taliban's official magazine, the jihadist group devoted significant space to Al-Qaeda leaders and pro-Al-Qaeda clerics eulogizing its former emir, Mullah Mohammad Omar. The Taliban's new leader, Mullah Mansour, then made a demand to Kabul in a message marking the Muslim festival of Eid-ul-Adha: "If the Kabul administration wants to end the war and establish peace in the country, it is possible through ending the occupation and revoking all military and security treaties with the invaders," Mansour said. Peace negotiations are not moving forward in Afghanistan. Even with very limited goals for its role in the peace process, the US will have to rethink its strategy for achieving a negotiated truce with the Taliban that itself is facing a growing ISIS challenge.

In Syria, any real strategic success will require, first, a very difficult, and highly unlikely, decision by the US and its Coalition partners to support the military removal of Assad, which is the primary aim of most of the insurgents that the U.S is trying, without much success, to recruit to fight ISIS. A large part of the lack of US success fighting ISIS is that "moderate" and not-so moderate insurgents in Syria are much more focused on removing Assad. Transformation of or reconstituting governance in Syria, Iraq, Yemen, Libya and other countries in the Middle East, creating civil order out of chaos, that somehow brings together Sunnis, Alawites, and Kurds, restoring a functioning economy in Syria and other such challenges all are contingent on factors that are not in US control.

The strategic challenge in Iraq, with as much as a third of its territory controlled by ISIS, also is "nation-building" that somehow brings together Shiites, Sunnis, and Kurds in a "creative" governance model that, first and foremost, resolves national and local sectarian and ethnic divisions. Thus far foreign policy experts in the US and elsewhere have not attempted to define how such a "creative" governance model would be structured or could work. In the meantime, Iraqis are joining the masses of refugees from other Middle East and African countries who are trying, by any means possible, to escape their chaotic worlds and migrate to Europe. And that exodus is just beginning as more Middle East meltdowns create thousands more refugees daily, mostly from Syria and Iraq.

Strategies for stabilizing the future of Iraq, Syria, Yemen, Libya or any other Middle East country have to go far beyond just success in the war against ISIS, which will be an enormous challenge in itself. ISIS is only one cause of instability in the region and only one source of spreading sectarian and ethnic violence. Iraq cannot create effective national security forces without addressing sectarian and ethnic divisions. No form of US air campaign and train-and-assist missions with US combat advisors will have lasting success if Iraq remains divided along sectarian and ethnic lines. And only a much more stable Iraq can limit the future role of Iran, with or without a P5+1 nuclear agreement.

Adding to the complexity of the political challenges across the Middle East is the need to provide a peaceful solution to the "Kurdish problem" in Syria, Iraq and also in Turkey and Iran. All of these spectacular political feats will have to occur in the midst of sectarian tensions and conflicts and periodic outbreaks of terrorism in Lebanon, Egypt and the Arab Gulf states that can push public sentiment in these countries to extremes of pessimism, despair and hostility.

The fact that the United States has agreed to work with Turkey to create an "ISIS-free zone" in Syria near the Turkish border north of Aleppo has no apparent strategic underpinnings. It is also unclear how this narrow area on the Turkish border will operate and whether Syrian Kurds in their People's Protection Units (YPG), the most effective forces fighting with the United States against ISIS in Syria, will have any role in the ISIS-free zone. We have very little information about where and the extent to which the Assad/Alawite-led faction is losing ground in Syria and what kind of support continues to be provided to Assad by Iran and Hezbollah.

A Sunni Arab coalition of Islamist groups called the "Army of Conquest" has emerged in Central-Western Syria that includes the Al Nusra Front, the Al-Qaeda affiliate in Syria. Even though Al-Nusra has been fighting ISIS, it also regards the US as a foreign enemy, which exemplifies a US problem in Syria and the complexities of the situation there. The "Army of Conquest" has support from Jordan, Saudi Arabia, Qatar, and the UAE. This anti-Assad effort may have tacit US support and even some possible CIA support activities. Like most everything else going on in Syria, the success of this Syrian insurgent group and its aims, other than removal of Assad and battling ISIS, remain quite opaque.

There is no way for the American public to really understand what actually is going on in Syria, even people with a passion for research. The options available to the US going forward not only are difficult to fathom for the American public relying on the news media they are mostly incomprehensible. Strategies for the US to deal with ISIS or the chaos in Syria, Iraq, Yemen and elsewhere in the Middle East are rarely discussed in the presidential election campaign. The Obama administration has made no references to the scale or complexity or time-frame for dealing with myriad challenges in the Middle East. No matter who is elected president, there will be no good or obvious foreign policy options.

The White House, Congress, and the intelligence community have not provided the American public with any meaningful milestones to measure progress in dealing with 15 years of terrorism in the Middle East and the scale and type of resources that will be required in the future. The really bottomline bad news, as confirmed by testimony presented by Defense Secretary Ash Carter and Chairman of the Joint Chiefs of Staff and Army Gen. Martin E. Dempsey before the House Armed Services Committee, is that the US has no counterinsurgency strategy for dealing with ISIS. In fact in their Congressional testimony, neither Carter nor Dempsey addressed the role of counterinsurgency to contain Iranian influence in Iraq, Syria, Yemen and elsewhere. Likewise, US cooperation with its Arab allies as an element of US counterinsurgency strategy was not mentioned at all.

The testimony of Carter and Dempsey confirmed that: ISIS in fact presents a "grave threat" in the Middle East and worldwide; ISIS must be denied safe havens and its financing and social media messaging disrupted; and Coalition partners in the fight against terrorism need advice, assistance, training and equipment. Understandably Dempsey stressed the need for patience and that progress will take a long time, especially since presently the US is responsible for most of what needs to be done in the Middle East and North Africa to fight ISIS and other terrorism. That news in itself should have been a wakeup call for Congress, the American public and, not least of all, presidential candidates.

The US needs a new US strategy for counterinsurgency training for so-called "moderate" rebels to enable them to become the main force opposing expansion of ISIS in Syria. The Pentagon's efforts to-date highlight the shortcomings of its intelligence and planning, and the failure of counterinsurgency strategies in the Middle East that have consumed billions of taxpayer dollars with nothing to show for it. Now the Pentagon says that it is drawing up plans to significantly revamp its training-and-assist program for "moderate insurgents" in Syria to include placing them into safer zones, providing better intelligence and improving their combat skills. The Pentagon was forced to make these changes after Jabhat al-Nusra, an Al-Qaeda affiliate, recently attacked many of the first 54 Syrian graduates of the US military's training program who were unprepared for the attack, had no local support from the Syrian population, and no intelligence about the attackers. The Pentagon belatedly admitted that they knew from the beginning that their mission to train insurgents "was going to be difficult."

US and international rhetoric says that halting the mass migration of refugees from Syria and elsewhere in the Middle East will require a comprehensive international effort to bring peace and stability to areas that those refugees are now fleeing. In reality, bringing stability to these areas will require a strategy that, since the US and its Coalition partners refuse to put boots-on-the-ground, gathers up very large numbers of local insurgents and trains them to become an effective fighting force, with US and Coalition air support. For this purpose a $500 million train-and-equip program was authorized by Congress in 2014 to generate more than 5,000 Syrian insurgent fighters. The program was supposed to be run by US Special Forces, with help from other allied military trainers, separate from a parallel covert training program for insurgents run by the C.I.A.

The Pentagon and the White House had no idea of where the trained insurgents would be sent after training. In fact they didn't have any "direct command and control with those forces once we do finish training and equipping them when we put them back into the fight," said Brig. Gen. Kevin J. Killea, chief of staff for the American-led military operation fighting the Islamic State. "If I had to point to a place where we could explore better lessons learned, that would be it." That unclear and confusing admission came after the Syrians training insurgents and several of the trainees were killed or captured by the Nusra Front.

The lack of any strategy for and discernible progress in combating ISIS in Syria and elsewhere in the Middle East means that the US has to build the next phase of its COIN operations virtually from scratch based on painful lessons learned. Any such COIN strategy will be complicated by the results of the Iranian nuclear deal which provides financial resources to amplify Iran's proxy wars, including in Syria that Iran views as its "35th province." Congressional testimony from the Pentagon has not addressed whether and how Iran or Russia fits into a US anti-terrorism strategy in Syria and the Middle East.

The US COIN strategy going forward in Iraq will require that the US and its Iraqi partner will be able to attract, hold, train and engage large numbers of Iraqi Sunnis. In the last 15 years, US forces have learned a tremendous amount, especially during the Anbar Awakening, about the dynamics of what works and doesn't work to recruit and engage Iraqi Sunnis in the fight against Al-Qaeda and ISIS, and also what it takes to minimize the tensions between Shiite forces and Kurdish forces. For the foreseeable future, Iraq will have to continue its reliance on Iran-supported Shiite militias in the fight against ISIS, but the Iraq strategy has to include a plan to, if not reduce that dependence, integrate Shiite militias into Iraqi Security Forces (ISF) that will have to be trained in counterinsurgency. Carter-Dempsey testimony to Congress made no mention of US train-and-assist activities in Iraq.

As members of Congress debated the P5+1's proposed nuclear deal with Iran, the Joint Comprehensive Plan of Action (JCPOA), and the adequacy of its provisions to block Iran's uranium enrichment, plutonium separation and covert paths to a nuclear bomb for the next 15 years, in reality the overriding issue has been Iran's trustworthiness. Almost absent from the Iran nuclear deal debate, however, was discussion of the fact, covered in detail in the aforementioned State Department report, that Tehran remains the world's leading sponsor of terrorist groups, including through its Islamic Revolutionary Guard Corps-Qods Force (IRGC-QF), the Lebanese Hezbollah, Iraqi Shia militant groups, Hamas, and Palestine Islamic Jihad. The State Department report further accuses Iran of "prolonging the civil war in Syria, and worsening the human rights and refugee crisis there."

While unquestionably Al-Qaeda and other terrorist groups remain credible threats, the growing threat from ISIS has become of paramount importance in the Middle East.

For years US counterterrorism efforts have focused on defeating Al-Qaeda, without much success. The group that carried out the 9/11 attacks has grown as an international threat primarily operating through regional affiliates such as Al-Qaeda in the Arabian Peninsula (AQAP). Since 2014, the US intelligence community has shifted its focus to ISIS as the primary driver of terrorism in the Middle East based on: its major territorial gains in Syria and Iraq; the flow of foreign fighters from Muslim and non-Muslim countries to join ISIS; the development of affiliates like Ansar al-Sharia in Libya and Ansar Beit al-Maqdis in Egypt's Sinai Peninsula; its effective global social media campaign to attract jihadist recruits; and its highly successful methods for financing its organization and activities through extortion networks, crime, taxing local populations, smuggling and sale of oil, antiquities, and drugs.

US counterterrorism strategies and methods have not been modified to deal with ISIS even though it has been in existence since 2004 when it arose as Al-Qa'ida in Iraq (AQI). The Department of Homeland Security (DHS) has a major domestic and international program for "countering violent extremism" (CVE) but there's no way for the American public to know anything about its effectiveness vis-à-vis ISIS other than, thank goodness, America has experienced very few instances of violent extremism attributable to the dissemination of inflammatory messages by ISIS or any other terrorist organization. Nevertheless, Congress is currently considering legislation that would create a whole new bureaucracy within DHS to deal with and coordinate CVE.

With approval of the Iran nuclear deal, and lifting of sanctions against Iran, it will gain access to tens of billions of dollars from blocked accounts and, sooner rather than later according to Iran's pronouncements, from substantial additional oil sales. We know that Iran will spend a large part of this money on its domestic priorities. What no one knows, however, is how much of the more than $100 billion pouring into Iran's coffers will be spent on support for its extremist and terrorist proxies in the Middle East, Gulf region, and elsewhere, including building affiliate bases in Latin and Central America. US foreign policy and national security strategies must have strategic answers ready to respond to Iran's increased financial ability to support insurgencies and extremist groups in Syria, Iraq, the Gulf States, and Latin America, and proxy groups such as Hezbollah and Hamas.

By any measure, President Assad qualifies as the Syrian version of Adolph Hitler. In addition to killing hundreds of thousands of Syrians, he has driven millions of Syrians out of the country to migration destinations in Europe. Most Syrians today avoid dangerous and potentially deadly water escape routes and proceed over land through Turkey to the Balkans, Central and Northern Europe. Although Assad hasn't loaded Syrians into freight cars to convey them to concentration camps, the end result is comparably destructive for displaced persons and refugees and, for many of them, deadly or psychologically damaging. A substantial slice of Iran's funds from sanctions relief will go to boost the survival of Assad's regime, including support for a growing number of foreign Shiite fighters and pro-Assad militias in Syria and Lebanese Hezbollah which has deployed at least 5,000 fighters in Syria. Iran probably would continue shipments of more than fifty thousand barrels per day of crude oil to Syria, more than a billion dollars worth annually.

As for Iran's investment in influencing (controlling?) Iraq, the timing of sanctions-relief funds for Iran couldn't be better. For the past year, Iraq's only effective self-defense against ISIS, that already controls a vast Iraqi territory, has been the Hashd al-Shabi (i.e., Popular Mobilization Units or PMUs), militias commanded by the Iranian-backed Badr Organization and other PMUs that are US-designated terrorist groups with direct command and logistical ties to Iran's Revolutionary Guard Corps's (IRGC) Quds Force. Removal of sanctions is likely to result in Iran and its IRGC becoming Baghdad's main security partner, undermining US efforts to strengthen the Iraqi Security Forces (ISF).

Funds flowing to Iran from sanctions relief, therefore, will compete with about $1.6 billion of US funding for Iraq under the Train and Equip Fund and will establish Iranian proxies as the dominate military and political force in Iraq as it heads toward provincial elections in 2017 and parliamentary elections in 2018. This is not new news for Iraq since already in 2010 Vice President Joe Biden predicted that Iran would spend at least $100 million to strengthen its Iraqi proxies. In other words, funds from sanctions relief for Iran could undermine Iraq's independence.

Hezbollah also would be a primary benefactor of sanctions largesse for Iran. In addition to funding the group's weapons, training, intelligence, and logistical activities within Lebanon and for defending Assad, the additional funds would benefit Hezbollah's regional and international operations in support of Shiite militias in Iraq and Yemen, Yemen's Houthi rebels, and international terrorism in Latin America and Asia. An infusion of sanctions cash also will enable Iran to expand recruitment of foreigners and equip them for combat.

In Yemen, the Saudi/UAE-led coalition fighting to reinstall President Abdu Rabu Mansour al-Hadi continues to blame Iran for backing opposition forces led by Houthi rebels and supporters of former president Ali Abdullah Saleh. The lifting of sanctions against Iran is likely to mean that the Houthis will receive more funds from Tehran. Increased Iranian support for the Houthis and further destabilization of Yemen in itself is enough to seriously upset Saudi Arabia, other Sunni-ruled kingdoms and sheikhdoms in the Gulf. Bahrain, for example, ruled by Sunnis, has a majority Shiite population. Shiites constitute a majority in the Eastern Province of Saudi where the Kingdom's main oil fields are located.

Iran's nuclear deal with Western powers has received, at best, a lukewarm reception from Gulf States. Saudi Arabia, in particular, is concerned by the potential political shift of political and military power in the Middle East and Gulf region in favor of Iran. The Saudis are especially worried about the release of more than $100bn of Iran's frozen funds that will allow it to fund its proxy wars in Syria, Yemen, and elsewhere, and also enable Iran to accelerate development of and flood the energy market with cheaper oil and also gas.

The media in Jerusalem and elsewhere in the Middle East, however, has been publishing more positive messages about the potential of the Iran nuclear deal to dramatically shift Middle Eastern geopolitical tectonic plates in ways that will change relationships between Saudi and Russia, Turkey and Saudi, and even could result in Sunni Arabs needing Israel more than they ever anticipated. It is very difficult to know how much credence to attach to this seemingly optimistic view.

One of the first indications of this possible shift is Riyadh signing a $10bn investment deal with Russia despite the fact that both are competing for oil markets and business in Europe and elsewhere and both are in opposite camps on the Assad regime in Syria. In return Moscow will work with Saudi to develop nuclear energy. Media reports also have said that the ultra-rich Prince Waleed Bin Talal is "secretly" planning to go to Israel to dialogue with the Israelis at the request of Saudi's King Salman. Saudi and Israel, that have never had official diplomatic relations, share a common opposition to Iran.

Another thing that Israel and Saudi have in common is that Saudi (and Egypt, Jordan or the United Arab Emirates) was omitted from one of President Obama's recent addresses about the nuclear deal in order to highlight the Kingdom's opposition. King Salman did reluctantly capitulate on the nuclear deal during a visit to Washington. Israel's opposition to the deal was singled out by Obama in his address dozens of times but now Obama and Netanyahu have reached an understanding about the nuclear deal and are moving forward to deal with related and other security issues. For very different reasons, both Saudi Arabia and Israel see Iran and its proxies (Hezbollah and the Houthis) as their main terrorist threats and enemies in the future.

For Saudi, Iran's economic threat also is very real. For example, just one day before the nuclear deal was signed, Iran's oil-shipping company, with the world's largest fleet of supertankers, announced its intention to return to European and international markets. Iranian companies already have signed agreements worth billions to construct 800 miles of pipelines to export gas to Europe from the country's massive South Pars field.

Unofficial word indicates that Saudi and Israel have signed a joint security cooperation agreement that includes Israeli "technical aid" to protect key Saudi targets. One wonders (pure speculation) whether Saudi has negotiated access to Israel super-secret, coveted dome technology. Unofficial reports even indicate that Saudi Arabia has agreed to let Israel use its airspace as a shortcut to attack Iran if necessary. The word from Riyadh is that Saudi and Israel are completely coordinated on all matters related to Iran. Uncorroborated rumors also have suggested the possibility that Saudi oil giant Aramco is planning a pipeline that would run through Israel to provide easy export of Saudi oil to Europe. In addition to benefits to Israel, this could be a Saudi counter-measure aimed at offsetting pipeline projects from both Russia and Iran to European markets.

Despite critical common interests, the Saudis are unlikely to say much officially about their relationship with Israel. Both countries have publically admitted to a series of secret meetings over the past year focused on Iran. Ironically, even though both countries are collaborating on agreements and plans to protect each other in the event of attack, Riyadh still refuses to publically recognize Israel's right to exist. More than merely an excuse that admission is contingent on creation of a Palestinian state. Hopefully, in the foreseeable future, the growing ties among Israel, Saudi, Egypt and Jordan will pave the way for Palestinians to come to the bargaining table.

In addition to a change of leadership in the Palestinian Authority, this will require the Saudis to delete references to a so-called right of return in their proposed peace agreement and removal of several other lines in the sand that are not responsive to Israel's security concerns. Again hopefully, thanks in part to the Iran nuclear deal, growing security, economic, energy and technical cooperation can lead Saudi, the Gulf states and Israel to establish normalized relationships.

In the future, the main challenge for the US in battling ISIS anywhere in the Middle East or elsewhere is not just President Obama's reluctance to commit boots-on-the-ground, it is defining the core mission of an effective COIN strategy for ISIS containment. Central to the debate about the core mission of counterinsurgency (COIN) has been whether the US should engage in "nation-building" or as it is sometimes called "stabilization." In addition to its role in counterterrorism, there's no argument that COIN can include humanitarian assistance, but the red line has been drawn by Obama on COIN engaging in rebuilding a state or attempting, overtly or covertly, to reshape governance in host countries.

In Petraeus's writing of the *2006 Army and Marine Corps Field Manual (FM) 3-24, Counterinsurgency*, it states, "Soldiers and Marines are expected to be nation-builders as well as warriors." He applied this concept to Iraq in 2007 when he became commander of US forces. Nation-building, however, has not been part of the Obama doctrine for military engagement in Iraq or elsewhere in the Middle East. The president's position is "the end of long-term nation-building with large military footprints."

About 18 months ago, the US military finally published a revision to its 2006 COIN manual known as *Field Manual (FM) 3-24*. The new manual was named *Joint Publication (JP) 3-24*. As some critics have pointed out, JP 3-24's assumptions at the strategic level about the role of US counterinsurgency in restoring the legitimacy of "host nations" were unrealistic and flawed. COIN efforts to build or rebuild the legitimacy of "host" national governments are futile and doomed to failure when the national regime is dictatorial, brutal, corrupt, instrumental in fueling sectarian conflicts and otherwise unpredictable in the near- or long-term.

COIN should not be in the business of attempting to engineer political and institutional transformation in "host countries" such as Syria or Iraq. It's not simply a matter of the significant levels of US political and financial commitment that would be required. No matter how much the US invests, the process and outcome would be completely unpredictable. The military-civil commitment and other support required probably would take generations, not just years, which understandably is more than the American public, and political leaders of any party, especially in an election year, are willing to support.

Perhaps for these reasons, COIN JP 3-24 relies on platitudes to describe "nation-building" activities connected to COIN without providing any guidance for planning and implementation, for example: "providing incentives to host governments to initiate reforms"; "encouraging elites in host governments to address local grievances"; "improving US interagency coordination and collaboration"; "support for the COIN strategy of host nations"; and "COIN should address the root causes of insurgent's grievances." In Syria, Iraq, Libya and Yemen, ISIS has risen in power vacuums and probably cannot be contained or expunged until, if not "nation-building," "creative measures" are implemented to bring about "stabilization." In Iraq, as proposed elsewhere, that "creative measure" should be collaboratively planned decentralization of the central government, drawing on lessons learned in the Great Awakening.

ISIS rose up in a power vacuum in Syria caused by the Assad regime's retreat from large portions of eastern Syria and the collapse of Iraqi security forces in the Sunni west of Iraq. Disenfranchised, frustrated, angry local populations hostile to government forces have allowed ISIS to hold large swaths of territory in both Syria and Iraq.The United States has never clearly articulated its desired outcome in Syria or its strategy for achieving the outcome it is seeking or how it would engage Russia and Iran in the process. In both Syria and Iraq, the US has no choice other than improving efforts to engage and support local tribes and insurgents against ISIS, including more effective use of Coalition Special Forces as frontline advisors in safe havens, computer-based intelligence, and airpower to degrade ISIS's logistical and operational capabilities.

It's startling and dismaying to witness the number of experienced, highly credentialed people in the US military-civilian decision-making establishment that have been so wrong in their strategic judgments about Iraq, Afghanistan, Syria, Libya and elsewhere. Some of the notable exceptions, who were right at least some of the time, like Petraeus, McChrystal, and Gates, often had to fight an uphill battle with the White House and their own military and national security bureaucracies. Thanks to their admirable efforts, however, valuable counterinsurgency lessons learned in Iraq, Afghanistan and Syria are available for integration into next generation counterinsurgency mixed with additional doses of 20-20 hindsight:

US military leaders involved in planning counterinsurgencies in chaotic conflicts need to have Plan B in place for the aftermath of regime failures and changes. With the notable exceptions of the occupations of Germany and Japan after 1945, the United States has a long tradition of bungling the conclusions to wars, from the American Civil War, to the Korean War and the Vietnam War, the Gulf War and the more recent military interventions in Iraq and Libya.

The strategic and other assumptions, including measures of success, governing military and political policy-making for any Middle East or other country under siege by Islamic or other extremists need to be very clearly and explicitly articulated so that members of Congress can exercise due diligence without rose-colored glasses. Political and military leaders up and down the chain of command have tended to paint rosy pictures of successes and challenges being overcome in Middle East countries in spite of the fact that their military and political initiatives are faltering or failing. Worse, current and former intelligence officials claim that top Pentagon officials pressured intelligence analysts in CENTCOM to alter their reports to show more positive results in the fight against ISIS.

Every version of COIN manuals and thinking has emphasized the importance of "nation-building" as a key component of counterinsurgency. Easier said than done as proved in Afghanistan and especially Iraq after Saddam's downfall in April 2003. The problem, as illustrated by the Office of Reconstruction and Humanitarian Assistance and then by the Coalition Provisional Authority, the US may have the military resources to take down Islamic terrorists but too often lacks the capabilities to build "governance" and "legitimacy" of "Host" countries and their localities after the downfall of their governments. In Afghanistan after the Taliban's downfall, a power vacuum was filled by corrupt warlords and then a resurgent Taliban.

Unless the job of reconstruction is handled by professionals who really know how successful "city building" or "nation-building" is done, and also possess local cultural and other knowledge and linguistic skills, the mission is likely to end up a fiasco. As a core NexGen COIN strategy, "nation-building" needs to be subordinated to collaborating with local tribes and other local people to create protected communities with local governance that transcends sectarian conflict. Training of local counterinsurgency and support personnel and teams should emphasize using their brains and skills to see, understand and leverage opportunities for developing local engagement and resources.

US forces should rely on soft power and the right kind of messages in addition to firepower to deal with extremist insurgencies in any country. In many instances these messages should be delivered by US soldiers who have learned to communicate with locals and build trust. In this context, there are serious limitations to using drone strikes to eliminate terrorist leaders and for other purposes that frequently kill civilians and turn others into angry enemies of the US

In spite of the resistance by Obama to boots-on-the-ground, as Col. MacFarland proved so clearly in Ramadi, there is no substitute for ground-forces (or ideally local police trained by US soldiers) embedded in neighborhoods for the purpose of controlling terrain. The Ramadi Great Awakening story is one of small bases of US operations where locals are trained and stationed for their own protection while being responsible for the security of neighborhoods and winning hearts and minds. In these small bases, there's an important role for special operations forces as frontline advisors, who also are involved in training local insurgents.

The idea that when US and Coalition forces overthrow a regime, the best plan is to pull out US forces as quickly as possible, so that the country cleansed of bad leaders can take responsibility for its problems, has not worked. Assuming that COIN goals include stabilization, sectarian and ethnic reconciliation, US and Coalition forces had better plan to stay or think about not getting involved in the first place. Recruiting locals for engagement in counterinsurgencies is almost impossible if they believe that their American or other "allies" soon will head for the exits. As Col. MacFarland points out from his experience in Ramadi, it's critical for US forces to convey that their counterinsurgency efforts, including "governance building," includes staying for the long-haul, whatever it takes. Otherwise US and Coalition partners are wasting their time.

ISIS and Al-Qaeda are there for the long haul and locals know it.

The American public and Capitol Hill need to understand and appreciate the critical importance of counterinsurgency commitments in Middle East and North African countries that have staying power. The alternative will be future wars at much greater human and financial costs, and very likely the failure of too little and too late.

The US should fight fewer wars but will have to engage in calculated combat when necessary to prevent having to play warfare catch-up. There is no reason to believe that the Islamic State will let up on its drives to control territory, especially those with valuable energy and other assets. Since ISIS's targets for territorial expansion are more or less chaotic countries with corrupt and broken political systems, US counterinsurgency involvement in these countries brings the risk of perpetual warfare requiring the commitment of resources that can't be predicted at the outset or even at any future point.

Unconventional or conventional wars without any exit strategy or even the illusion of an end are the products of strategic and political mistakes and not realistic, sensible and sane choices. We've had mistakes like that under different presidents in 2003 in Iraq and 2009 in Afghanistan where the issue became the right number of troops when it should have been the strategy driving the wars. Neither troop surges nor limitation of troops have proven successful because they didn't produce results that could be labeled a "win" and because, in both instances, no end-games and strategies to achieve them had been defined at the outset or even along the way.

As the context for planning NexGen COIN, the Obama administration or the future occupant of the White House and its NATO partners should conduct a comprehensive strategic assessment of the status of security in every Middle East and North African country and the US borders with Mexico and Canada to: project various scenarios of what is likely to evolve in the next few years in order to develop strategies that mitigate risks and the cost of options for interventions; and test the potential value of NexGen COIN and its *protected safe havens* in Syria, Iraq, Afghanistan, Libya and other countries with weak or failing governments faced with the ascendency of ISIS and Islamic extremists.

This strategic review also should play an important role in educating the American public about the nature of disorders and disarray in the Middle East that compares with or probably even surpasses anything in recent historical memory for civil wars and interstate chaos, other than going back to the Thirty Years' War in the first half of the seventeenth century. Another recent factor, which also has to be viewed in its historical context, is the intention of Russia's President Vladimir Putin to become more involved in Syria's civil war to bolster Assad's regime. What is not commonly known is that Russia and Syria have been linked for more than a century. During the Cold War, Damascus was one of Moscow's few allies. Since the launch of the Syrian Revolution in 1966, Russia was one of Syria's strongest allies and suppliers of arms. Russia has been shipping arms, air defense systems, helicopters, and fuel to Syria for decades. Tartus, Syria, is home to Russia's only naval facility in the Mediterranean region.

Russia's recent intervention in Syria becomes even more troublesome for the US and the West because Russia is constructing a compound for its troops and improving one of Assad's airbases for airplanes that presumably one day will attack ISIS. Thus both the US and Russia, separately, will be at war with ISIS in Syria at the same time. No one can forecast how this scenario will play out over time. The US, and the next phase of its counterinsurgency strategy in Syria, now faces Russia, Iran and Iran's proxies like Hezbollah supporting Assad against ISIS and other insurgencies attempting to overthrow his regime.

In this context, NexGen COIN would create networks of technology-enhanced protected safe havens for insurgent training and humanitarian purposes, and to contain the expansion of ISIS. It is cautious and restrained unconventional warfare that relies heavily on intelligence, rather than on the exercise of blunt power. It is guided by very specific strategies and goals, and assumes that counterinsurgency is accompanied by diplomacy, "nation-building" programs and even covert action that is judiciously deployed.

NexGen COIN will require additional training for special operations forces to serve effectively as frontline advisors/CyberWarriors.

They will have a much greater and more important role in fighting terrorism in the Middle East, along the US border and elsewhere than in past history, especially with the shift to bottomup decision-making, including co-piloting UAV strikes, and the arming of special ops with cognitive computing and the full spectrum of US intelligence resources.

The proposed NexGen COIN strategy applies to any country in the Middle East, Asia or Latin America that is under siege by violent extremists including, but not exclusively, ISIS. The main US commitment will be to create networks of bases – protected safe havens -- designed to provide training for insurgent allies, vetted by trusted locals, and safe places for humanitarian assistance for displaced persons. Each of these protected safe havens would be managed by frontline advisors, special forces and Rangers, who use the latest intelligence, cognitive computing and communications technology to enable data-driven decision-making that brings together, in real-time, all relevant information from their ground operating environment and other sources of the US intelligence community.

The only way to speedup more successful military action against ISIS in Iraq, Syria and elsewhere is to empower more innovative and creative bottomup decision-making by US Special Forces in frontline advisory roles. US battlefield history in Europe and Asia are full of examples of adaptive leadership that succeeded in winning battles with only small contingents of boots-on-the-ground. In the proposed cognitive technology-enhanced bottomup decision-making system, all strategic and tactical decisions for each protected safehaven and network of protected safe havens will be made by frontline advisors, including UAV reconnaissance and airstrikes, without being overridden by rules of engagement. Frontline advisors will be the trusted, tactically responsive eyes on the ground together with their trained teams of vetted local insurgents.

Experienced teams of Special Forces or Rangers operating as frontline advisors will be able to query a cognitive computer system for answers needed in real-time that include intelligence delivered by drones. Frontline advisors will be able to share control of drones with remote co-pilots. In addition, frontline advisors will perform the multiple roles of combat leaders, intelligence analysts, insurgent trainers and advisors, forward air controllers, protected safehaven community developers and managers, managers of humanitarian aid and all aspects of assistance to displaced persons seeking help and shelter, and managers of internal and external community relations.

The US already possesses cognitive computing systems that would enable frontline advisors to access, query, interact with and use vast amounts of structured and unstructured data being collected on battlefields and nearby locations to identify enemy targets and to manage all aspects of networked protected safe havens. These advanced cognitive systems will learn from every action by frontline advisors and be able to instantaneously compare their selected strategies and actions with prior ones and their outcomes, and offer decision options for potentially more effective strategies and actions to counter ISIS or other enemy targets or to accomplish any other objectives.

These cognitive systems not only will include the capability for two-way communication with drones (UAVs), frontline advisors will be able to co-manage weaponized drones together with remote pilots located in the US. These UAVs also will be connected to the cognitive computing system to ensure that their intelligence, surveillance, reconnaissance (ISR) and targeting activities are effectively driven in real-time by Big Data and the system's analytics capabilities, and the UAVs and their pilots have learned from all previous drone missions and campaigns in the region. The drones and their frontline advisors and pilots will keep watchful eyes on and analyze any evidence of Iran's and Hezbollah's changing footprints and activities in Syria and the activities of the "Army of Conquest" in relation to ISIS, Assad and Iranian proxies.

CHAPTER 21

NexGen COIN: Protected Safe Havens

Before and after the 2003 invasion of Iraq, the Middle East has been in turmoil, which will continue no matter who is elected president in 2016. In 2015, the right combination of US military and diplomatic policy for the Middle East is still elusive. Syria, Afghanistan, Tunisia, Egypt, Libya, and Yemen are experiencing continuous acts of terrorism and civil wars. Lebanon and Jordan are full of refugees with millions more in Turkey. Supported by Iran, Lebanon's Hezbollah is fighting for the life of Assad's regime in Syria. Iraq, Russia, Syria and Iran are now sharing intelligence, presumably in a common battle against ISIS. Iraq already has strong ties with Iran in the fight against ISIS.

President Obama refuses to endorse additional military interventions in the Middle East. He has relied on targeting Islamic extremists with drone strikes in Afghanistan, Pakistan, Somalia, Yemen, Libya, Iraq and Syria. Successful drone strikes have included ISIS's No. 2 figure in Iraq, Haji Mutazz, who was killed outside of Mosul on August 18, 2015. On September 30, 2011, the US-born radical Islamic cleric, Anwar al-Awlaki, was killed by a drone strike in Yemen. Placed at the top of a CIA kill list in 2010 by the Obama administration, al-Awlaki was involved in the 2009 Christmas Day airline bombing attempt in Detroit and a 2010 plot to blow up US-bound cargo planes. Obama's most famous assassination decision, executed on May 2, 2011, by

SEALS rather than a drone: Osama bin Laden who (surprise!) turned out to be not only the ideological leader of Al-Qaeda but its day-to-day manager of terrorism operations worldwide.

The Obama Administration and its NSC are well aware of the limitations of drone strikes against extremist leaders as states in the Middle East are crumbling and collapsing. They know that Iraq, Syria, Libya and Yemen are the products of governments that, even though they have had international recognition, have ruled through the repression of ethnic and sectarian minorities by corrupt elites. Call it the Arab Spring or by some other inspiring name, armed nonstate actors, including ISIS, have been determined to capitalize on the chaos and disintegration of state governments in the Middle East and rule them across and without national boundaries.

ISIS eventually may disappear or be transformed in the future. But no matter what happens to ISIS or countless insurgencies in the Middle East, the former nation states within which these insurgencies have emerged cannot be brought back to life in any recognizable political forms. What does it all mean? First of all, it means that the future of the Middle East involves political, social, economic and demographic forces over which the United States and other outside powers have little control or perhaps even influence. For the next generation, at least, instability and unpredictability will be the rule in the Middle East. The impacts of any US policies themselves will be quite unpredictable. With the possible exception of the nuclear agreement with Iran, it will be very difficult in the years ahead for the US to play an exceptional leadership role in the Middle East.

The US already has faced the historical fact that, at great human and financial cost to itself, it probably can inflict more serious warfare damage in the Middle East than conceivably do good. While facing some serious questions from Western allies about its failure years ago to take appropriate action on Assad's sectarian bloodbath, US foreign policy fundamentally calls for making as few costly mistakes as possible on questions of military intervention in the Middle East. With or without US military interventions, however, for the foreseeable future increasingly destabilized Middle East countries will be subjected to proliferating insurgencies. The US's only choice is to develop a NexGen COIN response that draws on the well-documented lessons learned in its counterinsurgency warfare history and leverages the technological superiority of its private and public sectors.

The Islamic State emerged in the aftermath of the US invasion of Iraq in 2003. Abu Mus'ab a-Zarqawi, who shared Bin Laden's ideology and trained with Al-Qaeda in Afghanistan before 9/11, led an Islamic extremist organization in northern Iraq when the US invaded. Called Al-Qaida in Iraq (AQI), it attacked Shia targets as well as Coalition and Iraqi government targets with the goals of destabilizing Iraq and fomenting a civil war. AQI split with Osama bin Laden's Al-Qaeda organization. Zarqawi was killed in a US airstrike in 2006. The emergence of the US-backed Anbar Awakening, or Sons of Iraq, weakened AQI. Zarqawi's successors "rebranded" AQI as the Islamic State of Iraq and al-Sham (ISIS), which refers to a territory that roughly corresponds with the Levant.

Al-Qaeda's goal of forming a global network of Muslims to carry out attacks against the West and confront the US and other secular powers preceded the emergence of ISIS. ISIS evolved rapidly under its new leader and self-proclaimed caliph, Abu Bakr al-Baghdadi, especially after the 2011 revolt against the Assad regime in Syria expanded into a civil war. ISIS took full advantage of the chaos in Syria and established a base of operations in Syria's northeast. During this time US forces had withdrawn from Iraq. A weakened Baghdad was faced by intensifying sectarian strife. Iraqi Prime Minister Nouri al-Maliki pursued a hard-line, pro-Shiite agenda. This further alienated Sunni Arabs throughout the country. ISIS capitalized on this turmoil and weakness by adding Iraqi Sunni tribal leaders to its cadres and even former Iraqi military officers who wanted to regain the power that they enjoyed during Saddam's era.

None of this was anticipated or acted on by US intelligence at the time. The ISIS capture of Fallujah and Ramadi in January 2014 came as a shock. Indicative of the failure of intelligence, from the Pentagon to the field, it was believed that US-trained Iraqi security forces would contain the ISIS threat. On the contrary, mass desertions from the Iraqi army enabled ISIS to capture Mosul, Tikrit, al-Qaim, and numerous other Iraqi towns, and move toward Baghdad. By the end of June 2014, ISIS had renamed itself the Islamic State, proclaimed the territory under its control to be a new caliphate, and attracted some 15,000 foreign fighters from 80 countries around the globe, including the US

Just about every US military leader and CIA official involved in the Iraq war has written about the disastrous decisions made in 2003 by the Coalition Provisional Authority (CPA) to ban former members of Saddam's Baath Party from positions in the Iraqi government and military leadership that created a vacuum filled by AQI and Shia militias backed by Iran. US forces in Iraq had considerable success against AQI from 2009 to the end of 2011 when the last of US troops left Iraq. AQI took advantage of the military vacuum left by US withdrawal. Prime Minister Maliki's sectarian actions alienated Sunnis who increased their support for AQI. At the same time, Syria's 2011 uprising helped AQI's expansion. AQI joined the fight in Syria under the name of ISIS. Fighting Assad, gaining Syrian supporters, foreign fighters, money and supplies, in 2014 AQI moved aggressively to control territory in western Iraq. No extremist group has taken as much territory more quickly and attracted more foreign fighters.

In June 2014, after seizing territories in Iraq's Sunni heartland, including the cities of Mosul and Tikrit, ISIS proclaimed itself a caliphate with both political and theological authority over the Muslim world. Widely publicized battlefield success and a skillful use of social media attracted thousands of foreign recruits to ISIS. But this expansion also led to a rupturing of the relationship between Al-Qaeda and ISIS. The AQI-Al-Qaeda conflict was over the Syrian Al-Qaeda affiliate, Jabhat al-Nusra, that Al-Qaeda wanted to remain independent. Zawahiri also insisted that Baghdadi's ISIS organization only operate in Iraq. In other words, the rift between AQI-ISIS and Al-Qaeda was over who made the key strategic decisions. Today, ISIS and Al-Qaeda's branch in Syria, the Nusra Front, continue fighting each other for control of Syrian territory.

In addition to threatening the stability of Syria, Iraq and the Middle East, ISIS's goal of a global caliphate continuously fosters sectarian and religious conflict and humanitarian crises throughout the region. The flow of foreign fighters into Syria, and the experience that they gain on the battlefield, is a threat to countries around the world, but especially the US and Europe when they return home. ISIS also is building alliances with extremist groups in other countries such as Libya, Egypt and Afghanistan that make them increasingly dangerous.

ISIS is determined to replace Al-Qaeda as the leader of a global movement to establish an Islamic caliphate. Many splinter groups from Al-Qaeda and its affiliates are pledging their loyalty to ISIS. Islamic and jihadi groups in Egypt, Libya, Gaza, Tunisia, Indonesia, Malaysia, the Philippines and the Boko Haram in Nigeria have pledged their loyalty to or in various ways are showing leanings toward ISIS. A number of prominent AQAP leaders and increasing numbers of AQAP fighters also have been attracted to ISIS. It will take time for ISIS to break the bonds of top leaders of Al-Qaeda's affiliates that have sworn *bayat*, a religiously binding oath of fealty, to Zawahiri and to other leaders in Al-Qaeda's global network. Since Zawahiri's disavowal of ISIS combined with what almost sounds like an olive branch, however, Al-Qaeda affiliates have been hedging their bets.

Loyalty to Zawahiri among Al-Qaeda affiliates is strong. For example, when Qasim al Raymi recently became the new emir of AQAP, after his predecessor, Nasir al Wuhayshi, was killed in a US drone strike in mid-June 2015, he reaffirmed his allegiance to "the eminent sheikh, the beloved father," Ayman al Zawahiri, and reiterated his *bayat* to Zawahiri. "I pledge allegiance to you, to listen and obey, in times of difficulty and prosperity, in hardship and in ease, to endure being discriminated against and not to dispute about rule with those in power, and to wage jihad in the cause of Allah the Almighty."

The civil war raging in Syria that involves ISIS, Al-Qaeda, and numerous insurgencies fighting Assad's regime, Alawites and Hezbollah has displaced more than ten million Syrians and about 4 million have left the country. Sectarian divisions get deeper every day. The Islamic State's territory now stretches across hundreds of miles, from the outskirts of Aleppo in Syria into central Iraq, where it shares a border with the Kurds in the north and Baghdad in the south. Much of that area is sparsely populated desert, but overall ISIS already has millions of people under its control. Those who are "enemies" flee or are killed. For the rest, mostly Sunni Arabs, ISIS provides some precarious stability, predictability and basic services. Thus, by strategic plan, ISIS and its sundry affiliates are becoming increasingly entrenched and dangerous in the Middle East. The main ISIS goal, establishing a global "caliphate," would involve the collapse of Syria, Iraq, Yemen and other states, and the elimination of their borders.

Which group, ISIS or Al-Qaeda, poses a greater threat to the US homeland or Europe or countries in the Middle East is not worth debating. Any one of them that can get access to WMD will try to figure out how to use it. Up until recently, Al-Qaeda in the Arabian Peninsula (AQAP), that provided 15 of the 19 members of the 9/11 terrorist team, has been viewed by US intelligence as a greater threat for a mass attack on the US homeland than ISIS. AQAP already has been responsible for three attacks against the US. Ibrahim al-Asiri, AQAP bomb-maker and trainer of bomb makers, is near the top of the FBI's list of the most dangerous terrorists in the world. AQAP was the mastermind behind the *Charlie Hebdo* terrorist attack in Paris.

In addition to WMD, terrorism concerns are growing in the US and Europe with each terrorist incident. For example, a young Moroccan man recently was prevented from carrying out a plan to kill passengers on a Paris-bound express train. In spite of the fact that enhanced security and surveillance measures had already identified the man, he was only one of thousands of Europeans who had come on the radar of authorities as potential threats after traveling to Syria. The sheer number of militant suspects and the vast number of potential targets presents European officials with a nearly insurmountable surveillance task. In Paris alone, 1 million passengers use high-speed trains daily and 3 million use suburban trains. In France there are 3,000 train stations with 40 million passengers and 100,000 trains daily. Passenger and baggage screening is impossible.

There is virtually no defense in the US or Europe against soft targets like trains. In Europe, there are thousands of Europeans of Islamic descent, soon to be joined by millions of Islamic refugees, who will have to be in security and surveillance databases as potential threats. Unpredictable terrorism by radicalized and disenchanted Muslims is the wild card in Europe and, to a lesser extent, the US. Dealing with this threat will require both first-rate intelligence and security procedures and the capability of European countries and the US to effectively act on it with a sense of urgency. Europe's refugee crisis was not anticipated before it happened starting in mid-2015. The flows of refugees could increase astronomically with further destabilization in Syria, Iraq, Afghanistan, Libya and elsewhere. The European refugee crisis greatly amplifies the terrorism threat in Europe and works to the advantage of ISIS and Al-Qaeda.

One of the most serious outcomes of terrorism and warfare in Middle East and North African countries has been the vast numbers of refugees trying to cross the Mediterranean and land routes through Greece, Macedonia, Serbia and Hungary to get to Germany and Scandinavia. In recent years it was inevitable that, sooner or later, huge numbers of Syrian refugees would head for Europe. As yet another example of the failure of decision-making in Western countries pertaining to the Middle East, nothing was done to prevent this disaster from befalling both Syrian civilians and European countries. Prevention of the migration crisis from Syria, for example, would have required European countries to commit to ending the civil war in Syria, which neither the EU nor the US were prepared to do, and engaging with the UN, the US and other international humanitarian agencies to plan an integrated political-humanitarian solution.

The unending flow of migrants from the Middle East and Africa, that could amount to many millions in the near future, for good reasons has become a major issue for EU countries. The massive flow of migrants is unlikely to taper off without a strategy, which as yet has not been discussed by the EU, designed to provide protected safe havens for displaced persons in the Middle East and North African countries. By comparison, resettlement of 1.7 million Vietnamese refugees after the Vietnam War will look small.

Every day stories emerge of desperate people fleeing chaos and violence in the Middle East and North Africa only to encounter even more violence as they attempt to migrate to safety in Europe. Turkey erected a controversial border fence to keep refugees out. Thousands of Syrians cut through the border fence and crossed into Turkey, fleeing intense fighting in northern Syria between Kurdish fighters and ISIS. The news media showed thousands of Syrians passing babies and their belongings over the barbed-wire fence. Turkish troops gathered up the refugees, preventing them from moving further into Turkey. Turkey already has taken in more than two million refugees since 2011. For hundreds of thousands more refugees, Turkey is the main transit zone to Europe.

Is ISIS intentionally trying to drive Syrians out of Syria? We don't know the answer to that question but it's clear that ISIS intends to squeeze both rebels and Assad's forces in order to build its "caliphate" that straddles the Syria-Iraq border. ISIS has prevented fuel shipments from reaching rebel-held parts of northern Syria, grounding ambulances, paralyzing medical centers and shutting down every business that needs fuel. On the other side, Assad has been targeting Syrian medical centers, forcing these facilities to shut down. International aid groups have been trying to attract US and Coalition attention to the fact that the Syrian government is using barrel bombs to destroy medical facilities in opposition-controlled areas. ISIS is creating humanitarian problems of comparable scale and severity.

AQAP, Al-Qaeda and ISIS may have differences in tactics but not in goals. All of these Islamic extremist groups need maximum coordinated pressure and surveillance from the intelligence, security, military and law enforcement communities in the international community. The refugee crisis in Europe also vastly increases the incentives for and critical importance of devising ways to reduce the number of displaced persons, refugees and asylum-seekers in Middle East and north African countries that will attempt to flee or migrate to Europe. This will require a next generation of coordinated COIN efforts on an unprecedented scale that combine counterinsurgency and provision of much greater safety and security – protected safe havens -- for people living in cities, towns and other communities in Syria, Iraq, and other Middle East countries.

Although this NexGen COIN strategy includes components that resemble "nation-building," it much more resembles and underscores the potential importance of the decentralization strategy proposed for Iraq that builds on lessons learned in the Anbar Awakening, including containment of Islamic extremism and, at the same time, broad participation in community development programs and projects. In each Middle East and North African country, the dynamics of the political and societal context for a NexGen COIN counterinsurgency strategy that aims for containing ISIS and other terrorism and, at the same time, supports and promotes stabilization and reconciliation realistically faces serious headwinds.

The NexGen COIN strategy's pessimistic assumptions include: for the foreseeable future the Assad regime will oppose a national stabilization and reconciliation solution; in Libya the central government is in a conflict-ridden "transition" and has limited or no value for stabilization and reconciliation; the national government in Iraq has a limited but potentially important support role if it can manage Sunni and Shiite conflicts; Yemen and Afghanistan have few if any assets within their borders that can be leveraged for stabilization and reconciliation. In each of these countries, the potential for long-term success in containing and fighting ISIS and other extremists will depend on real-time data- and intelligence-driven NexGen COIN operations and decisions that continuously identify and leverage every potential positive element of local culture, politics, and conditions that might contribute to stabilization and reconciliation.

In every area of Iraq, Afghanistan, Libya, Yemen, Syria, Egypt and elsewhere in the Middle East and North Africa where ISIS is recruiting supporters and fighting, local situations typically are so complex as to defy a formulaic response by any country considering intervention. Even figuring out who the evolving "bad guys" are in various parts of these Middle East and North African countries can be challenging and confounding.

When such decisions are made remotely, for example, Saudi and its allies attacking Houthis by air in Yemen with US targeting support, the results can backfire very badly and most of those killed are innocent civilian bystanders. The Saudi-led bombardment of Yemen that began in early 2015 has resulted in thousands of civilian deaths. UNICEF says that nearly 10 million Yemeni children need urgent aid. In the midst of the chaos, Yemen's branch of Al-Qaeda loyal to ISIS has been thriving on the fighting between Houthis, Hadi loyalists and Saudi-Gulf Cooperation Council (GCC) forces.

As Syria continues to disintegrate, rival jihadists, insurgents and ISIS battle in the rampant chaos and confusion. In Aleppo, Syria's former industrial and economic capital, insurgents are on the offensive against Assad's forces and supporters that include Iran-supported Hezbollah and Shiite militias. Insurgent opposition to Assad includes the al-Nusra Front (The Front for the Defense of the Syrian People), supposedly (but denying it) Al-Qaeda's affiliate in Syria. Al-Nusra recently captured insurgents from Division 30, the name given to a contingent of "moderate rebels" being trained in northern Syria by the US. Other rebel groups claim that they don't know anything about Division 30. Which insurgent groups will eventually "liberate" Aleppo from Assad's forces is anyone's guess.

What has Saudi Arabia done for Syrian refugees? The reports are mixed. One report, to which Saudi did not respond, says that Saudi has enough air conditioned tents, over 100,000, used to house pilgrims on the way to Mecca, which could house as many as 3 million Syrian refugees. Responding to criticism that it has not done enough to help Syrian refugees, Saudi Arabia's foreign ministry said that it has received nearly 2.5 million Syrians since 2011. None of the six states that form the Gulf Cooperation

Council (Saudi Arabia, Oman, United Arab Emirates, Kuwait, Bahrain and Qatar) has signed the UN convention on refugees, which has governed international law on asylum since World War II.

Gulf states say they have taken in hundreds of thousands of Syrians since the Syrian civil war began. The Kingdom also claims to have provided about $700 million in humanitarian aid to Syrians and through international relief organizations to countries hosting Syrian refugees. Saudi Arabia definitely has a key role to play in resolution of Syria's civil war. In Yemen, Saudi and the GCC coalition of Arab states have proven that they can organize a large-scale commitment of troops and aircraft to battle jihadists and ISIS. In March 2015 Saudi mobilized fighter jets from Egypt, Morocco, Jordan, Sudan, the United Arab Emirates, Kuwait, Qatar and Bahrain in a joint operation in Yemen against the Houthi. The US provided intelligence and logistical support. Even Pakistan joined the coalition by providing warships. Saudi has proven that it can bring together a formidable coalition aimed at military containment of extremists. Now it's time for Saudi to reach across the great sectarian divide and exercise its diplomatic muscle in Syria aimed at stabilization and reconciliation in the Middle East.

In an interview in May 2015, Gen. McChrystal said: "... the US is mistakenly viewing ISIS as a traditional foe that lines up on the battlefield." But a more interesting McChrystal comment was: "In reality, I view ISIS as a symptom, not the problem. The real problem is this meltdown in the region that lets an organization that is really as obnoxious in their doctrine and behavior as ISIS is" (add the word "succeed"). McChrystal went on to say that: "The US-led coalition should look at what is allowing ISIS to grow and the methods it is using to propagate itself. I do think we are taking an approach that says maybe if we bomb enough or do enough commando raids or give enough weapons to our allies, that will solve the problem. I think it's a bit more complex."

McChrystal went on to say: "America thinks it has the technological edge because it has aircraft and precision weapons, but in reality ISIS is leveraging technology effectively. They are terrifying the region. People believe that ISIS is behind every door and under every bed," he said. "They are not a traditionally hierarchical kind of force that needs the traditional chain of command. They are just able to move quickly, and we should take some lessons from that." Reflecting the concepts in his book, "*Team of Teams: New Rules of Engagement in a Complex World*," McChrystal argues for building a "team of stakeholders" that is "an effective coalition," created out of all of the groups fighting ISIS, that all share the same strategy, and are prepared to stay in Iraq for a long time. Although his focus is on Iraq, no doubt McChrystal would apply the same concept to Afghanistan, Syria, and Yemen.

McChrystal doesn't say what that strategy should be other than a big, long-term military commitment, and leadership that fosters an adaptable military organization that shares information and empowers decision-making at all levels. Sounds familiar and certainly is not revolutionary. The key conceptual component that McChrystal advocates, which also fills today's business literature, is changing the military organization's style of leadership. McChrystal asks the relevant question: What if you could combine the adaptability, agility, and cohesion of a small team with the power and resources of a giant organization? One of the best examples of that strategy in recent times has been Col. MacFarland's brigade in Ramadi that he divided into small teams to perform specific operational missions, backed by all of the support in Iraq that he could muster, with some difficulty on the spur of the moment.

The Saudi intervention in support of the contested Yemeni government of President Abd Rabbuh Mansur Hadi, who fled Aden and went to Saudi, does not represent a strategy for Yemen endorsed by the US. In fact, the US does not appear to have a Yemen policy as indigenous militia groups, reminiscent of Libya, take advantage of the failed state to further their own tribal and sectarian agendas. Houthis control the north and other parts of Yemen and fighters linked to AQAP are surging in the south. The US continues to rely on UAVs and other airborne man-hunting to track down and strike terrorist leaders. A drone strike in Yemen, for example, killed the leader of AQAP and, a few days later, so far as we know, F-15 jets in Libya killed Mokhtar Belmokhtar who, in 2013, planned the seizure of an Algerian gas plant in which 38 foreign hostages died.

Chaos and a humanitarian crisis continue unabated in Yemen. Like the villages in Vietnam, Yemen is being destroyed to "save it." It would seem that the occasional killing of militant leaders is the most the Obama Administration and the US expect to achieve in Yemen. Killing terrorist leaders, however, is the narrowest imaginable mission for counterterrorism. Counterterrorism in the Middle East and North Africa needs to have a strategy specifically designed for each country, focused on containment of extremists, including ISIS, that leverages local factors and resources and that, as recommended by McChrystal, combines the adaptability, agility, and cohesion of a small team with the power and resources of a giant organization

In Afghanistan, it is the Taliban, and not ISIS, that at the moment is the main cause of security concerns. The Taliban have been based in Pakistan -- in Quetta, Peshawar and Karachi -- since the US-led invasion in 2001 toppled their regime and forced them to flee. Since the transfer of security control from NATO to Afghan forces at the end of 2014, Afghanistan has had a relentless continuation of Taliban violence. Taliban leaders direct their terrorist operations from Pakistani soil, sending gunmen and suicide bombers, weapons and money across the border to support Taliban summer offensives. President Ghani has thrown down the gauntlet. Earlier this year, Ghani sent Pakistani Prime Minister Nawaz Sharif an eight-point proposal in which he said that both countries were engaged in an undeclared war and that Pakistan had to take strong action against the Taliban, including placing Taliban leaders under house arrest and controlling their movements.

President Ghani's strong demands were long overdue, but also come at a time when leaders of the Afghan Taliban are struggling with leadership turmoil since the revelation that their leader, Mullah Mohammad Omar, has been dead for over two years. The Taliban have been trying to cement ties to Al-Qaida and other extremist groups and are dealing with the fact that some of their members have been attracted to the brutal tactics and aims of the Islamic State as it tries to extend east from its bases in Syria and Iraq. In Afghanistan, just this year, insurgent violence has resulted in more then 5,000 civilian deaths. Mullah Akhtar Mansour, named as successor to the deceased Mullah Omar, has been endorsed by Al-Qaida chief Ayman al-Zawahiri. One of Mansour's deputies is Sirajuddin Haqqani, a leader of the violent Haqqani network, also linked to Al-Qaida. Pakistan's powerful Inter-Services Intelligence (ISI) spy agency supports Mansour.

In Afghanistan, for the moment at least, the Taliban appear to have the upper hand. But the current situation for the Afghanistan government qualifies as a military-civil disaster. The attrition rate and casualties for Afghan forces are at all time highs. The main attraction to the Taliban by local populations is that corruption in national and local governments is so pervasive. Many ISIS recruits simply may be disgruntled Taliban trying to get some attention and respect. Otherwise there is not much difference between ISIS and Shiite militias in Afghanistan in terms of violence, crimes and retaliation against Sunnis, violence against women, pillage and other humanitarian crimes.

So what happens next? Anyone's guess is as good as another. As cynical as it may sound, without a fundamental and strategic change of governance in Afghanistan probably the most ruthless, vicious extremist group will win various regional wars. Intensification and spread of sectarian war seems likely. US distrust against intervention currently is so strong that it is unlikely that even genocide would bring the US full-bore back into an Afghan battleground. In the meantime, the US response to extremism in Syria, Yemen, Libya and elsewhere in the Middle East and North Africa also appears weak and incoherent. Perhaps, however, behind the scenes, in the vast labyrinthine maze of US intelligence and national security, invisible to the public and the media, and perhaps even to Congress, effective anti-terrorism strategies targeting Middle East and North African countries as well as ISIS actually may be on the drawing board. Let's hope so!

Unlike conventional warfare in a single country, it is extremely difficult to communicate to the American people, and even to informed members of Congress, happenings on the ground in Syria, Yemen, Libya, Afghanistan, Turkey, Lebanon, and Jordan. As for Congress, the task of communication is especially challenging in light of what former Secretary of Defense Gates refers to, in his fascinating, surprisingly candid memoir *Duty*, as an "uncivil, incompetent, micromanagerial, parochial, hypocritical, egotistical, thin-skinned …" Congress and its "kangaroo-court environment." Perhaps as a bitter reflection of his own personal experience, Gates' criticism is excessive, but nonetheless it vividly conveys the communication challenges during and in-between Congressional hearings on national security, especially in a highly partisan political environment, which certainly won't improve much as the 2016 election approaches.

As ISIS gains ground and strength, adds more terrorist fighters to its cadres every day, we can expect both Congress and a multiplicity of presidential candidates to ratchet-up their political rhetoric over US foreign intervention in the Middle East and ISIS containment strategies and policies. The debate could prove to be especially interesting since, hopefully, US counterterrorism strategies will be in the process of an accelerating transformation in the midst of what increasingly will look like all-out warfare in Iraq, Syria, Yemen, Libya and Afghanistan. For more than a decade the United States has been planning and adapting its counterterrorism and counterinsurgency activities in military, intelligence and law enforcement agencies to deal with Al-Qaeda. After all of that, a completely different terrorist group suddenly emerges, and ISIS supplants Al-Qaeda as the greatest jihadist threat from Afghanistan to the Middle East and North Africa.

The ideology and goals of ISIS, its strategies and tactics, may seem similar to Al-Qaeda but ISIS requires a different form of counterinsurgency than the US has been developing for a decade and a different containment strategy. "Containment" has to occur both on the ground and by undermining the jihadist appeal through social media to Muslim millennials: "counter-radicalization" has to be an integral part of the next generation of the US counterinsurgency strategy. COIN did not anticipate a "counter-radicalization" dimension of next generation COIN. The evolution of COIN understandably did not include or anticipate the potential value of the Internet and cognitive computing for implementing the all-important intelligence function of COIN and also the role of social media in both ISIS radicalization and "counter-radicalization."

Regime Change: National Security in the Age of Terrorism, written hastily by this author at the end of 2003, discusses: the US's trillion-dollar intelligence, military and law enforcement operations built post-9/11 primarily aimed at deterring Al-Qaeda; dozens of US governmental organizations producing thousands of reports on terrorism that might include strategies or ideas about how to be effective in preventing new terrorist attacks on US soil and elsewhere in the world, but did not include any proposals for containing the spread of terrorism from Pakistan to the Middle East; what COIN refers to as the "root causes of terrorism" (without reference specifically to ISIS which did not exist at the time); and containing or combating terrorists in the Middle East that were dedicated to establishing their own theocratic or other form of governments for captured territories. What was clear, even 12 years ago, was that traditional US anti-terrorism strategies and tactics were not working in Afghanistan, Iraq, northern Africa and elsewhere. Almost incomprehensible at the time, there was no evidence that the US and its vast intelligence community were adapting its counterterrorism strategies to deal with emerging terrorist organizations in the Middle East and South Asia.

Twelve years ago, at the end of 2003, as *Regime Change* was written, Al-Qaeda's financing from global sources was thriving. The lack of an effective global mechanism for preventing Al-Qaeda's money laundering was not started in the U.S. until 2004 and evolved over the years into an international system for intercepting terrorist financing backed by the UN, the EU, and cooperating governments. What was not anticipated, however, was the emergence of a terrorist organization like ISIS that didn't need or rely on outside financing.

As a terrorist organization that captures and holds territory, ISIS has taken over oil assets in eastern Syria and oil-producing operations in Iraq that enable it to generate millions of dollars per day in revenue to finance its operations. But that's not all. When ISIS seized Mosul, a city of 2 million people, it looted the provincial central bank and other smaller banks. And as it has been doing in Palmyra, Syria, and elsewhere, ISIS is plundering antiquities to sell on the black market along with jewelry, cars, livestock and whatever else it captures from residents and businesses. When ISIS takes over a city or town, they literally tax everything, including electricity and water supplies. They control most of the major transportation arteries in western Iraq and charge tolls on all of them.

The only potential competition at the moment that ISIS may have in the Middle East is Iran. Both Iran and ISIS want to be hegemonic powers in the Middle East and beyond. Iran wants to reestablish the Persian Empire; ISIS is committed to establishing a caliphate. Both Iran and ISIS concur that Israel should be destroyed. Both Iran and ISIS use terrorism to fulfill their goals of empire. Both Iran and ISIS are working with or against insurgent groups to overthrow governments in the Persian Gulf.

ISIS has not (yet) sought to create a nuclear program, but eventually they will be able to acquire nuclear weapons, and will be a far worse security challenge than Iran for the US and the rest of the world. The US is attempting to contain Iran's nuclear threat with the Joint Comprehensive Action Plan (JCAP). The US has no ISIS WMD containment plan. There is no agreement in Washington about a next-generation COIN strategy to deal with the expansion of ISIS. Achieving these goals will require extraordinary American leadership that educates the American public while dealing with many complex policy challenges. The Iran nuclear deal has been a crucial test case of the capacity of the US to provide international leadership on vital global security issues.

CHAPTER 22

NexGen COIN: Frontline Advisors/CyberWarriors

Since at least November 2014, Army General Martin Dempsey, chairman of the Joint Chiefs of Staff (JCS), had been telling lawmakers and the media that what he referred to as "more complex operations" in Iraq, such as efforts to retake Mosul or secure the Syrian border, may require deploying a limited number of additional American military advisers in action with Iraqi soldiers. While President Obama had ruled out combat "boots on the ground," a series of defeats in Iraq made it obvious that Iraq needs forward US advisers.

While Dempsey stressed the urgency of the Islamic State's threat to the US and its allies, he rebuffed criticism from US lawmakers, such as Republican Senator John McCain of Arizona, that the US was not arming anti-Islamic State coalition partners quickly enough or creating no-fly zones over parts of Syria to protect civilians and rebels.

It was apparent from testimony by the Pentagon at these and other Congressional hearings that the US had no strategy for defeating and degrading the Islamic State in Syria that also deals with serious military threats posed by Assad's military forces and especially its air force.

Notwithstanding resistance in Congress and among the American public to more "boots on the ground" in Iraq, Syria and elsewhere in the Middle East, one thing that US military and civilian decision-makers could agree on is that training and assisting Iraqi, Syrian, and other indigenous forces is an urgent challenge for US and Coalition forces. US efforts thus far have failed. In each of these efforts, the US has provided or promised to provide advisors for train-and-assist programs. The key question, however, is not whether but how to deploy US advisors in the most effective ways from Afghanistan and Iraq to Syria and possibly in other terrorism trouble spots today and in the future. Russia's latest phase of military support for Assad's regime makes an answer to this strategic question much more complex and urgent.

A key component of the answer, from lessons learned from Vietnam to Afghanistan and also in Iraq and Afghanistan, is that advising from the rear doesn't work, especially for the purpose of building and rebuilding insurgent forces that are supposed to fight ISIS. In September 2014 President Obama said that he would consider requests to forward deploy US military advisors with Iraqi troops "on a case by case basis." He has not made a similar commitment for Syria although frontline advisors have to play the key role in training "moderate insurgents." Without experienced teams of forward advisors (Army Special Forces or Rangers or Marines Corp. Forces Special Operations), adaptable terrorists like Al-Qaeda or ISIS typically can gain significant intelligence and other advantages on the ground that they have learned how to quickly exploit for deadly attacks.

To be absolutely clear at the outset, frontline advisors certainly qualify as "boots-on-the-ground," but as discussed here are not envisioned as conventional "boots on the ground." Frontline advisory roles would not be without dangers, but their primary role would be that of "special ops/CyberWarriors" focused on development and operation of networked protected safe havens that, sheltered by no-fly zones, function as pivotal components of regional and local ISIS containment strategies. These NexGen COIN special ops/CyberWarriors would be the leaders, organizers and managers of networks of protected safe havens in Syria, Iraq and possibly other Middle East countries.

In other words, this is not just conversion of one part of the Turkish "ISIS-free zone" to a safe haven, but rather creation of as many as needed, and a great many highly skilled special ops/Cyberwarriors will need to be trained, urgently. Key population centers and their environs, for example, would qualify as protected safe havens. That's exactly what happened in Ramadi and Anbar that Col. MacFarland and the "Ready First" Brigade found was under Al-Qaeda control in 2005.

Besides providing and collecting critically important human intelligence, NexGen COIN's frontline advisory teams need to be armed with forward air control decision-making authority and the ability to guide drones which not only track ISIS and a wide range of factors on the ground, but also provide real-time tracking of civilians trying to escape death and chaos, needing medical care, food and other help. The capability of frontline advisors to call on UAV and other precision airstrikes as needed will enhance the morale of local counterinsurgency forces in addition to putting significant pressure on ISIS, while helping to minimize (but, unfortunately, not altogether eliminate) civilian casualties.

Forward advisors will function as the brains, eyes, ears and voices of patrols, knowing and acting on when, where and how Coalition reinforcements of all kinds need to be provided. In addition to shaping and driving insurgent troop tactics, assisted by wireless devices connected to remote cognitive computing and analytics systems, forward advisory units always will be thinking and making decisions about how to create both enhanced local military and civil capabilities. This is exactly what Col. MacFarland and his staff did in Iraq's Anbar Province without the benefit of the kind of advanced information technology envisioned in NexGen COIN.

Implementation of NexGen COIN strategy, which aims for a continuum of both fight and rebuild in Iraq, Syria and elsewhere, will take place within networked protected safe havens. As a primary mission of forward advisory teams, local military-civil capacity-building will be significantly reinforced by continuous intelligence and data feeds, including from advanced drones. Drone development and use for military and commercial purposes is just in its infancy analogous to the early stage of smartphones.

Hundreds of millions of dollars are being invested in the US by private equity funds that envision widespread commercial and governmental drone applications. Military uses of drones in support of frontline advisors and protection of safe havens can provide ideal testbeds for drones and their software platforms without concerns about FAA approvals. The data and intelligence provided to frontline advisors by drones integrated with their own experiences and other sources of intelligence will be essential for NexGen COIN's bottom-up decision-making process. Leveraging these advanced technologies, frontline advisors in networked protected safe havens will operate as teams of teams as advocated by Stanley McChrystal.

America and the rest of the world are crossing a critical frontier in the evolution of computing and entering the era of cognitive systems. Most visibly was the victory of IBM's Watson on the television quiz show Jeopardy! Post-Jeopardy scientists and engineers at IBM, SAS and other companies are pushing the boundaries of information technology to create machines that sense, learn, reason, and interact with people using cognitive computing systems to provide decision-making insights and advice. NexGen COIN proposes to leverage "cognitive systems" in order to enable frontline advisors to make much better decisions in the frontlines of counterinsurgency and in their roles as developers and managers of protected safe havens. Frontline advisors will be able to harness "Big Data" that enables them, in real-time, to integrate the experiences and insights of frontline advisors anywhere in Syria and in any battle zone in the world by asking questions of a machine that is continuously learning from and analyzing every relevant action and interaction of frontline fighters.

Frontline advisors - CyberWarriors will be able to ask natural language-based questions of remote cognitive computing systems, get relevant replies in real-time and engage in Q&A until satisfied with the system's responses as they relate to local battles and a host of other OE and community situations. Cognitive computing systems will be able to continuously and instantly learn from all frontline advisors' experiences and queries, which will be integrated on the backend with massive amounts of relevant structured and unstructured information ("Big Data") provided by intelligence, counterinsurgency and other information sources.

Rather than depending on conventional top-down feeds from intelligence agencies, frontline advisors/CyberWarriors themselves will be able to function like quasi-independent mobile intelligence agencies. Frontline advisory units, with drone (and back-end analytics) support, will become the primary sources of counterinsurgency intelligence collection and analysis. Thus the focus of strategic intelligence collection and dissemination by the intelligence community will become effective support for tactical engagement with ISIS by insurgent forces in protected safe havens and also in the process of local military-civil capacity-building.

Even as frontline advisors/CyberWarriors apply what they have learned firsthand through experience in battles, and from a cognitive computing system, inevitably there will be trial and error, but most decisions and advice will not be shooting from the hip. The interactions between frontline advisors and their teams and the cognitive computing system will be stored for analysis and incorporated into evolving NexGen COIN/cyberwarfare learning and doctrine. NexGen COIN/cyberwarfare learning and experiences will be accessible by approved parties in real-time, rather than being incorporated at some later date into the next edition of an Army counterinsurgency field manual. Of course NexGen COIN cyberwarfare also will be available for teaching and training purposes at various US military installations that are training cadres of frontline advisors.

When the Army Irregular Warfare Center (AIWC) closed in 2014, after eight years of working to educate soldiers on counterinsurgency, it highlighted the fallacy of reliance on "Doctrine." Counterinsurgency doctrine had very little impact on

Iraq heading downhill or Iraqi military strategy. No matter what the Army did to try to refine its knowledge about counterinsurgency and it applications, there remained a persistent disconnect with the realities and decision-making of warfare on the ground in Iraq and elsewhere. NexGen COIN will change all of that because special ops trainees for frontline advisory roles will have available to them in real-time and be able to query the same cognitive computing system being used by frontline advisors in Syria or elsewhere.

The Army Special Operations Center of Excellence, the Army Peacekeeping and Stability Operations Institute, and the US Army John F. Kennedy Special Warfare Center and School, at Fort Bragg, North Carolina, picked up from where AIWC left off. But counterinsurgency training didn't simply need a new home and military curriculum, it needed to be integrated into real-time cyberwarfare operations and decision-making guidance for frontline CyberWarriors in Iraq, Syria and elsewhere who, as an integral part of their day-to-day missions, using state-of-the-art, secure wireless communication technology, will be enabled by NexGen COIN to create and interact with a next-generation counterinsurgency curriculum, from the bottom up.

In addition to their military advisory role, Army SF, Rangers and MARSOC developing protected safe havens on the frontlines in the Middle East will perform advisory and other functions that otherwise would be performed by civilian personnel. Not only are State Department and other government agencies usually unable to provide sufficiently skilled personnel as needed in fluctuating frontline situations, frontline advisors have to be able to call the shots on what they see is needed for governance and economic development purposes to complement their ISIS containment and protected safehaven development efforts.

As illustrative support for utilization of predictive analytics and Big Data to anticipate ISIS military activity, US researchers recently announced that they have used artificial intelligence to better understand ISIS military tactics. These analysts established a causal link between air strikes and roadside bomb attacks. The algorithmic system that analyzed several thousand recorded incidents of ISIS activity in the second half of 2014 found spikes in the use of improvised explosive devices (IEDs) when ISIS experienced a spike in air strikes and a simultaneous shift away from large US infantry-style operations. These researchers also discovered an increase of vehicle-borne bombs prior to large infantry operations by ISIS. Also, a sharp increase in arrests by ISIS following Syrian air strikes were interpreted as retaliatory attempts to weed out Syrian intelligence agents who might have played a role in the targeting of enemy air strikes.

In summary, instead of periodic up-dates of counterinsurgency manuals and courses traditionally provided at various military training centers, frontline advisors guiding forces fighting ISIS need efficient decision-making support in real-time provided by a cognitive computing system that can learn, interact with, and be queried in natural language by these frontline advisors. Just as people in business and government are working with, adapting and learning from cognitive computing to extend the decision-making capabilities of humans, the military has to "train" cognitive computing systems to use artificial intelligence and machine learning to "think" and learn continuously about all aspects of counterinsurgency environments in which frontline advisors operate, while drawing on Big Data repositories that contain everything worth knowing about most facets of frontline combat environments anywhere in Iraq, Afghanistan, Syria, Libya or elsewhere.

The NexGen COIN cognitive system supporting frontline advisors from Iraq and Syria to Yemen and Afghanistan will ensure that these advisors understand and integrate all relevant aspects of local cultures, customs and mindsets into their decisions. The same cognitive system will be able to interactively teach frontline advisors at least rudimentary local language skills that include Arabic, Farsi, Pashto, Urdu and local dialects.

The United States Special Operations Command (SOCOM) will have to review and approve all aspects of the proposed protective safehaven strategy. SOCOM would be responsible for training assigned forces and ensuring their readiness to carry out frontline advisory missions in any country. In addition, DOD's Cyber Command also would have a key role as part of its responsibility "to provide integrated cyber capabilities to support military operations and contingency plans." The NexGen COIN frontline advisory strategy becomes a significant new dimension of "cyber warfare."

Utilizing a cognitive computing system, predictive analytics and Big Data, every action and decision by frontline advisors will be able to draw on all of the expertise available from any government, military, diplomatic or think-tank source. Every decision made by frontline advisors will be measureable in terms of inputs and outcomes, including near- and long-term contributions to providing security and protection for soldiers and civilians in protected safe havens or the potential risks involved in these decisions.

A NexGen COIN goal is to take the guesswork out of frontline or other decision-making that can save or lose lives. The NexGen COIN cognitive system will provide real-time assessments of jihadist physical and logistical sanctuaries, actions taken to disrupt or destroy them, and analysis of outcomes. The cognitive computing system's performance and effectiveness as a frontline advisory decision-support system will be continuously and thoroughly evaluated, including how well frontline advisors and machines are working together.

Information streams from a NexGen COIN cognitive computing system to frontline advisors will: provide analyses about how the local conflict is trending and, based on those assessments, alternative ISIS containment scenarios; suggest ways to cut off ISIS support and eliminate sanctuaries; and recommend improved ways to protect the local population and bolster the local government's functionality and legitimacy. All of this decision support will happen in real-time. In addition, NexGen COIN will learn from all interactions with frontline advisors and continuously get better at decision-support.

Frontline advisors will operate in both the physical and digital worlds. Data-driven guidance will specifically support advisors in their missions to attack, weaken, dismantle, and destroy ISIS and other enemy bases and networks in ways that minimize negative consequences for local populations and their infrastructure. NexGen COIN will be able to able to evaluate the efficacy of safehaven decisions in relation to any component of ISIS's provincial or community governance structures that are being either supported or replaced by protected safe havens.

NexGen COIN data-mining and analysis provided to frontline advisors, drawing on countless sources of relevant intelligence, will not only support specific tactical battle decisions but will incorporate insights into the root causes of ISIS's strengths in local contexts, including specific aspects of failed governance, endemic corruption, economic disparities, and sectarian violence. NexGen COIN also will identify key actors and groups, motivations, tactics, levels of grass-roots and other support, etc., and make recommendations for strategies and tactics that might weaken and delegitimize local leaders that should be removed or circumvented for one reason or another.

After learning as much as possible pre-deployment about sectarian and tribal issues, Shiite militias and the ways in which, for example, Iranian influence manifests itself, with the invaluable aid of NexGen COIN frontline advisors will be learning post-deployment what they need to know to perform their jobs effectively. A 7x24 interface and interaction between combat advisory teams and local insurgents will be crucial for generating essential trust between them. One of the biggest and most complex challenges for frontline advisory teams, for which there is no proven formula or even special training, is functioning as buffers between Sunni and Shiite units. NexGen COIN will provide a continuous stream of real-time suggestions for guiding interactions between frontline advisors and local insurgents that incorporate all of the known information about these insurgents and indigenous sectarian groups, past experience from these interactions, and outcomes of previous interactions that were based on recommendations by NexGen COIN.

The 450 military advisers that the US plans to send to Iraq should become one of the first contingents of frontline advisors that have an in-depth understanding of their frontline CyberWarrior roles and every aspect of the political and military situation in Iraq, Syria or elsewhere. Although the current US commitment of military advisors is focused on Anbar Province, and probably one day also will encompass Mosul and Ninewa, in the foreseeable future trained frontline advisors also will have to be assigned to develop protected safe havens in other countries where some of these frontline advisors from Iraq might train their counterparts, with the invaluable assistance of NexGen COIN.

NexGen COIN will provide real-time training support for frontline advisors anywhere in the Middle East that provides interactive access to all of the lessons learned by frontline advisors elsewhere, strategically and in the minutest detail. Just imagine if Col. MacFarland could have used NexGen COIN before he and his brigade were deployed to Anbar Province and afterwards. and if frontline advisors in the future could ask "Big Data" versions of "MacFarland" or "McChrystal" questions through a NexGen COIN cognitive system.

Frontline advisory teams will become key participants in rewriting the manual for US rules of engagement and figuring out how to reverse conventional top-down US command-and-control battlefield decision-making. They will perform these tasks while coping with some of the biggest military and national security challenges facing the US in the Middle East and along the US border with Mexico.

Another role for frontline advisors will be managing the performance of private military contractors that can either effectively support or unexpectedly degrade their mission. The number of private military contractors has grown dramatically along with troop levels. Between June 2014 and mid-2015, the number of private military contractors in Iraq, for example, has grown from between an estimated 1,700 to more than 6,500. The proposed NexGen COIN protected safehaven strategy will seek to minimize reliance on contractors to manage logistics.

None of these proposed frontline advisory roles and activities will need any additional presidential authorization. Proposed changes in counterinsurgency strategy and operations will have to be addressed by the Pentagon, the NSC, and the CIA. Basically the goal is optimum utilization of 21st century analytics and communication technology in counterinsurgency operations by frontline advisors/CyberWarriors aimed at creating and operating protected safe havens as part of a strategy to contain and defeat ISIS.

Integrated ground-air data collection systems will feed data to NexGen COIN for processing. Battlefields, cities and towns, and vast stretches of desert in Iraq can be implanted with microscopic sensors: that send data flows instantly up to drones; drones relay the data and video feeds to satellites; satellites transmit the data to some of the world's most powerful cognitive computing systems that integrate and analyze it along with structured and unstructured data from other sources; the ground-air data collection system tracks, analyzes and reports in real-time the enemy's every activity and movement; and the information will be available for natural language queries by frontline advisors/ CyberWarriors. Even battery charging for super-smartphones in the hands of frontline advisors/ CyberWarriors will be done wirelessly, enabling "always on" coalition forces, advisors and their seamless interactivity.

ISIS is getting plenty of attention from American CyberWarriors and defense analysts. We can assume that they are using "Big Data" analytic techniques to learn about and predict behaviors before, during and after battle situations. We also can assume that analytic software firms that supply cognitive computing tools to various national defense communities also are playing a big (and profitable) role in providing the means to collect, store, integrate, analyze and interpret streams of structured and unstructured data. The real tests of the value of "Big Data," advanced analytics and cognitive computing platforms, however, will be the benefits for frontline advisors in their multiple roles at the point of engagement with ISIS and other extremists, and the enhanced value of feedback that they can provide, from the bottom up, that can be mined and processed in ways that has value for planning and managing the entire spectrum of counterinsurgency warfare in any location in the Middle East.

With the aid of "Big Data" analytics, frontline advisors can become the key intelligence analysts in the military services dealing with ISIS and other terrorist groups. Drawing on "Big Data" analytics technology that ingests huge amounts of structured and unstructured data from countless sources, the frontline advisor/ CyberWarrior can search for real-time guidance and answers either as an individual or as a node in a NexGen COIN network.

In addition, analytics software will continuously learn about frontline advisors' usage of their wireless-enabled devices in order to improve his or her process of search and to provide algorithmic support for connecting the dots and other real-time decision-making. Implementing this NexGen COIN concept will not require development of yet another technology solution in a US Army that already is struggling with some 3500 IT systems, each with its own security that prevents sharing across IT systems. Technology corporations already have the necessary cognitive computing systems and analytics software that can be adapted for the proposed frontline advisory uses. Frontline advisors in the Middle East and elsewhere should not have to wait for predictive analytics and "Big Data" to be harnessed across the Army's byzantine tech infrastructure.

Currently an heroic effort is being made by the Army to create a predictive analytics system -- the Enterprise Management Decision Support tool (EMDS) – that enables data in its 3500 IT systems to be collected, synthesized and stored in one environment for data analysis and management by the Army active component, the Army National Guard, and US Army Reserves. This EMDS system has a long way to go to achieve its goals, none of which today include enabling frontline advisors to be more effective fighting ISIS and other radical extremists.

Irrespective of the counterinsurgency strategy adopted for the future battle against ISIS, America's drones will continue to play a pivotal role waging long-distance war and gathering intelligence through their video screens. This is not a new conclusion. For years it has been clear that armed surveillance drones have been one of America's best weapons against the Taliban in Afghanistan and ISIS and other jihadists in the Middle East.

There is no question that the US will field a great many more unmanned combat aircraft for use in counterinsurgency in the future. They will possess more stealth in order to penetrate air defenses, have longer range and more sophisticated technology to identify and track targets. In addition, a variety of smaller drones will be used to swarm battlefields and evade air defenses. Although smarter drones combined with smarter missiles will be important technology components of future COIN warfare, the most important innovations will occur in the software and cognitive systems elsewhere. Drones feeding data to cognitive systems will support the complex mission of frontline advisors in the Middle East, Gulf region and North Africa. Military R&D will rely heavily on defense contractors and Silicon Valley companies to develop this technology.

Killing one jihadist leader at a time is not the primary NexGen COIN aim of arming frontline advisors with smart drone support. Unmanned aerial vehicles (UAV) and modern satellite tracking combined with GPS technology are being used extensively in battlefields. But it is the integration of this technology with cognitive computing systems and with human intelligence (HUMINT) that will make the decisive difference in the value of this technology for decision-making on the frontlines of fighting ISIS and other terrorists.

Success in all facets of counterinsurgency requires that HUMINT, enhanced and enabled by cognitive technology, becomes the paramount source of frontline advisor's decision-making. Today no more than 20 percent of the information gathered by the US intelligence community is HUMINT. Excessive reliance on Signals Intelligence (SIGNIT) and other technologies for intelligence gathering grossly underestimates the importance of HUMINT at the frontlines for combating ISIS and other terrorist groups.

NexGen COIN will play a key role for the US military by creating the right mix of human intelligence and technologies like smart drones and cognitive computing systems.

The increasing use of smart drones means that the Air Force has to train a sufficient supply of drone operators to deal with their inevitable burnout. Unfortunately, drone operators have been burning out faster than they can be replaced. The Air Force has had to cut back on drone flights even as military and intelligence officials are demanding more in Iraq, Syria, Yemen, Libya, Somalia and elsewhere.

The Air Force is facing a crisis in training and replacing MQ-1/9 drone operators that are leaving the Air Force in droves. It's not just a shortage of pilots. In addition to the pilots who "fly" the MQ-1s and MQ-9s, there are sensor operators who work the cameras and other intelligence-gathering hardware onboard the unmanned aircraft, and maintenance crews who have to fix the drones. Worst of all, the analysis of drone video surveillance is last generation. Drones still require hundreds of intelligence analysts who have to comb through thousands of hours of video surveillance footage in order to understand what flight crews are watching. Every hour of flight requires hundreds of man-hours of support.

How could Pentagon and Air Force officials simply watch as a significant number of the 1,200 pilots operating drones complete their obligation to the Air Force and indicate that they will opt to leave? How could a drone pilot training program be setup that is designed to produce only about half of the new pilots that the service needs? How could the Air Force simply watch as undermanned and overworked drone pilots burn out in alternating day and night shifts, without academic breaks or even the chance of promotion? The Air Force's excuse is the unexpectedly rapid emergence of ISIS. But more to the point, the US decision not to increase ground forces was not accompanied by a decision to increase drone operators to keep up with increasing reliance on drone surveillance and strikes. Starting early in 2014, Predator and Reaper drones have conducted thousands of sorties, missile and bomb strikes in Iraq alone.

The Air Force also did not sufficiently take into account mental health stresses among drone operators. Drone operators in Nevada flying Predator and Reaper drones via satellite links while living at home with their families have experienced PTSD-type stresses as they move back and forth every day and night between delivering death and rejoining their family activities. The fear of accidently causing civilian and coalition casualties has been another major cause of stress and PTSD.

Drones (or unmanned aerial systems (UAS)) can perform mapping, surveillance, inspection, delivery and other functions from the air. Army UASs fly millions of flight hours each year with almost 90 percent of those hours logged in combat situations in Iraq and Afghanistan. A containment strategy for ISIS and Al-Qaeda that relies on drones providing data is not that much different from drone deployments at the US border with Mexico designed to intercept illegal immigrants and, hopefully, also terrorists.

Along the border with Mexico, at least one UAS already is in use in ways that resemble applications for ISIS containment in Iraq and elsewhere. This UAS, named Falcon, has an eight-foot wingspan, weighs just 9.5 pounds, is powered by an electric motor, carries two swiveling cameras, visible and infrared, a GPS-guided autopilot, can fly for an hour and is easy to operate. Imagine a frontline advisor putting coordinates, desired altitude and airspeed into a laptop, clicking GPS targets (obtained from a cognitive computer source) on a digital map, and launching a Falcon or a facsimile by simply hurling it into the air.

Not only has the US military deployed more than 15,000 military drones to carry out a wide variety of missions, at least 50 other countries are using drones and all of them are investing heavily in drone R&D and expanding manufacturing capabilities. A huge number of companies worldwide are in various stages of the drone business. Some of the most recognizable names include Boeing, Lockheed Martin, AeroVironment and other defense contractors, and recently even Facebook and Google.

The Defense Advanced Research Projects Agency (DARPA) has challenged researchers to build drones that mimic the size and behavior of bugs and birds. Part of the inspiration may have come from AeroVironment's UAVs used by DOD to provide real-time reconnaissance, surveillance and communications that include a 6.5-inch tall, 2/3 ounce nano-hummingbird prototype aircraft that flaps wings for propulsion and control. Instead of ground sensors, imagine winged, lethal, multi-legged drone bugs swarming around the perimeter of and within ISIS territory and able to differentiate terrorists from civilians.

NexGen COIN for frontline advisors will include support for processing, analysis and dissemination of video-based intelligence gathered by drones integrated with intelligence from other sources. This capability already exists, for example, Palantir Defense by Palantir Technologies enables search of full motion videos and integrating the analysis with HUMINT, unstructured message traffic, telephony, documents, network data, sensor data, and structured data in order to discover links and facilitate data-driven decision-making.

It can be assumed that, sooner or later, ISIS and other terrorists also will have mini-drones and that the next phase of warfare with terrorists will pit ultra-smart US and enemy mini-UAVs against each other in the Middle East and elsewhere. US counterinsurgency strategy needs to redefine concepts of ISIS containment to include human-controlled and autonomous drones engaged in drone warfare, including drone "suicide" missions on both sides. In this seemingly sci-fi scenario, networked frontline "cyber-communities" organized and manned by frontline advisors and their trained tribal allies would use networks of linked drones and cognitive computers that can track everything that moves in ISIS- or Al-Qaeda-controlled territory. "Big Data" would include and integrate drone video, enemy cell phone tracking, and every facet of military, insurgent and other human behavior and physical terrain within and around ISIS containment territories.

CHAPTER 23

NexGen COIN: Empowering Bottom-up Leadership

The Pentagon's inspector general currently is investigating reports that United States Central Command (USCOM) officials may have falsified intelligence assessments of progress in the US-led campaign in Syria and Iraq against the ISIS in order to provide a more optimistic account of progress to the White House and Congress. USCOM is responsible for American bombing campaigns and other efforts against the Islamic State.

All the more reason for NexGen COIN to enable frontline advisors to have real-time access to all of the intelligence pertaining to their own battlegrounds with ISIS, and to be able to merge it with, compare and test it against their own assessments. NexGen COIN bottomup leadership means that 21st-century information and communication technology will enable US and Coalition frontline advisors/CyberWarriors to effectively perform the role of integrated battlefield command and control centers supplied with data- and intelligence-driven decision-making guidance.

As General McChrystal says in his book, *Team of Teams*, in Libya he faced the "unexpected revelation that our biggest challenges lay not in the enemy, but in the dizzyingly new environment in which we were operating, and within the carefully crafted attributes of our own organization." In Libya, North Africa, and other complex Middle East operating environments (OE), too little has been known and understood by US counterinsurgency teams about these OEs. In addition, the military's standard operating procedures (SOPs) often have proven irrelevant to frontline combat needs in these OEs.

Read Emma Sky's thoughtful and disturbing memoir, *The Unraveling*, about her experiences as the indispensible advisor in Iraq where military leaders depended on her knowledge of the region and Iraq to make their most important military and civil decisions. In a real sense Sky was the marvelous, improbable genie operating out of the box that NexGen COIN's artificial intelligence capability will try to emulate for frontline advisor's bottomup decision-making and the role played by Sky serving the advisory needs of Generals Odierno and Petraeus. Every military officer and frontline advisor should have an "Emma Sky" at his or her side 7x24 when fighting ISIS and setting up protected safe havens in any Middle East country.

At least 17 intelligence agencies make up the US "intelligence community" with an annual budget approaching $100 billion. Only five of these agencies actively gather intelligence and the rest merely refine and distribute it. None of the literature about US counterinsurgency engagement in Libya, Syria, Iraq, Afghanistan or Yemen provides much reassurance about the capabilities of our military and national security intelligence experts to really understand what actually is happening, in real-time, at any geographic level, and to supply top-down or bottom-up decision-makers with immediate, near-term and longer-term recommendations for action, and then track and evaluate the outcomes. Spending $100 billion of taxpayers' money annually, the most technologically advanced country in the world should be able to harness advanced information technology to supply each top-down or bottomup decision-maker with their own "Emma Sky." NexGen COIN can provide an even more omniscient and reliable alternative.

NexGen COIN's technology gathers, analyzes and transmits information instantaneously to, between and within small battlefront groups and will enable frontline advisors, who also function as battlefield analysts, to use their "super-wireless" devices to query remote cognitive computing systems that continuously supply increasingly relevant data, having algorithmically learned from the results of its applications. Cognitive computing support systems will enable frontline advisors/CyberWarriors to perform their multiple roles like masters of improvisation and efficiency, while facing an enemy that itself is adroitly maneuvering in dispersed but digitally connected networks.

As McChrystal reported about his own experience with the consequences of digital interconnectivity in Iraq: "... we saw the rise in interdependence manifested almost daily. An operation in one city would lead almost instantly to a chain reaction of Al-Qaeda in Iraq (AQI) actions and civilian responses across the country ... An operation on one side of the country would spontaneously incite reactions from a cell on the other side that we did not even know existed ... Social media could spark riots in minutes. Militant videos could incite insurgent recruitment in a matter of hours or set off a series of effects that topples a government."

The same person that creates a counterinsurgency combat plan needs to be able to manage its implementation in collaboration with other stakeholders and not have to wait for approvals passed through a chain of command. By the time such approvals arrive from the chain of command, a COIN plan often is irrelevant or counterproductive. As McChrystal admitted based on his own Iraq experiences: "We could not predict where the enemy would strike, and we could not respond fast enough when they did." When dealing with an agile, adaptable enemy like ISIS, the leaders of NexGen COIN teams have to be able to leverage their own battlespace experiences and knowledge in order to avoid costly and fatal mistakes.

This means that the nation's military and intelligence organizations have to restructure the flows of and intricate safeguards for information sequestered in their silos in order to serve the urgent needs of, and enable bottom-up decision-making by, frontline advisors. Frontline advisors have a need for continuously adjusted holistic views of their combat OEs that fuse intelligence and perceived operational realities. That imperative takes precedence over SOPs for every other level in the COIN chain of command. It doesn't mean simply substituting one intelligence silo on the frontline for another remote one. On the contrary, information sharing interactions and interdependencies will grow exponentially, thereby empowering bottom-up leadership.

Military and national security strategists and planners frequently use terms like complexity, uncertainty, and unpredictability to describe COIN OEs, but US COIN solutions do not yet incorporate information and communication technologies designed to deal with manifestations of these challenges in Iraq, Syria, Libya or elsewhere. If just tiny increments of time and small lapses in decision-making can spell the difference between success and failure of anti-terrorist combat missions, clearly the fastest possible pace of access to integrated quality intelligence becomes imperative.

As the next battle for liberating Ramadi from ISIS grinds on in the summer of 2015 and both Libya and Afghanistan become more important centers of ISIS activity, the challenges and unpredictable complexity of these counterinsurgency OEs underscore the critical importance of much better human and machine intelligence. ISIS has mastered urban guerilla warfare. The OE in the battle of Anbar in 2015, which probably will drag on into 2016, exemplifies the unpredictability of battling ISIS with hybrid Iraqi and local troops and the importance of granular intelligence that can instantly identify asymmetric challenges and assess options for containment of and responses to ISIS. NexGen COIN will provide virtually complete OE awareness within and outside of Mosul, Ramadi and other cities in Syria, Iraq, Afghanistan, Yemen and elsewhere.

The recent Taliban takeover of Kunduz in northern Afghanistan, dealing a stinging blow to the country's security forces, resembles the ISIS offensive in Mosul. In both cases, US-backed security forces supported with training, equipment and airstrikes crumbled in the face of assaults by much smaller insurgent contingents. In the aftermath of both defeats, more questions are being asked of Afghani leadership. A consensus among US military experts is that the chains of command in both Iraq and Afghanistan are so politicized and corrupt that improving motivation for combat forces is virtually impossible. This is not a new conclusion. It is well-documented that the Afghan government and its defense ministry are disorganized and corrupt. However, the consequences of Mosul's takeover by ISIS and Kunduz by the Taliban are different. Mosul as an Islamic State stronghold threatens other Iraqi cities. Kunduz is not a threat to neighboring provinces.

Occupied by ISIS since June 2014, Mosul is a city of over 1 million people (after more than a half million fled). No one in Washington or anywhere is talking about "liberating" Mosul, but some day the US will have to possess the ground and air intelligence capabilities that would make it possible to engage and defeat ISIS in Mosul. This will not happen without a large ground force of well-trained and equipped troops and transformation of Baghdad's governance and its Shia civil and military domination, and concurrent decentralization of area governance in Iraq so that the people of Mosul will support the removal of ISIS, return to and remain in the city.

BIBLIOGRAPHY

Since the Islamic State (ISIS) exploded into the public eye in 2014 with its shocking brutality and speed conquering Middle East territory, it has succeeded in attracting recruits globally in startling numbers. Many experts have written books, given papers, participated in webinars and conferences, and analyzed and dissected ISIS and its violent extremism sufficiently to leave little to the imagination.

Even with all of that has been written and said, we still don't really grasp the potential for this comparatively new Muslim "caliphate" and its international network to expand in the Middle East, North Africa, around the world and extend its reach to the United States. Recent ISIS terrorist attacks in Paris, Beirut and on a Russian jet confirm that, in addition to conquering massive territories in Iraq and Syria, ISIS already is expanding its violence from the Middle East to Europe and globally. For the selected group of authors included in this bibliography, none of these terrorist events are unexpected surprises.

Authors of the books selected include current and former US military and national security leaders, top officials in the nation's intelligence community and some of the world's most knowledgeable experts on counterinsurgency strategies and operations. Their books urge and contribute to rethinking modern military strategy and COIN. These authors are not just scholars and intellectuals in their ivory towers, but experts that have experienced first-hand and thoroughly digested lessons learned in Vietnam and Indo-China, Syria, Iraq, Afghanistan, Libya, the

Philippines, Indonesia, Thailand, Chechnya, Pakistan and North Africa. They understand the dynamics of local insurgencies and geopolitical trends.

Most important, these authors possess an in-depth understanding of the ways in which the US has developed and applied various strategies for dealing with terrorism, ISIS and insurgencies worldwide, and the reasons for successes and failures. Reading any of the books recommended below is guaranteed to change the way that readers think about modern warfare, the war on terror, Al-Qaeda, the Islamic State (ISIS) and counterinsurgency.

Clark, Wesley, *Winning Modern Wars: Iraq, Terrorism and the American Empire*, 2003.

Clay, Steven, *Interview with Col. Sean MacFarland*, 2008.

Gates, Robert, *Duty: Memoirs of a Secretary at War*, 2014.

Gordon, Michael R. Gordon and Trainor E., Bernard, General, *The End Game: The Inside Story of the Struggle for Iraq from George W. Bush to Barack Obama*, 2012.

Kaplan, Fred M., *The Insurgents: David Petraeus and the Plot to Change the American Way of Warfare*, 2014.

Kilcullen, David, *The Accidental Guerrilla: Fighting Small Wars in the Midst of a Big One*, 2009.

Marston, Daniel, *Counterinsurgency in Modern Warfare*, 2008.

McChrystal, Stanley A., *Team of Teams: New Rules of Engagement for a Complex World*, 2015.

Morell, Michael, *The Great War of Our Time: The CIA's Fight Against Terrorism -- From al Qa'ida to ISIS*, 2015.

Nagl, John A., *Institutionalizing Adaptation: It's Time for a Permanent Army Advisor Corp*, 2007.

Nagl, John A., and Schoomaker, Peter J., *Learning to Eat Soup with a Knife: Counterinsurgency Lessons from Malaysia and Vietnam*, 2005.

Panetta, Leon, *Worthy Fights: A Memoir of Leadership in War and Peace*, 2014.

Patrikarakos, David, *Nuclear Iran: The Birth of an Atomic State*, 2012.

Schuchter, Arnold, *Regime Change: National Security in the Age of Terrorism*, 2004.

Sky, Emma, *The Unraveling: High hopes and Missed Opportunities in Iraq*, 2015.

Stern, Jessica and Berger, J.M., *ISIS: The State of Terror*, 2015.

Weiss, Michael and Hassan Hassan, *ISIS: Inside the Army of Terror*, 2015.

Wright, Lawrence, *The Looming Tower: Al-Qaeda and the Road to 9/11*, 2007.

INDEX

9/11 Commission   127-8, 238

A

Abdu Rabu Mansour al-Hadi   283
Afghanistan   xv-xviii, 12-15, 26-9,
    32-40, 87-90, 99-106, 110-
    13, 117-18, 126-9, 237-9,
    256-8, 264-5, 267-8, 287-8,
    305-9
Al-Qaeda   x-xiv, 4-5, 103-5, 118-
    21, 123-9, 137-40, 147, 153-
    8, 163-5, 182-4, 194-6, 237-
    9, 277-80, 295-301, 308-9
Al-Qaeda in Iraq (AQI)   xiii, 4, 135,
    153, 239, 329
Al-Qaeda in the Arabian Peninsula
    (AQAP)   137, 183-4,
    280, 299
Alawites   x, 21, 49, 274-5, 299
Aleppo   25, 42, 50, 176, 276,
    299, 303
Ali Abdullah Saleh   183-5, 187-
    8, 283
Alliance for Prosperity   218, 226
Anbar Awakening   13, 34, 107,
    153, 159-60, 162-3, 166-7,
    279, 296, 302
Arab Spring   xiii, 61, 73, 76, 113,
    137, 185, 295

Army of Conquest   277, 293
Authorization for Use of Military
    Force Against Iraq   139
Ayatollah Ali Khamenei   55, 65,
    67-8

B

Baath Party   145, 297
Bab-el-Mandeb Strait   184
Badr Organization   107-10, 282
Baghdad   ix, 5, 42, 108-9, 132,
    139-42, 145-7, 153-4, 159,
    161-5, 169-72, 176, 243,
    254, 296-7
Bahrain   23, 30, 60, 62, 72-4, 82,
    137, 182, 184, 283, 304
Barrio 18   215-16
Barzani, Masoud   141, 176
Benghazi   194-202, 204-5
Biden, Joe   135, 282
Bin Laden, Osama   4
bottom-up leadership   327, 330
Bush, George W.   18, 124, 130,
    132, 148, 334

C

Calle 18   216, 225
Campbell, John F.   29, 36, 100

cartels 6, 210-14, 216, 219-27, 229, 246-8
CENTCOM xx, 139, 288
Central America 6, 210-12, 214-20, 222, 224-9, 231, 246-7, 281
Central America Regional Security Initiative (CARSI) 226
Clark, Wesley 124, 334
clear-hold-build strategy 260
Clinton, Hillary 18, 103, 133, 197-8, 201, 204, 220
Coalition Provisional Authority (CPA) 138, 145, 160, 297
cognitive computing systems 272, 293, 314-15, 317, 321-4, 329
corruption. 104, 118, 226, 259, 262
counterinsurgency field manual 252, 265, 315
counterinsurgency in Iraq 158
counterterrorism 33-4, 79, 99, 102, 119-20, 126, 128, 169, 181, 189, 239, 252, 280-1, 306, 308-9
Country Reports on Terrorism 8, 274
CyberWarriors 180, 240, 248, 291, 311-12, 314-16, 321, 327, 329

D

Damascus ix, xiii, 52, 61, 269, 291
debaathification 138, 144-5, 161
Defense Advanced Research Projects Agency (DARPA) 266, 326
Defense Department 37, 113, 198
Dempsey, Martin E. 260, 277

drones 53, 71, 115, 136, 159, 252, 293, 313-14, 321-6

E

Egypt xvii, 4, 6-7, 11-13, 20-1, 47, 50, 75-83, 182, 184, 186, 202, 207-8, 284-5, 298
El Salvador 210, 215-19, 223, 225-6
Erdogan, Recep Tayyip 23, 63, 245, 259

F

Field Manual (FM) 3-24 285-6
frontline advisors xvi, 106-7, 139, 167, 180, 240-1, 248, 251, 260, 263, 266, 272, 291-3, 311-23, 326-9

G

Galula, David 116, 239
Gates, Robert 15, 99, 114, 334
Germany 46, 84-6, 88, 90, 96, 169, 242-3, 257, 287, 300
Ghani, Ashraf 27, 37-8, 101, 268
Grand Ayatollah Ali al-Sistani 151
Guatemala 214, 216-18, 223, 225-6
Gulf Cooperation Council (GCC) 60, 69, 73, 187, 303

H

Hadi al-Amiri 107, 109
Hamas 8, 66, 79-82, 280-1
Hezbollah xiii, xv, 3, 16, 42, 48-9, 52, 61, 64-6, 109, 137-8, 212-14, 245-6, 280-2, 293-4

Honduras 215-16, 218, 223, 225-6
Houthi 23, 65-6, 69, 183-4, 187-8, 191-2, 282-3, 304
Hussein, Saddam 5, 107, 123-4, 138, 140, 160, 169, 172

I

intelligence, surveillance, reconnaissance (ISR) 293
Iran xvii-xviii, 22, 42-3, 45-6, 49-52, 55-74, 107-9, 137-40, 181-3, 185-8, 236-8, 244-6, 279-85, 293-5, 310
Iraq xiii-xx, 3-5, 104-18, 120-6, 129-51, 158-63, 165-73, 252-5, 257-65, 267-70, 274-7, 279-82, 285-8, 294-302, 307-13
Iraq Liberation Act 124
Iraq Study Group 161
ISI 4-5, 307
ISIS-free zone 42, 175, 210, 248, 276, 313

J

Jamaat al-Tawhid wa'al-Jihad 161
JCPOA 56-60, 280
"Jersey girls" 238
Joint Chiefs of Staff (JCS) 311
Joint Comprehensive Plan of Action (JCPOA) 280
Joint Force Commanders (JFC) 264
Justice and Development Party (AKP) 23, 259

K

Kerry, John 52, 77, 237, 244
Kilcullen, David 116, 144, 239, 334
Killea, Kevin J. 279
Kirkuk 109, 141, 166, 172, 176-7
Krepinevich, Andrew 106
Kurdistan Regional Government 166, 171-2, 176
Kurds xvii-xix, 23-6, 28, 41, 108-9, 134, 139-41, 145, 148-9, 151, 159-60, 165-6, 171-8, 259, 274-6
Kuwait 8-9, 60, 62-3, 73, 82, 109, 137-8, 145, 184, 188, 304

L

Lebanon xvii, 3, 16, 65, 69-70, 74, 81, 89, 124, 137, 182, 212-14, 241, 250-1, 294
Libya xv-xviii, 12-14, 19-20, 77-8, 83, 89, 101-2, 112-13, 194-7, 202-9, 253-4, 286-7, 294-5, 305-8, 327-8

M

MacFarland, Sean xix-xx, 13, 134, 153, 334
Mara Salvatrucha 215-16
McCain, John 77, 146, 311
McChrystal, Stanley 33, 99, 254, 314, 334
Mexico 6, 119, 126, 210-12, 214-29, 231, 238, 240, 246-8, 290, 320, 325
Moqtada al-Sadr 132
Morsi, Mohamed 75, 79

Mosul 3, 5, 9, 25, 28, 108, 116,
136, 144-5, 151, 159, 177,
297, 310-11, 330-1
MS-13 211, 216, 225
Mullah Mansour 275
Mullah Mohammad Omar 27,
275, 306
Muslim Brotherhood 7, 75-80

N

Nagl, John 115, 144, 154, 334-5
narco-refugees 222
National Security Agency (NSA)
15, 238
National Security Council (NSC)
39, 53, 114, 122-3, 165, 239
NATO xix, 22-3, 35, 40, 50, 53-4,
87, 93, 99-101, 124, 194-5,
203, 205-7, 268, 290
Netanyahu, Benjamin 49
nuclear deal xvii, 15, 55-6, 58,
60-9, 72, 118, 137, 151, 245,
279-81, 283-5, 310
nusra Front xii-xiii, 5, 277, 279,
298, 303

O

Obama, Barack 18, 114, 130,
235, 334
Odierno, Ray 132
operating environments (OE)
x, 327

P

Pakistan 13, 20, 26-8, 35, 68, 94,
103-4, 115, 127-9, 182, 184,
186, 212, 268, 306-7
Palestine Islamic Jihad 280
Panetta, Leon 335

Pentagon xi-xiii, xv, 15, 27, 41,
101, 105, 112, 116-17, 124,
134, 144, 165, 195, 278-9
People's Protect Units (YPG) 276
Petraeus, David 99, 115, 132,
144, 148, 154, 239-40, 252,
265, 334
predictive analytics xvii, 251, 266,
272, 316, 318, 322
proxies xvii-xviii, 15, 22, 26, 55,
57, 61, 64-6, 69-70, 143,
181-2, 281-2, 284, 291, 293
Putin, Vladimir 22, 44, 63, 244-
5, 291

Q

Qaddafi, Muammar 194
Quds Force 64, 68, 108-9, 282

R

Ramadi xvi, xix, 13, 20, 28, 34,
106-7, 136, 153-60, 162-4,
250-2, 254-5, 257, 289, 330
refugees. 16, 82-5, 89-91, 94-6,
186, 222, 303-4
Rouhani, Hassan 55, 58, 74
Russia vii-viii, xiv-xv, xvii-xix, 6,
11-12, 15-22, 41-54, 63,
143-4, 174, 236-7, 244-5,
247, 283-4, 291
Russian Federal Drug Control
Service (FSKN) 247

S

Saddam Hussein 5, 107, 123-4,
138, 140, 160, 169, 172
safe havens xv, xvii, 16-18, 66,
92, 105-6, 155, 240-1, 243,

251, 263, 290-4, 301-2, 312-16, 318-21
Safronkov, Vladimir 247
Sanaa ix, 183-5, 187-9, 192
sanctions xi, xvii, 8, 15, 43, 45-6, 56-8, 60-6, 68-71, 113, 151, 187, 212, 245-6, 281-3
sanctuary cities 227, 229-30
Saudi Arabia xiv-xv, xvii-xviii, 20-3, 43-6, 49-50, 60-2, 65, 68, 70, 72-4, 181-4, 186-93, 245, 283-4, 303-4
Sayyid Ammar al-Hakim 141
Sinaloa cartel 210-11, 223
special forces xvi, xx, 15-16, 25-6, 29, 60, 69, 78, 108, 110, 116, 118, 128, 167, 292
Stevens, Chris 195, 198, 200
Suleimani, Qassem 107, 109
Syria vii-xx, 7-26, 41-4, 47-53, 63-7, 88-92, 135-9, 172-5, 177-80, 241-6, 257-63, 274-83, 286-7, 290-305, 307-14

T

Tal Afar 153-4, 157, 159, 162
Taliban 26-9, 32-40, 87, 99-101, 103, 112-13, 117-18, 128-9, 256-7, 261-2, 268, 275, 288, 306-7, 330-1
terrorist and narco-terrorism free zone 248
Tripoli ix, 199, 201-3
Turkey xvii-xix, 9-10, 16-17, 21-4, 26, 41-6, 49-50, 63, 84-5, 91-4, 172-5, 177-80, 241-2, 259, 301

U

United Arab Emirates (UAE) 23, 70, 73
United Nations xix, 16, 36, 82, 120, 148, 190, 192, 214, 249
United States Special Operations Command (SOCOM) 317
U.S. State Department 198
USS Cole, bombing 127, 185

V

Vietnam War 115, 287, 301

W

Wahhabism 71-2, 182
weapons of mass destruction (WMD) 123
West Point 115, 239
White House xvi, 11-12, 15-18, 23, 25-6, 102-3, 111-12, 114-15, 122-5, 127-8, 165, 190-2, 194-5, 197, 254
Wilayat Sinai 13, 78

Y

Yemen xv-xviii, 12-15, 29-31, 64-6, 68-70, 72, 137, 181-92, 245, 253-4, 257-8, 274-7, 282-3, 294-5, 302-8
YGP 173, 179

Z

Zarqawi, Musab al- 4, 161
Zawahiri, Ayman al- 127, 307
Zetas 214, 216, 219, 223, 225